T0330175

Regional Development in Russia

Regional Development in Russia

Past Policies and Future Prospects

Edited by

Hans Westlund
Swedish Institute for Regional Research, Östersund, Sweden

Alexander Granberg
Council for the Study of Productive Resources, Moscow, Russia

Folke Snickars
Royal Institute of Technology, Stockholm, Sweden

IN ASSOCIATION WITH THE SWEDISH INSTITUTE FOR REGIONAL RESEARCH

Edward Elgar
Cheltenham, UK • Northampton, MA, USA

Published by
Edward Elgar Publishing Limited
Glensanda House
Montpellier Parade
Cheltenham
Glos GL50 1UA
UK

Edward Elgar Publishing, Inc.
136 West Street
Suite 202
Northampton
Massachusetts 01060
USA

Reprinted 2002

A catalogue record for this book
is available from the British Library

Library of Congress Cataloguing in Publication Data

Westlund, Hans.
    Regional development in Russia: past policies and future prospects / Hans Westlund, Alexander Granberg, Folke Snickars.
    Includes index.
    1. Regional planning—Soviet Union. 2. Soviet Union—Economic policy.
I. Granberg, Aleksandr Grigor'evich. II. Snickars, Folke, 1944– III. Title.

HT395.S69 W47 2000
338.947—dc21

                                                          99–044608

ISBN 1 84064 269 6

Printed and bound in Great Britain by Bookcraft, Bath

Contents

Figures

Tables

Glossary

ASPC	automated system of plan calculations
CEMI	Central Economic–Mathematical Institute
CIS	Commonwealth of Independent States
CNIEIugol	Central Research Institute of Economic Studies in Coal Industry
Comecon	Council for Mutual Economic Assistance
CSB	Central Statistical Bureau
FFFSFS	Federal Fund of Financial Support of the Federation Subjects
GDP	gross domestic product
GOELRO	State Committee on Electrification
Gosplan	State Planning Committee
Gosstroy	State Construction Committee
Gubernia	county, pre-revolution administrative region
IEC	Inter-republic Economic Committee
IEOIP	Institute of Economics and Organisation of Industrial Production
Krai	administrative region
Narkomaty	all-Union people's commissariats
Narkomtyazhprom	People's Commissariat for Heavy Industry
Oblast	administrative region
RF	Russian Federation
RSFSR	Russian Soviet Federated Socialist Republic
SOPS	Council for the Study of Productive Forces
Sovnarkhoz	Regional Economic Council
SSR	Soviet Socialist Republic
SSSR	Union of Soviet Socialist Republics
TPC	territorial production complex
USSR	Union of Soviet Socialist Republics
Uyezdy	pre-revolution administrative district
Volost	pre-revolution administrative district
VSNH	All-Union Council for the National Economy

Contributors

Aleko Adamesku is professor in economics at the Council for the Study of Productive Forces (SOPS) in Moscow.

Murat Albegov is professor in economics at the Central Economic-Mathematical Institute (CEMI) in Moscow.

Alexander Granberg is professor in economics, head of the Council for the Study of Productive Forces (SOPS) and member of the Russian Academy of Science. He has been adviser to the Russian President Boris Yeltsin.

V.V. Khistanov is professor in economics at the Council for the Study of Productive Forces (SOPS) in Moscow.

Boris Shtoulberg is professor in economics at the Council for the Study of Productive Forces (SOPS) in Moscow.

Folke Snickars is professor in regional planning and head of the Department of Infrastructure and Planning at the Royal Institute of Technology (KTH) in Stockholm. He has been President of the European Regional Science Association and main editor of the journal *Papers in Regional Science.*

Hans Westlund, is doctor in economic history and researcher at the Swedish Institute for Regional Research in Östersund, Sweden.

Preface

The joint Swedish–Russian research project which is described in this book has its origin in scholarly contacts established almost 20 years ago. During the Cold War, cooperation in research, like other forms of cooperation between East and West, was exceedingly limited. However, efficiently functioning research cooperation did occur in certain international bodies located on neutral soil. The International Institute for Applied Systems Analysis (IIASA) in Vienna was – and is – such a body.

Systems analysis is a practicable method for studies in a number of different fields, including regional science, which was abundantly represented in the IIASA during the first half of the 1980s. It is no exaggeration to say that a large proportion of the cooperation between Swedish and Russian regional scientists which occurred then and goes on today is based on contacts originating from the IIASA. The most pertinent example is a series of books which were published with reports of issues and methods in regional policy in both East and West. The first one was the 1982 volume on *Regional Development Modelling: Theory and Practice* which was edited by Murat Albegov, Åke E. Andersson and Folke Snickars. This book was one of the first in the postwar period which showed to the international research community some of the research methods and policy tools which were developed for the territorial planning in the USSR. The contacts which were established have continued primarily under the auspices of the regional science association. One example of the continuation of the contacts is that, when the European Regional Science Association's 33rd Congress was held in Moscow, on 24–27 August 1993, it was organised in collaboration with the Department of Infrastructure and Planning at the Royal Institute of Technology (KTH) in Stockholm.

The congress in Moscow formed the starting point of the project on regional development in the Soviet Union which is reported in the current book. The main responsibility for the Moscow congress was carried by Alexander Granberg, member of the Russian Academy of Science, head of the Council for the Study of Productive Resources (SOPS) and at that time also adviser to the Russian President Boris Yeltsin. Alexander Granberg approached Folke Snickars, head of the Department of Infrastructure and Planning at KTH, at that time President of the European Regional Science Association, with a proposal that a Swedish–Russian research project should be arranged on regional development and regional policy during the Soviet epoch, and also under the new conditions created by the transition to democracy and a market economy. The fact that the archives of SOPS, like many other Soviet archives, had been opened for research would enable light to be shed on the regional development of the Soviet Union in a long-term perspective. It was decided at a meeting between Alexander Granberg, Folke Snickars, Börje Johansson and Hans Westlund that the last-named should be entrusted with the main responsibility for seeking finance and performing such a project.

Finance for the project was secured from the Swedish Council for Planning and Coordination of Research (FRN) and the Swedish Institute for Regional Research (SIR). The project, like many others in the field of East–West collaboration, has taken a long time, but we believe the time expended on this book in the end has been used fruitfully.

This book does not merely give new perspectives on regional development during a remarkable period of history in an empire which accounted for one seventh of the earth's land surface, nor does it merely discuss the conditions requisite for a modern regional policy in the new Russia. It is also a document from 'the people who were there' – that is to say from those who were trying, in the circumstances then prevailing, to develop a regional science research which never achieved practical application and never could have done so under the planned economy. Like other fields of scholarly work, Soviet regional science was cut off from the Western world and thus forced to find its own way. Scholars and planners created economic–mathematical models for a social system in which such models could not be applied. This, too, is a story which merits elucidation.

The book's introductory chapter, 'The Soviet paradox: imbalanced equalisation and balanced divergency', has been written by Hans Westlund, and describes the long-term regional development of the Soviet Union, emphasising the way in which regional disparities evolved. It has been customary in studies of these developmental processes within the Soviet Union for regional specialists in various disciplines to cite Williamson's (1965) hypothesis of the so-called 'reversed U-curve', which states that during a country's industrialising phase the regional disparities increase at first, but that with the passage of time the trend goes into reverse and the regional disparities diminish. Previous research has been based on data from 1956 onwards, showing an increase in regional disparities. Scholars therefore drew the conclusion that the Soviet Union had not yet reached the stage of development where these disparities begin to diminish.

With the help of data from the period prior to 1956, however, the analysis shows that regional disparities during the Soviet epoch evolved in the form of a U *the right way round.* Regional disparities were diminishing until the mid-century point and started to rise only after that. This pattern of events is interpreted in the light of the industrialisation strategy which was being applied. Massive investment in heavy industry required the exploitation of geographically dispersed supplies of raw materials, which reduced regional disparities of production. After the Second World War, however, when the Soviet Union began to switch little by little to more balanced industrialisation, light industries were located increasingly in the most developed regions of the West. Westlund points out that this turn of events was paradoxical. Imbalance of economic structure went hand in hand with regional equalisation, while the shift towards a balanced economic structure brought increased regional disparities. Westlund therefore argues that from many standpoints the Soviet Union must be regarded as a special case – and not only in political respects. No other geographically united state has had such internal differences of economic developmental level, culture, ethnicity and so on. Factors such as these influenced Soviet development strongly and have an impact even today on the prospects for regional development in the new Russia. The chapter is a revised and expanded version of an article entitled 'The limits of spatial planning. Regional experiences of the Soviet epoch', from *Papers in Regional Science*, vol. 77, no. 3, 1998 and is published by permission of that journal.

Chapter 2, 'Soviet regional policy', has been written by Boris Shtoulberg, Aleko Adamesku and V.V. Khistanov, all of whom are professors at SOPS, and Murat Albegov, professor at the Central Economic–Mathematical Institute (CEMI) in Moscow. The chapter consists of four sections. In the first section, 'Main stages of regional policy', Soviet policy towards the regions is broken down into six periods during which central direction and a degree of decentralisation have alternated. Section 2, 'Organisation of territorial management', describes briefly the administrative systems during the various periods. The third section, 'Soviet philosophy of territorial planning', discusses the general objectives of the Soviet state's economic policy and how these were pursued in territorial planning. The authors emphasise the dominance of centralised economic–sectoral policy over decentralised, regionally focused policy during most of the Soviet Union's period of existence as being crucial to any understanding of regional development patterns. This section also includes a discussion of the reasons why regional research, despite the hundreds of different research bodies, actually played a very remote role in practical policy. The conflicting interests, bottleneck problems and political priorities of the various sectors and regions weighed far more heavily than recommendations based on scholarly grounds. Section 4, 'The role of economic science in industrial and territorial policy', provides a summary of the main intellectual streams in Soviet regional economic research. In this section Murat Albegov traces the roots of the economic research to the pre-revolutionary period and shows how the traditions have been retained over the whole 50-year period from the revolution to the fall of the Soviet Union. He starts by pointing at the repressive role that the Stalin period had on economic science. He then reports on the peculiar developments which took place during the 1960s, when the research which later provided L. Kantorovich with the Nobel Prize was performed (linear programming models, input–output tables, analyses of territorial production complexes). He asserts that the economists fiercely attempted to provide the planned economy with principles which would help in the enormous need for coordination which existed both between sectors and between regions. One of his points is that the decision to use computer models to find the optimal resource use in the economy was a strategy to remove some of the power from the sectoral ministries with their rejection of the usefulness of scientific analysis as a support for economic policy. Performing objective calculations would be a strategy in the big game which was played between the sectoral ministries and Gosplan, and between the Moscow centre and the regions. In the world of regional economic analysis two centres competed in the Soviet Union, Moscow and Novosibirsk, the Novosibirsk centre attaining much of its scientific status from thorough studies of the economic development prospects in Siberia.

Chapter 3, 'Regional development and regional policy in the Gorbachev period', was written by Alexander Granberg. The chapter opens with an analysis of the exchange of goods between the republics prior to the Soviet Union's collapse. The wide disparities of production between the republics are elucidated here in concrete fashion. The great Russian republic was clearly the leading net exporter to the other republics. Converted into world market prices the disparities between the Russian republic's trade surplus and the deficits of the other republics (except Turkmenistan) are revealed to have been even greater than they were in terms of the Soviet price system. Under the Soviet system of non-market-determined prices, this did the Russian republic no favours at all. Because imports did not require any balancing measure in the form of exports, being a net importer was an advantage for every republic. Granberg calls attention to the strong economic interdependence between the republics of the former Soviet Union and the severe disruptions of the republics' economies which a dissolution of the economic networks would bring about. On this view, and given the existing economic structure, only the republics producing the most raw materials and power will be able to profit from the former Soviet Union's integration into the world economy. At the end of the chapter the author goes on to describe how the Union disintegrated economically when the administrative system began to collapse, while at the same time it was still sufficiently strongly rooted politically to prevent the emergence of functioning markets.

In Chapter 4, 'Regional development and regional policy in the new Russia', Alexander Granberg provides an exhaustive account of the present regional situation in Russia and discusses the various forms of economic policy *vis-à-vis* the regions which have begun to emerge. After a scrutiny of such factors as demographic developments, production and incomes, Granberg divides up the Russian regions according to the various types of problem: economic, geopolitical, ethnic and environmental. As regards the emergence of the new regional policy, Granberg lays special emphasis on two problems which permeate Russia in all fields: (a) the Russian state's lack of adequate resources to implement the regional policy decided upon, and (b) the fact that the juridical system and other institutional factors have not yet been adapted to the new Russia; in the present context this applies particularly to the relationships between state and regions, between the centre and the periphery. However, the predominant trend is for the regions to get increased economic self-government.

Chapter 5 is entitled 'Collapse or a new dynamism?' and has been written by Hans Westlund. Russia's resources and deficiencies, and the factors favouring unity and disintegration and their respective strengths as we enter the new millennium are discussed in the light of the present economic policy crisis and the growing regional cleavages in Russia. The growing regional disparities and the weakening of the centralised state constitute a threat in themselves to the country's unity. Against this it is urged that Russia, unlike the Soviet Union, is to a very large degree homogenous in ethnic and religious terms. Except for certain areas of Northern Caucasus, including Chechenya, a few regions of the central Volga district and on the border with Mongolia, Russians form the clearly dominant population group. The Russian Orthodox Church forms another unifying factor and a dividing line *vis-à-vis* Russia's Asiatic neighbours. In this way the disjunctive tendencies at certain levels are confronted by very change-resistant, unifying structures which have to be taken into consideration in any overall assessment.

Westlund singles out the historical absence of small business as a crucial problem of economic development in Russia. Russian industry prior to 1917 was dominated by large-scale enterprises, while the Russian peasantry had hardly emerged from the paralysing grip of serfdom. To homo sovieticus, the 'Soviet Man' shaped by the Soviet state, the enterprise mentality was inconceivable. Thus the absence of small businesses is more than a short-term juridical problem – the lack of a comprehensive code of Western-style commercial and business law in Russia. It is largely also a question of a shift of mentality, which may require more than a generation to accomplish. The author's conclusion is that even though doomsday prophecies of Russia's collapse are probably mistaken, the modernisation of the Russian economy will proceed considerably more slowly than the optimists have predicted.

The title of the book is *Regional Development in Russia*. It presents aspects of the history of spatial policy and regional development in the territory which formed the Soviet Union. It provides future perspectives on the core of this area which is made up by the historical Russia. The forecast made in the book is that there will be a Russia of regions in the future. Russia has everything to gain from bringing the regions to work in defining and designing their futures. The cultural ties among Russians will vouch for the long-term coherence of the country. The sooner a system of interlinked economic regions can be established where interregional trade will prevail the better for the welfare of the Russian population. The political challenge is for the centralist views traditionally held by actors in the Moscow hub to be replaced by promotion of regional diversification. The future of Russia is in mobilising its regional resources.

The editors wish to express their warm thanks to all who have contributed to the realisation of this project: Berit Örnewall, in charge of the project's administration at FRN; Professors Murat Albegov, Boris Shtoulberg, Aleko Adamesku, V.V. Khistanov, Börje Johansson, Ulf Olsson, Dr Lennart Samuelson and Dr Vladimir Wedensky. Dr Natasha Plevako assisted in the work in the Russian archives. Dr Galina Terentieva of SOPS, Ms Margareta Grill of SIR and particularly Mr Geoffrey French undertook translating tasks along with linguistic and formal editing. Kent Eliasson and Magnus Johansson of SIR copy-edited the typescript. Thanks are also due to other staff of SOPS, SIR and the Department of Infrastructure and Planning at the Royal Institute of Technology.

HANS WESTLUND
ALEXANDER GRANBERG
FOLKE SNICKARS

1. The Soviet paradox: imbalanced equalisation and balanced divergency

Hans Westlund

INTRODUCTION

From the end of 1917 until the end of 1991, the greatest attempt the world has ever seen to transform a society through central planning was going on in Russia and the other parts of the former Soviet Union. The allocation mechanisms of the market were to be replaced by planning, and the 'dictatorship of the proletariat' was to protect the socialist society from the emergence of new market influences. The collapse of the Soviet Union in late 1991 was the ultimate proof of the failure of this gigantic endeavour.

The USSR experienced remarkable economic growth from the 1920s until the early 1960s, in spite of Stalin's terror and the heavy damage and losses sustained during the Second World War. For several decades the Soviet Union was the only real competitor to the United States, and in many former colonial countries 'socialism' in some sense became the official policy of the new independent states. Planning, although not in the Soviet sense, became a generally accepted instrument of national development after the Second World War in both the developed Western world and the developing countries. The Western world seemed to be moving some steps away from pure market capitalism, while during the Khrushchev era it seemed as if the USSR might be going to adopt a more market-oriented policy. The Dutch Nobel prizewinner Tinbergen formulated his convergency theory, which predicted continued *rapprochement* between the capitalist and socialist systems.

However, the predictions of the convergency theory turned out to be wrong. The Soviet system did not or could not shift little by little towards a market economy. After the politically turbulent 1960s the Western world found itself in a transitional phase in which, as the relative importance of manufacturing industry in the economy decreased, the industrial value-system was slowly superseded by 'post-industrial' values. Planning was no longer a universal panacea for solving the economic and social problems of capitalism but 'merely' a means of collecting and processing information for investment decisions concerning the housing and transport infrastructure.

With the answers supplied by history, it is easy to identify as the main explanation for the ultimate breakdown the inability of the centralised planning system to manage the transformation from raw material-based and other heavy industrial production to production to meet consumer demand. The lopsided growth strategy chosen in the USSR was unable to switch over to balanced economic growth. The world's largest planning apparatus lacked the prerequisites for modernising the Soviet economy. The Soviet experience demonstrated – more starkly than has been seen anywhere else – the limits of planning.

The limits of planning are not an issue of general economic development alone. To a large extent they are also a question of spatial development. Certain 'principles of location of productive forces', based on Engels' *Anti-Dühring* and a short note of Lenin's (1918), became a part of the official Soviet state doctrine (Dyker, 1983, p. 114). There was already a policy with extensive regional implications even from the time the USSR was founded in 1922.

The history of the USSR contained many contradictions, for example between the different stages of the official policy, between the official policy and what really happened, and – not least – between the diverse development patterns that emerged in the various parts of the vast Union. Regional planning and development in the USSR was not only a matter of spatial differences within the Union. It was also a matter of what kind of policy (or policies) *vis-à-vis* the regions were formulated and decided on during the various phases of the Soviet epoch; this involves a consideration of the executive authorities utilised for implementing policy in the regions and the extent to which the policy selected actually was implemented.

PLANNING VERSUS 'PRODUCTIVE FORCES' IN SOVIET REGIONAL DEVELOPMENT

Soviet policy for the regions can broadly be said to have been as old as the Soviet Union itself. Lenin himself stressed on several occasions the importance of the economic development of the widely dispersed peripheral regions of the new Soviet state (Koropeckyj, 1967). The reasons of course were that the differences in both economic, cultural and other respects between the most advanced European regions and most of the rest of the Soviet Union were probably greater than in any other territorially united state and that these differences formed the most important internal threat to the solidarity of the Soviet state. The Soviet Union 'inherited' Russia's former colonial empire, and this circumstance constituted the foundation of the special type of regional policy which came to be framed under the command economy. However, it is important to distinguish between *regional policy* and *regional effects of the policy* conducted. Pallot and Shaw pointed out in 1981 that there were only two periods when the leadership had shown serious interest in regional development – immediately after the Revolution and during the 1960s and 1970s. 'For most of the Stalin period, the Soviet Union seems not to have had a clearly defined policy on regional development' (Pallot and Shaw, 1981, p. 68*)*. But of course the policy of the Stalin epoch did have regional *effects*.

Centralised Pluralism versus Territorial Planning

The two five-year plans of the interwar years can be evaluated in different ways. On the one hand there is the officially depicted heavy investment in electrification of the 'whole' country, in 'new economic regions', in the building of the Turkestani–Siberian railway, in the Stalin canal, and so on and so forth. There is no doubt that large resources were poured into backward regions and that these investments produced tangible results. On the other hand the investments made in the Moscow, Leningrad and other western industrial regions were also on a very high level.

The location of the Russian munitions industry during the interwar years furnishes a telling example of how locational advantages such as extensive infrastructure, a trained industrial workforce and other external effects outweighed the factors favouring the establishment of production far from the national frontiers. Despite the pressure from the military for a change in the location of the munitions industry, most of the new plants were placed in the advanced western parts of the Soviet Union and especially in the militarily and strategically highly unsuitable Leningrad region (Tsaplin, 1990).

Seventy per cent of the output of the mechanical engineering and metallurgical industries came from Leningrad and the Ukraine prior to the Second World War (Schiffer, 1989, p. 191). It was only the massive effort to intensify industrialisation east of the Ural Mountains through such measures as the physical transfer of entire factories, enforced by the necessities of the Second World War, that swung the balance of power between centre and periphery to the advantage of the latter. During the three and a half years for which the third Five-Year Plan was operative prior to the German attack in June 1941, 35 per cent of investment went to eastern regions (Tsaplin, 1990). After the war, however, when direct removals of factories came to an end and 'normal' investment in the periphery was resumed, the shift in the relative distribution of industrial production ceased, many evacuees returned home, and the situation stabilised at the new level (Dobb, 1966, p. 442; Schiffer, 1989, pp. 28 and 197).

Growth through spatial expansion was also the lodestar which guided Khrushchev's heavy investment in agriculture during the second half of the 1950s. New, enormous and previously untilled areas of the Russian interior were to be opened up to cultivation, and food shortages were to become a thing of the past. Khrushchev's failure was perhaps the worst example of the shortcomings of the spatial expansion principle because in this instance it was not only economic efficiency criteria that were ignored but also the conditions of natural geography and climatology.

SOVIET ECONOMIC STATISTICS: A PROBLEMATICAL SOURCE

The problems involved in using Soviet economic statistics for research purposes are well known. Official time-series of key socioeconomic variables are missing over long periods. The figures which have been published officially have often been selected and converted to indices or percentages, so that direct comparisons in time and space have been rendered impossible. In those cases where annual figures have in fact been published, they have been at a highly aggregated level both structurally and territorially.

Another of the familiar problems with official Soviet production statistics is that, until 1950, 1926/27 (before the launching of the five-year plans) was used as the index year. The fact that the relative prices in the most rapidly expanding sectors were falling sharply during the 1930s means that growth was overvalued (Nove, 1986). Overall, any assessment of the trend of total production in the Soviet Union is difficult because of the absence of market pricing. Professor Anders Åslund, for example, has pointed out that the low quality of many Soviet goods makes comparisons with other countries' production values irrelevant.

The problems noted above are among those which anyone desirous of studying developments at Union level has had to contend with. However, anyone who wants to study regional developments in the Soviet Union, especially if endeavouring to apply a comparative perspective, has had to face even greater difficulties. Data which exist sporadically at Union level occur even more seldom at republic level and often not at all at lower regional levels (oblast, krai). In cases where there is some sparse incidence of data at oblast and krai level, comparisons over time are impeded by alterations in the regional boundaries and the fact that the alterations did not occur at the same point in time across the whole of the Soviet Union.

Obviously, the opening of the archives of Gosplan, the Central Bureau of Statistics, the Finance Ministry and other ministries has signified great positive changes for research into the economic history of the Soviet epoch. At the same time, however, there remain problems which can be characterised as interesting research tasks in themselves. This applies above all, perhaps, to the question of the extent to which, and during which periods, official economic data were manipulated selectively and with dubious index and percentage calculations. With regard to data concerning industrial production, there are no indications that scholars' previous assumptions concerning the reliability of the physical output figures were wrong (cf. Nove, 1986, for example pp. 293–4 and 392–9).

In the course of the present project, only a small random sample of the steel production returns in four different sources has been taken for the year 1934. This showed that the discrepancies between the official figures, the printed but confidential figures and the archive figures were minimal and cannot really be explained as anything other than computational errors (see Table 1.1).

Table 1.1   Steel and pig-iron production (in tons) in the Soviet Union, 1934, reported by six different sources

	Total Production		National Steel 'Trust'	
	Steel	Pig-iron	Steel	Pig-iron
I.	–	–	3 763 782	6 081 560
II.	9 563 300	10 438 100	3 763 200	5 981 000
III.	9 517 000	10 413 000	3 763 000	6 084 200
IV.	9 565 000	10 428 000	3 763 200	6 081 500
V.	9 565 000	10 440 000	–	–
VI.	9 693 000	10 428 000	–	–

Sources: Russian State Archive of the Economy (RGAE), Moscow. I: File 4086, cat. 2, doc. 887. (Steel trust, annual report.) II: File 7297, cat. 28, doc. 310. 'Heavy Industry in the USSR, 1934'. (People's Commissariat for Heavy Industry. Dept of accounts and economy.) (Secret classified printed book.) III: File 4372, cat. 33, doc. 355. Control Figures of Production for the People's Commissariat for Heavy Industry. (Gosplan.) IV: File 4372, cat. 33, doc. 358. Reference book in black, metallurgic, iron industry for 1928–34. (Gosplan, metallurgic dept.) V: File 1562, cat. 8, doc. 1440. Reference book in colour and metallurgic industry, 1935. (Gosplan, statistical office.) VI: Official statistics. Statistical abstract. (Moscow, 1936.)

However, relatively big problems seem to remain for the researcher aiming at regional comparisons, even after the opening of the archives. Although quantities of primary material and working tables are now available, especially at republic level, it is evident that many essential socioeconomic data simply do not exist in collected form at lower levels than the republics. The reasons are probably to be found in the fact that during the entire Soviet epoch, heavy industry came directly under the authority of the respective central ministry. The strongly sectorised heavy industry was an all-Union matter and therefore there was simply no need for regional compilations of planning targets and production results. A coherent picture of the development of production in the Soviet epoch at different regional levels can therefore only be obtained by means of very exhaustive scrutiny of the sources in the ministries' (people's commissariats prior to 1946) archives. However, more detailed studies made of various sectors of Soviet economic development since the opening of the archives have given access to records which can shed much light on what actually happened below the macro level of which at all events we do believe ourselves to have a fairly correct picture.

The Khrushchev period represented a brief exception to the almost total dominance of the sector policy. The *sovnarkhozy* system introduced by Khrushchev brought increased regional influence over economic decisions. The system was based on a new division of the Soviet Union into economic regions which sometimes cut across the republic boundaries. For the production of statistics it meant primarily, however, that the Russian Republic's 'autonomous' republics and oblasts were arranged into a number of economic regions for which a certain amount of official data were published. After 1965, however, the publication of figures for these economic regions dwindled considerably after they lost their functions in the new wave of centralisation which marked Brezhnev's accession to power.

To sum up, therefore, we can say that, even though many archives are now open for study, great difficulties remain when making use of the available sources in 'Western' scholarly fashion. Non-market pricing and the difficulties of making comparisons with international prices constitute an almost insoluble problem because of qualitative differences which are hard to assess. On the other hand the manipulations of price-index base years can probably be corrected after thorough studies of price history. The conclusion is that the material available on the economic development of the USSR is far from ideal, but it is all that exists. *If we want to study economic developments in the Soviet Union this is the material which we must consult, but results based on these sources must always be related to the distortions and deceptions which are built into them.*

In combination with the general problems attaching to Soviet statistics, this means that time-series will always be biased in one way or another, even in the future. Comparative historical regional research will probably have to resort largely to the methods employed during the Soviet epoch, that is regional cross-sectional analyses at different points in time. Even if, there too, non-market pricing brings problems which give rise to thorny points of interpretation, cross-sectional analyses will at any rate avoid the difficulties to which the indexing has given rise.

THE LONG-TERM DEVELOPMENT OF REGIONAL DISPARITIES

Methods and Measures Employed in Studies of Regional Disparities

The most frequently employed summary measure of the difference in incidence of different variables between the regions of the Soviet Union has been the *coefficient of variation*, that is the standard deviation as a percentage of mean value. The coefficient of variation is a simple and robust measure for calculating distribution within a population. When it is employed for estimating regional disparities within a country, it also, in principle, makes international comparisons possible as well. Thus, because a large proportion of Soviet statistics – in consequence of the problems of double counting, relative price changes, non-market pricing and poor quality – are unsuitable for making comparisons with other countries, a relative measure such as the coefficient of variation often becomes the only possible method if the results are also to be capable of being used for international comparisons.

However, the use of the coefficient of variation as a measure of regional differences is not problem-free. The main reason is that 'regions' are usually administrative units of a country, with wide dissimilarities with respect to both population and area. This brings special problems in studies of the Soviet Union. As was observed above, in many cases only data at republic level can be found in the archives. Bearing in mind that the Russian Republic extended from the Baltic to the Pacific Ocean, constituted three-quarters of the area and contained about half of the Soviet Union's total population – and that the population of the Ukraine formed about 20 per cent of the Union's – a serious bias is obviously implied in the fact that two republics account for such an overwhelming proportion of the population and area, while the other (after the Second World War) 13 republics together had less than one-third of the population and only just over one-fifth of the area. Therefore, for example, a calculation of the coefficient of variation of production per head in which such dissimilar magnitudes as the Russian Republic and the Baltic republics are given the same weighting will not be so easy to interpret.

With a view to correcting this bias, therefore, many scholars have chosen to weight the republics' values according to their populations when computing the coefficient of variation. By employing this procedure account is taken of the different size of the republics, and Russia's large proportion of the Union's population and production is allowed for. However, there is nothing which actually says that the weighted coefficient of variation must be a 'better' aggregate measure of the various regional differences within the Soviet Union than the unweighted coefficient of variation. The reason can be stated briefly: it will be at least equally misleading to make *one* republic govern half the value of the coefficient of variation (and *two* republics govern about 70 per cent of the value) as to give all the republics the same weightings. The disparate sizes of the Soviet republics are not a problem to be solved by applying weightings, if the aim is to produce an indisputable measure of the *regional* differences. The regional differences within the Russian Republic are probably at least as large as the differences between the republics. To allow this mean value for the whole of Russia to be the sole determinant of half the value of the coefficient of variation, as is the case if the latter is weighted, also means that the regional differences will not be well reflected and, as in this case, will appear to be considerably smaller than they actually are. On the other hand other regional divisions may very well hide the regional differences just as much.

Because the largest Soviet republics especially consisted of a relatively large number of regions, many regional differences are therefore concealed within the republics. In the main a state's size seems to have enlarging effects on the official 'regional' inequality. This was one conclusion drawn by Jeffrey Williamson in his celebrated study of 1965, and Williamson seems to have based this conclusion on a simple assumption that the geographical size co-varied with the regional differences. This also means that international comparisons of regional differences must take account of the 'scale' factor, the fact that large states cannot be compared straight off with small.

The conclusion is that weighted or unweighted coefficients of variation of conditions at republic level are definitely not the ideal method for assessing the long-term trend of regional inequality in the Soviet Union, but that there are not many alternatives to the methods discussed here until a very great deal of basic research has been done on the compilation of comparable historical data at oblast and krai level. However, if the comparisons over time are based on unchanged regions (such as republics), the results will shed light to some extent on how the spatial differences developed at these levels during the Soviet epoch.

More than 30 years have passed since the publication of Williamson's article. On an empirical foundation consisting mainly of regional income disparities within nations during the 1950s, he divided the disparities into groups in accordance with the stage theory which was so popular during the 1960s and whose foremost representative was W.W. Rostow. Williamson found that the regional disparities were small in countries which had not yet begun to industrialise; they were large in countries which found themselves in the midst of their industrialisation phase; and they were small again in countries which had already accomplished their industrialisation. Thus the size of the regional disparities in the countries during the 1950s could be described as a reversed U-curve, the position on the curve being determined by the countries' level of development. Williamson argued that this pattern also ought to be valid over time in the respective countries. All he had to support this thesis, however, consisted of data for industrial countries and data showing that the disparities were diminishing. But he had no empirical evidence for a phase of growing regional disparities over time.

Williamson's article came to exert an enormous influence on research into the development of underdeveloped countries and on studies concerned with regional comparisons. However, his theory and results have often become a general reference point, to such an extent that the reversed U-curve has been taken for incontestable truth, while calculations of regional disparities in different countries have been related, without any discussion of the problem, to the countries and stages in Williamson's study. Not even Williamson's observation (1965, p. 15) that the regional disparities seem to be larger in big countries than in small has led very often to any discussion of scale as a problem in comparative studies.

Williamson's method of measuring regional disparities by the coefficient of variation has also become the standard method in Western studies of regional development in the Soviet Union. The general criticism against those who have cited Williamson, however, is also applicable to many researchers. Koropeckyj (1972), Schroeder (1974) and McAuley (1979), for example, have remarked that the regional disparities in the USSR were actually somewhat smaller than they were at corresponding points in time in the United Kingdom, Poland, East Germany and Yugoslavia, without there being any discussion of the problem of different sizes of countries and regions and what effects this has on the coefficients of variation. One of the few exceptions is Spechler (1979), who discusses these problems thoroughly.

Lack of sources meant that Williamson (1965) did not have much to say with regard to development towards regional convergence or divergence in the Soviet Union. But he assumed that in this respect events followed the general pattern, since it seemed unlikely that growth would be sacrificed to secondary aims such as regional equality, but also that transport problems and the needs of military decentralisation, for example, would have had a degree of mitigating effect on the divergency process prior to the Second World War. Williamson also considered that the increasing official emphasis on regional development from the late 1950s onwards could be regarded as a sign of some 'serious attempt to reduce regional inequalities generated by the fabulous growth of three decades'.

Williamson's application of the U-curve even to developments in a command economy like that of the Soviet Union has been accepted uncritically by students of Soviet affairs. One example is Dellenbrant (1986, p. 57), who without substantiating his assertion writes: 'This theory [Williamson's] also fits the Soviet case. Regional differences were accentuated by the rapid industrialisation in the Soviet Union, and it was first around 1960, when the problem of overcentralisation was discovered, that the problems of regional development began to receive more attention.' Another example is Liebowitz (1991, p. 29), who writes: 'The Soviet Union, a state in the intermediate stage of development by Williamson's criteria, should have seen its regional gaps already on the decline. This has not yet happened.' It should be said in Liebowitz' favour, however, that he took note of Williamson's observation to the effect that the size of countries has an impact on how large the regional differences appear to be.

Thus a relatively large number of authors have discussed the Soviet Union's regional development in a comparative perspective. Williamson's method of measuring regional disparities by the coefficient of variation and his reversed U-curve have formed a benchmark. Because of the problems with statistical data, 'regional' level has usually had to be regarded as equivalent to republic level, and in fact it is only since 1956–58 that certain official figures at republic level have been more generally available.

Mainly because of lack of other data before 1956, this study is based on production data. Of course it is possible to measure many other aspects of regional disparities besides production. Numerous scholars have presented figures of regional-level agricultural production and of living standard indicators such as wages, disposable income, saving accounts, infant mortality, retail trade turnover, number of students and so forth (cf., for example, Wagener, 1972; Schroeder, 1974, 1979; Holubnychy, 1982; McAuley, 1979; Vogel, 1979; Spechler, 1979; Liebowitz, 1991). Events in the agricultural sphere are outside the scope of this chapter. As regards the various measures of living standards, these have in common the fact that, with a few isolated exceptions, data on them are only available after 1956. Until more detailed scrutinies of the archives have been made, calculations of regional disparities in living standards must be restricted to the period after Stalin.

In principle, data on production of services and their regional distribution are not to be found in collected form at all during the Soviet epoch. It seems practically self-evident that the service sector's regional variations were greater than those of industry and that data on the service sector would therefore have made the regional disparities of production greater than they appear to be on the basis of industrial production (Schiffer, 1989, p. 231).

The supply of data on industrial production (and national income produced) at regional level prior to 1956 is certainly not abundant either, but there are some compilations of data for certain years even so. Therefore, since the object of this chapter is to try to give a picture of the changes in regional disparities over the whole of the Soviet epoch, industrial production will be given pride of place. Obviously, there are other reasons for such an approach than those relating purely to sources. Production data measure the region's *own* contribution to its inhabitants' consumption, while various measures of living standards reflect mainly the desire of the central authorities for redistribution of consumption. This latter aspect will be touched on briefly at the end of the chapter.

A further limitation is that the empirical study in this chapter covers only interregional developments. As was remarked in the previous section, the supply of data at intraregional level was both sporadic and deficient, and considerable detective work is required merely in order to chart first of all what material exists or can be reconstructed.

The Problem with Different Regional Divisions

One of the few who have attempted to piece together the long-term trend of a number of socioeconomic variables at republic level is the late Ukrainian–Canadian economist Vsevolod Holubnychy. Table 1.2, which is based on data compiled by Holubnychy, shows the total industrial production per head of 13 of the 15 republics (figures for Estonia and Latvia are missing) for the years 1913, 1940, 1958 and 1965. The table shows on the one hand the enormous growth of industrial production which took place over the period of more than 50 years, although the figures may be exaggerated by the choice of index year. On the other hand the two coefficients of variation (CV) show that the relative gaps between the republics did not actually diminish at all between the year preceding the First World War and 1965. The tendency of the weighted coefficient of variation is clearly upward during the whole period, and especially in the last sub-period. The unweighted coefficient shows that the relative differences in industrial production decreased from 1913 to 1958 but that they increased thereafter. What is also interesting is that the relative gap between the Russian Republic and the average for the other republics widens greatly between 1913 and 1958, and that it only diminished very slightly up to 1965.

Table 1.2 suffers from the weakness that Latvia and Estonia, economically speaking the two most advanced republics after the Second World War, are not included. With these two republics, the coefficients of variation would definitely lie at a lower level, but they would probably have a stronger rising tendency since if anything the development of the two republics sharpened the polarisation within the Soviet Union. However, the gap between the Russian Republic and the other republics would diminish somewhat if figures for Latvia and Estonia were included in Table 1.2.

Table 1.2   Total industrial production (including small-scale industry) per head in 13 Soviet republics, 1913, 1940, 1958 and 1965, calculated in constant prices at level of 1926/27 and annual average growth rate

Republics	1913	Annual average growth (%) 1913–40	1940	Annual average growth (%) 1940–58	1958	Annual average growth (%) 1958–65	1965
Russia	130	22.6	923	14.8	3376	9.7	5671
Ukraine	120	14.1	576	10.8	1693	10.0	2884
Belarus	51	15.3	261	12.6	854	15.8	1801
Uzbekistan	67	14.6	332	4.0	572	20.2	1380
Kazakhstan	36	23.0	260	15.3	978	8.5	1560
Georgia	45	24.2	339	11.9	1067	7.8	1647
Azerbaijan	145	15.3	743	5.0	1417	3.7	1784
Lithuania	57	5.4	140	39.2	1127	17.4	2502
Moldova	25	18.2	148	22.5	748	15.7	1569
Kyrgizia	35	16.2	188	15.1	700	5.5	968
Tadzhikistan	12	18.2	71	9.0	186	12.6	350
Armenia	56	21.1	375	17.3	1540	13.6	3001
Turkmenia	39	15.4	201	8.8	520	1.8	587
CV(weighted)	0.332		0.403		0.466		0.606
CV (unweighted)	0.387		0.363		0.332		0.372

Source: Holubnychy (1982, p. 204).

Table 1.3 shows production per head of factory industry in the Russian Empire in 1908 divided into seven large regions. The regional differences are enormous, as expected, and the values of the two coefficients of variation are higher than the values for 1913 in Table 1.2. Although the data in the two tables are based on different sources and thus may have different bases of calculation, it is probable that the discrepancy for the weighted coefficient in particular is caused primarily by the fact that the divisions into regions are widely dissimilar. Whereas in Table 1.2 Russia is a unit corresponding to the Russian Soviet republic, the European parts of Russia in Table 1.3 are divided into regions which also contain other subsequent Soviet republics. The whole of Siberia and the Far East, on the other hand, is merged with the Asian republics into a single region. Despite these differences of demarcation, Table 1.3 confirms the enormous spatial differences in development which existed in the Empire when the Bolsheviks took power.

Table 1.3   Factory industry production per head (in roubles) in the Russian Empire, 1908, divided into seven large regions

Region	Production
Northwest and the Baltics	87
Central Industrial Region	78
Prievjiinskij Region	48
Southern Mountain Region	37
The Southwest	21
Rest of European Russia	19
Asian Russia	8
Total Russian Empire	*31*
CV(weighted)	0.787
CV(unweighted)	0.977

Source: Wagener (1972, p. 8).

Another division into regions appears in Table 1.4, which shows gross industrial production at current prices, divided over 19 economic regions during three years of the 1960s. Of these 19 economic regions, only three consist of republics. Russia is divided into ten regions and the Ukraine into three, but on the other hand the four central Asian republics are merged to form a single region. The three Caucasian republics too are merged to form a single region, and so are the three Baltic republics plus the Kaliningrad district. A comparison of the values for 1965 in Table 1.4 with those in Table 1.2 shows several notable differences. Production per head, measured in roubles, is more than twice as great in Table 1.2 if the three republics which appear in both tables are examined. In addition to the fact that the two tables are based on different sources it is probable that the main reason for the different levels is that Table 1.4 is calculated in current prices whereas Table 1.2 is calculated at 1926/27 prices, with upward index adjustments in 1952 and 1955.[1] However, since we are dealing here primarily with *relative* regional development, the different levels in Tables 1.2 and 1.4 are not a real problem.

Table 1.4   *Gross industrial production per head at current prices in 19 economic regions, 1960, 1965 and 1968*

Region	1960	1965	1968
Northwest Russia	1413.97	1735.01	2311.77
Central Russia	1325.92	1622.16	2197.17
Volga–Vyatka	735.49	1025.05	1503.20
Central Black Earth Region	499.42	766.30	1090.93
Volga (Povolzje)	718.98	1015.09	1445.72
North Caucasus	662.01	855.86	1157.98
Urals	971.97	1243.99	1803.95
West Siberia	646.16	915.57	1228.39
East Siberia	656.57	915.57	1310.45
Russian Far East	750.93	1015.09	1343.15
Donets–Dnepr (Ukraine)	936.06	1224.08	1610.64
Southwestern Ukraine	404.48	587.16	852.20
Southern Ukraine	682.98	925.53	1256.13
Baltic states and Kaliningrad	843.94	1253.94	1765.76
Transcaucausus	541.28	666.78	865.62
Central Asia	386.97	467.74	591.97
Kazakhstan	425.11	567.26	769.59
Belarus	481.37	726.49	1108.60
Moldova	386.02	597.11	834.04
Total USSR	*750.57*	*995.19*	*1358.13*
Max. in % of min.	366.29	370.93	390.52
Max. in % of mean	188.41	174.30	170.19
Min. in % of mean	51.43	47.00	43.59
CV (weighted)	0.429	0.382	0.379
CV (unweighted)	0.389	0.347	0.350

Source: Wagener (1972, pp. 22, 96).

Two disparities between the tables which are of greater significance, however, are that the coefficients of variation for 1965 lie at quite different levels, and that in Table 1.2 they show a rising tendency during the first half of the 1960s while in Table 1.4 they show a falling tendency. To some extent the first difference can probably be explained by the quite different regional division. It is true that the division into regions of Russia and the Ukraine shows wide differences within the two largest republics in terms of population, but these differences seem to be outweighed by the fact that the central Asian and the Caucasian republics have each been brought together in one region. For example, Table 1.2 shows that production per head in Uzbekistan in 1965 was nearly four times greater than in Tadzhikistan, whereas in Table 1.4 they are included in the same region. What remains to be explained, however, is the fact that the relative differences between the Russian Republic and the rest of the Soviet Union are considerably greater in Holubnychy's material, on which Table 1.2 is based, than in Table 1.4, which is based on Wagener's figures.

To a large extent it also seems possible to explain the differing trends of the coefficients of variation after 1958/60 in terms of differences in the regional breakdown. If the Russian and Ukrainian regions, respectively, are merged and compared with the other regions it is true that, for natural reasons, we get lower values of the coefficients of variation, *but with a slightly rising tendency*. Table 1.5 shows the different measures of dispersion recalculated for the eight large regions which then remain.

Table 1.5   Measures of dispersion of gross industrial production in eight large regions, 1960, 1965 and 1968

	1960	1965	1968
Max. in % of min.	231.42	268.08	298.29
Max. in % of mean	119.02	126.00	130.01
Min. in % of mean	51.43	47.00	43.59
CV (weighted)	0.256	0.260	0.272
CV (unweighted)	0.268	0.293	0.310

Source: Wagener (1972, p. 96).

The conclusion is that the regional breakdown had a great influence not only on the level of the relative regional disparities but also on their trends. Of course this is not really at all surprising. On the contrary, it is probably a general pattern that spatial differences can very well increase at one spatial level at the same time as they are diminishing at some other level. Different spatial classifications can thus both conceal and exaggerate existing regional differences.

Regional Disparities in Industrial Production: the Long-term Pattern

Figure 1.1 shows the coefficients of variation of the national income per head (excluding the service sector) produced in the 15 republics during the period 1956–94, based on data from five different sources. What is most interesting is the rising tendency of the coefficients of variation throughout the period 1956–94. (The fact that the coefficients appear to fall between 1978 and 1980 is probably attributable entirely to the data being taken from another source from 1980 onwards. The crucial point is that the data for the respective source show a rising tendency in all cases.) In short, it seems as though production per head, excluding the service sector, *relatively speaking* had an equal distribution between the republics in the middle of the 1950s but that thereafter the disparities only increased. In other words the very sharp increase in the disparities after the dissolution of the Soviet Union in 1991 has a long prehistory.

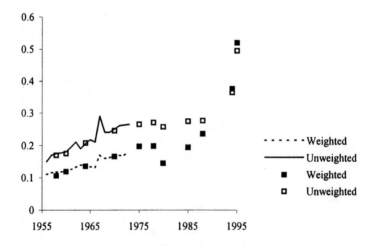

Sources: Lines, Olsson (1980, p. 309); spots, 1958–78: Spechler (1979 p. 26), 1980–88: Liebowitz (1991, p. 22), 1992: *Encyclopaedia Britannica* (1995), 1994: *CIA World Factbook* (www.odci.gov/cia/publications/95fact/index.html).

*Figure 1.1   Coefficients of variation of the national income per head
produced in the 15 republics, 1956–94*

A relatively coherent preliminary picture of the regional disparities at republic level during the Soviet epoch can thus be obtained with the help of the data in Table 1.2. Figure 1.2 summarises weighted and unweighted coefficients of variation for the period 1913–65. As has already been remarked, it is extremely interesting that the coefficients of variation do not display any clear tendency until after 1958. The fact that the unweighted coefficient of variation diminishes somewhat between 1913 and 1958 must be interpreted to mean that the small and economically 'backward' republics received investment which enabled them actually to reduce some of the advantage in production enjoyed by the Russian and other advanced republics. On the other hand, however, the fact that the weighted coefficient – in which the populous Russian Republic is weighted more heavily – rises slightly during the same period is a sign that the heaviest investment in the periphery took place *within* the Russian Republic, that is, in the Urals and Siberia.

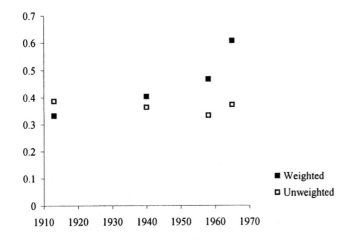

Source: Holubnychy (1982, p. 204).

Figure 1.2   Coefficients of variation of the total industrial production in 13 of the 15 republics, certain years, 1913–65

The increase during 1958–65 corroborates the increase which, according to Figure 1.1, had been going on since at least 1956. The removal of no fewer than 1523 industrial enterprises eastwards from 22 June 1941, the date of the attack by Nazi Germany, until November of that same year obviously implies a large-scale redistribution of production capacity between the centre and the periphery, which had lasting consequences. The major part of these relocations took place within Russia, however, so that it is uncertain how strongly the proportion between the republics was affected by the transfers of industries. However, the extensive destruction that occurred in Belarus, the Ukraine, western Russia and other parts of the western Union of Soviet Socialist Republics makes it extremely probable that the closing years of the war will have exhibited the lowest differences of production per head between the republics. The fourth Five-Year Plan of 1945–50 restored in principle the Soviet Union's production levels of 1940/41. Once reconstruction of the war-ravaged tracts of the Soviet Union had got under way, recovery in the western republics probably meant that the disparities between republics began to widen. But the question which this report will be unable to answer is whether the increased disparities amounted to a trend after 1945 and whether developments from 1956 onwards signify only a continuation of this long-term trend, or whether the recovery was followed by a number of years with stable ratios between the production capacities of the republics before the disparities between them began increasing steadily in the first half of the 1950s.

In a discussion on regional development in a command economy, it is of course impossible to neglect the command system. The five-year plans introduced in 1928 signified the start of the centralist policy in which sectoral questions came wholly to predominate over regional (Nove, 1986). The main features of this policy remained unchanged right through to the dissolution of the Soviet state, although a temporary and partial alteration of course did occur during the Khrushchev era (Shaw, 1985).

The aim of holding together a state comprising more than 100 nationalities had the effect of accentuating the centralising feature of the planned economy. On this view, all direct links between individual economic enterprises or regions implied a weakening of the central state and therefore of the Soviet Union. The Soviet method of securing control by the central power came to form one of the system's paradoxes: that which Nove (1977, p. 74) termed 'centralised pluralism' and consisted in the autarky of each respective ministry (Schiffer, 1989). 'Unable to rely wholly on other ministries for their supplies, each ministry tends to build its own supply system. ... Ministries fail to co-operate in the development and use of infrastructure, in resource exploitation, in production and research processes, and so on' (Shaw, 1985, pp. 403–4).

The spatially redistributable resources consisted of capital and labour. Raw materials, on the other hand, were locked in their geographical positions, and this trivial fact came to shape the methodology of Soviet regional policy. Simply expressed, what it amounted to was industrialisation by shifting labour and capital to where the raw materials were so as to extract them. From the centralist planning perspective in which 'everything' could be – and ought to be – controlled, economic growth became synonymous in some respects with territorial expansion. Growth via spatial expansion, in contradistinction to spatial concentration and more efficient exploitation of resources, may be said from this standpoint to have been the principal method of the Soviet Union's economic policy.

What has been said above may seem paradoxical, for of course a fundamental thesis of the ideology of the planned economy was precisely the idea of concentrating the means of production into efficient large-scale units, which were considered to be superior to the disharmonious and planless system of capitalism. This argument was applied particularly to the agricultural field, in which large-scale production in kolkhozy and sovkhozy was opposed to the irrationality of small-scale farming.

In order to elucidate these contradictions it is important to distinguish different levels of the policy adopted. At the *intra*regional level it can clearly be said that the planned economy concentration thesis was pursued. Agriculture was collectivised in large units and the industrialisation strategy was deliberately aligned towards the creation of few but large urban centres in each respective region, with few but large factories (Dyker, 1983). In terms of the *orientation of production*, too, there were tendencies towards concentration, especially in the case of heavy industry. An increased regional specialisation of production was in accordance with the socialist division of labour, which could be driven to such extremes that certain products were manufactured in only a single factory in the entire Soviet Union. At the intraregional and sectoral level it may be said that *space in itself* was re-garded as an obstacle to be eliminated. Space was an obstacle to planning and coordination, the control and direction of the socialist state. Therefore the achievement of the Soviet state's goals was facilitated by means of maximum intraregional and sectoral concentration.

However, it was impossible to apply the concentration principle at the *inter*regional level. The reasons for this have already been alluded to above. In the first place it would further reinforce the differences between the developed and underdeveloped parts of the Soviet Union and thus prepare the ground for the same problems to flare up as had plagued the European colonial powers, namely separatist and nationalist aspirations which in the long run would threaten the integrity of the Union. Secondly, but no less important, the Second World War had demonstrated the untenability from the defence standpoint of having the bulk of the Soviet Union's industries located in its western parts, which would be most under threat in the event of any new war. In the third place, raw materials and power resources were dispersed, and exploitation of them was regarded as a fundamental prerequisite of economic growth conditional on the diffusion of labour and capital.

The consequence was that the Soviet Union's economic geography broadly speaking came to be built up on the basis of a spatial concentration principle at intraregional and sectoral level but of a spatial dispersion principle at interregional level. This dichotomy can be discussed in terms of industrial–centralist organisational principles and networks respectively. The traditional socialist criticism of capitalism can be said to have been based in many respects on capitalism's alleged inefficiency when it came to taking advantage of the possibilities opened up by industrialisation. Socialism accordingly signified 'more' and 'better' industrialism inasmuch as feudal and petty bourgeois remnants would be abolished. In other words it became the task of the Soviet state to develop the 'progressive' aspects of industrialism such as the 'social character of production' by strengthening the hierarchical and centralist elements while also combating the 'backward' aspects of capitalism such as the 'anarchistic, unplanned market'. With the answer book in our hand we can show today that the Soviet Union took over an organisational principle which was certainly refined and developed under industrialism but in reality was founded on hierarchical principles rooted both in the slave society of antiquity and in the feudal system. But the feature of industrialism which was really novel from the organisational standpoint, the setting free of the market with its uncontrollable network of numberless transactions, was resisted. In this respect the Soviet Union in fact became a caricature of the backward aspects of industrialism at the same time as the possibilities of dynamic change were suppressed.

At the same time as the Soviet Union was pushing the hierarchical–centralist aspects of industrialism to the point of absurdity – in large measure in spatial respects as well at the intraregional level – there were, as has already been remarked, vital reasons of *realpolitik* for the 'decentralist' policy which was pursued at interregional level. However, if this 'decentralisation' was not to degenerate into independent local/regional development processes, it was necessary for the ties between centre and periphery to be knotted very strongly, through extreme specialisation of production, for example, but most of all through strict production quotas and delivery obligations in which everything was controlled by and redistributed via the central planning apparatus. The strongly sectoral character of the economic and organisational networks which evolved as a result of the ministries' autarky contributed strongly to the preservation of power at the centre and headed off any tendencies for local market-oriented networks to arise. Although the sectoral policy featuring ministerial autarky was successful in that it preserved central control of the economy, from the centralisation perspective it must nevertheless be regarded as a half-measure and a sign of inadequate control over the planning process (Shaw, 1985, p. 408).

At this point it is important to notice that the centralist sector policy's 'successful' battle against local/regional markets was so successful precisely because the network of capitalist markets was so underdeveloped in Russia and most other parts of the former Czarist empire. Even though socialism distorted economic forces in Eastern Europe seriously after 1945, the majority of these countries did have a capitalist tradition which to a large extent was lacking in Russia. This historical legacy did admittedly enable Eastern Europe to be 'socialised', but not 'sovietised', and today means that the conditions for a rapid and successful development of the market economy are probably considerably greater there than in most of the former Soviet Union.

An explanation for the break in the trend in the development of regional disparities is bound up with how significant Stalin's death and the destalinisation process were. If it is the case that the end of the Second World War constitutes the actual break in the trend, the most plausible interpretation is that the period 1913–45 was a single protracted period of war, terror and chaos in which economic progress was hampered by one shock after another. The end of the war then marks the inception of some sort of 'normalisation' when regional disparities began to increase as they are expected to do during a process of industrialisation.

If what happened instead was that the break in the trend occurred during the first half of the 1950s, this was probably connected with the more liberal economic development which followed Stalin's death. This latter interpretation makes the early five-year plans something more than widespread anti-peasant terror and economic chaos; they also formed an 'unbalanced' industrialisation process, based on centrally controlled, planned exploitation of raw materials and taking place outside the districts containing the old industrial nuclei. The absence, at inter-republic level, of the expected industrial concentration process becomes in this way a consequence not of repeated shocks but of the fact that industrialisation did not take place in accordance with the allocation mechanisms of market economics.

However, if the latter interpretation is correct, a new question presents itself: why did destalinisation necessarily signify a trend-like widening of disparities between the republics? In other words, it is not a question of seeking explanations for the growing regional disparities in general but for the disparities seeming to have begun growing at precisely this point in time. Thus explanations which in themselves are important sub-components, but which were barely starting to become operative just then, find themselves outside the frame. Among them, for example, are the demographic trends operating over the long term which are emphasised by several authors (for example, Schiffer, 1989, pp. 237–9; Dellenbrant, 1986, p. 147). The Muslim-dominated republics of Central Asia have long had a more rapid increase of population than the other republics, and this has had a directly depressing effect on production per head.

Probably the most important explanation for the break in the trend is the fact that the 'strategy' which formerly explained the *absence* of concentration, namely the unbalanced, centrally controlled exploitation of raw materials, could no longer be pushed on in its extremely unbalanced form. Calls for a diversification of the economy were growing, from a population which was demanding consumer goods after decades of sacrifice, but gradually the extremely unbalanced orientation of heavy industry also became in itself an obstacle to growth. The purpose of an unbalanced growth strategy on the lines of Hirschman's (1958) model may be expressed in simple terms as being 'that imbalance creates its counter-forces, which bring about balance at a higher level': that the growth branches create demand for the products of other branches, which causes the economy to move towards a (theoretical) equilibrium point between (for example) heavy and light industry. However, the Soviet planned economy to a large extent lacked these counterbalancing forces precisely because it was a planned economy which had very little need to take account of the demand forces at work in the nation. As long as 'all' that mattered was to produce coal and steel, the Soviet methods were extremely effective wherever they were applied in the Soviet Union. However, when it came to taking the next step, that is to creating diffusion effects, to diversifying the economy, the command economy became the worst enemy of economic progress.

The balancing phase of the economy simply proved to have a different spatial pattern from that of the preliminary diffusion phase. The Soviet economy was based on the principles of large scale, and for both political and economic reasons the balancing and diversification of the economy became concentrated on the largest urban regions, with Moscow in the lead. While the industrialisation of Siberia and the peripheral republics was governed by the incidence of raw materials and therefore became diffused geographically, the concentration of population and therefore (actual) demand was the most important factor underlying the localisation of the consumer goods industries and service sector.

According to this interpretation, in other words, the growing differences between the republics' production per head from the first half of the 1950s onwards would be a consequence of the fact that stage two of the unbalanced industrialisation by no means wielded the same propulsive forces for spatial diffusion as stage one had done. In spatial respects this meant that the local and regional diffusion effects from the new industries in the peripheral regions were less than they would have been in an economy in which the market had greater influence. The concentration of power in Moscow and the centrally controlled redistribution of resources for investment which took place in the Soviet economy were key factors in this process. It has also been shown that the command system failed to diffuse new technology across regions. Rates of diffusion of new technology within an industry were much slower in the Soviet Union than in industrialised Western countries (Amann et al., 1977; Escoe, 1995).

The long-term territorial planning which, admittedly, was developed from the 1960s onwards counted for little compared with the dominant short-term sectoral planning which sought, within each respective sector/ministry, to meet the set targets in a rational manner, given the irrationality of the system. The ministry in question would invest mainly where the biggest return was to be expected, and often this meant in the biggest towns, because of such factors as advantages of scale, availability of labour and possibilities for using existing infrastructure (Schiffer, 1989, *passim*; Dyker, 1983, p. 45; Pallot and Shaw, 1981, p. 224). In those instances where the investment had in view the exploitation of raw materials outside urban centres, ministerial autarky made for one-sided local/regional economies with a low degree of diversification. The traditional unbalanced Soviet investment strategy with its one-sided investment in heavy industry was therefore reinforced in spatial respects by the almost non-existent coordination between ministries and the absence of the above-cited intersectoral diffusion effects at local and regional level (Schiffer, 1989, *passim*). The general structural imbalances of the economy were accordingly supplemented by extreme spatial imbalances between and within the regions (cf. Dyker, 1983, p. 48). Even the much-discussed Territorial Production Complexes became in reality mere paper constructions within which each respective ministry minded its own business (Shaw, 1985, p. 408; de Souza, 1989).

But there is also cause to wonder whether there are other reasons for the increased disparities between the republics. One aspect of these reasons has been adduced above: the substantially higher birth rate in the Muslim-dominated republics. On a more general plane this might be expressed as a variant on the hypothesis of lack of 'industrial culture' which is often invoked to explain absence of economic growth in the Third World. The fact that the industrialisation of Siberia and the peripheral republics was pushed forward from above and administered in large part by Russians may have made native ethnic groups less interested in accepting to the full the industrial tradition brought by the 'foreigners'. One sign of this may be that a considerably larger proportion of the less developed republics' investment went into agriculture and other non-industrial sectors of the economy compared with the way investment was distributed in the leading regions. As a consequence of this, there are also great differences between the republics in the distribution of labour between the sectors. Whereas the Russian Republic in 1987 had 42 per cent of its labour force employed in industry and 14 per cent in agriculture, the proportions in Turkmenia, for example, were 21 per cent in industry and 41 per cent in agriculture (Liebowitz, 1991, p. 27).

Another consequence for the less developed republics was that immigrant Russians came to form a significantly larger part of the industrial workforce than of the population as a whole. In 1979 Tadzhiks formed 59 per cent of the population of Tadzhikistan but only 48 per cent of the industrial workers. In the most advanced industries Tadzhiks formed only 28 per cent of the workforce (Bromlei and Shkaratan, 1983, pp. 38ff., cited from Dellenbrant, 1986, p. 159f.). In Kyrgizia in 1988 the industrial workforce included only 25 per cent Kirghiz, whereas the latter formed 52 per cent of the population (Liebowitz, 1991, p. 27; *CIA World Factbook*, 1995).

In line with the above explanation it may be argued that in large parts of Siberia the native ethnic groups have been small, thereby making their attitude to the Russian 'industrial colonisation' devoid of significance. The fact that the industrialisation of Siberia can be described as an 'internal Russian' process ought in that case to have meant fewer problems than the industrialisation of the non-Russian republics. This ought also to have been a contributory factor in the growing gaps between the republics.

The hypothesis of lack of industrial tradition in the non-Russian Asiatic republics naturally cannot have validity only from the beginning of the 1950s. It can be argued, however, that the absence of industrial tradition ought to have a greater effect at the transition to stage two of Soviet industrialisation than the command-style forcing through of stage one. The more advanced the industry and the more diversified the economy, the greater the need for labour with high 'industrial culture'. Lydolph (1979, p. 472) has remarked, for example, that Soviet industry exhibits two spatially separated growth patterns: one with a concentration of 'skill-intensive' manufacturing in Moscow, Leningrad and the Baltic states, and another pattern with a growth of 'extractive industries' in Siberia and Central Asia.

The analysis so far has been carried out with the republics as regions. As has been observed, this division suffers from one weakness, the differing sizes of the republics in both geographical and population terms. In order to remedy this in some degree, alternative calculations of the coefficients of variation have been carried out in which the Russian Republic has been split up and the aggregate number of regions has been taken as 7 and 18 units, respectively.[2] The latter regional breakdown, into 18 regions, is the one officially applied during the 1960s. Figure 1.3 shows the changes in regional disparities in certain years from 1940 to 1975 with a breakdown into 18 regions. Figure 1.4 shows the corresponding changes from 1908 to 1975 with a breakdown into 7 regions with the whole of the Asiatic part of the Soviet Union forming one region. It should be stressed that the division into 7 regions in Figure 1.4 is not wholly consistent between 1908 and the other years.

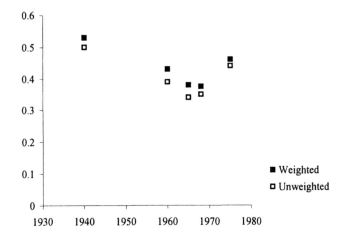

Sources: 1940: calculations based on Wagener (1972, p. 96) and Holubnychy (1982, p. 291); 1960–68: Wagener (1972, p. 96); 1975: Pallot and Shaw (1981, p. 160).

Figure 1.3   Coefficients of variation of the per capita national income in 18 economic regions, certain years, 1940–75

The two figures exhibit a similar pattern. The regional disparities show a declining trend until the middle of the 1960s and after that begin to rise. Thus the figures confirm the general picture of diminishing disparities as the analysis at the republic level showed, but with the crucial difference that the turning point at the 7- and 18-region level is not reached until the middle of the 1960s, that is a decade later than the turning point was reached at republic level. One reason for this difference might be that, up to the 1960s, the growth in the Asiatic republics (West and East Siberia and the Far East) belonging to the Russian Republic have an equalising effect on the disparities at regional level, while this growth took place within the Russian Republic and was therefore already contributing to increased disparities between the republics from the 1950s onwards.

A couple of conceivable contributory explanations for the sudden switch from diminishing to increasing regional disparities have already been discussed above. (The problem of spatially balancing an unbalanced growth strategy in combination with spatial differences of 'industrial tradition'.) A more direct explanation, however, might be that the spatial distribution of investment causes the spatial differences in production. Is it the case that, until the 1950s or 1960s, priority in investment was given to the less developed regions/republics and that thereafter it was directed increasingly towards the more developed regions? How has the distribution of investment between the regions/republics changed on the whole over time?

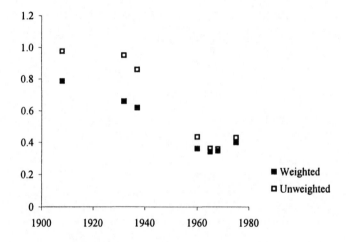

Sources: 1908: Wagener (1972, p. 8); 1932 and 1937: Tsaplin (1990, p. 81); 1960–75: Pallot and Shaw (1981, p. 160).

*Figure 1.4   Coefficients of variation of the per capita national income in
            seven large regions, certain years, 1908–75*

The answer is that both the relative distribution of investment and the relative distribution of production between the republics, expressed per head, have been very stable over time and that there is a clear covariance between the rankings of the two variables. Table 1.6 shows the republics' ranking with

Table 1.6   The republics ranked according to size of investment and production per head

Republic	Investment 1928–32	Investment 1946–50	Investment 1956–60	Investment 1970	Investment 1982	Ind. prod. 1940	Produced NI 1956	Produced NI 1967	Net Material Product 1978
Russia	1	3	2	4	1	1	4	3	3
Ukraine	3	5	4	9	11	3	6	5	6
Belarus	9	10	13	8	7	7	15	6	5
Uzbekistan	10	14	14	11	13	6	13	13	14
Kazakhstan	6	8	1	2	3	8	5	9	7
Georgia	5	4	12	13	8	5	12	11	10
Azerbaijan	2	2	6	14	12	2	7	12	11
Lithuania	–	12	6	6	5	–	8	4	4
Moldova	12	15	15	10	9	11	9	8	9
Kyrgizia	11	12	10	12	14	10	11	10	13
Tadzhikistan	5	12	10	15	15	12	14	14	15
Armenia	8	9	10	7	11	4	10	15	8
Turkmenia	8	7	8	5	6	9	3	7	12
Latvia	–	6	6	3	2	–	2	2	1
Estonia	–	1	3	1	4	–	1	1	2

Sources: Holubnychy (1982, pp. 204, 214), Dellenbrant (1986, p. 146), Olsson (1980, p. 309), Pallot and Shaw (1981).

respect to the two variables for selected years from the first Five-Year Plan to 1982. Russia and the Baltic republics are usually at the top of the rankings and the Central Asiatic republics (except Turkmenia) usually at the bottom. Caucasian republics such as Georgia and Azerbaijan have fallen in ranking, as regards both investment and production. With some exceptions, such as Kazakhstan, agreement between the republics' ranking for investment and production respectively is very good at adjoining points in time.

As was pointed out above, the distribution of investment was done on a sectoral base through the ministries. However, the investment was not solely directed by rational yield requirements. The long-term stability of the allocation of the investments between the regions should to a certain extent be explained by the regions' political strength. Both in the Soviet Union and in other command economies such as Poland, the strong industrial regions have traditionally had stronger political positions compared with, for example agricultural regions (Kowalski, 1986). The distribution of investment between the republics therefore appears capable of helping to explain the differences between their outputs during the periods both of declining and rising regional disparities, but on the other hand *the distribution of investment cannot explain the break in trend.* The results in Table 1.6 really show that, if the distribution of investment between the republics was crucial to the production disparities, these would not have changed appreciably during the Soviet epoch.

One factor with a strong link to the 'main explanation' cited above (transition from structurally unbalanced to balanced growth strategy) is the spatial disparities of productivity, generally speaking and during various structural phases. It is a plausible assumption that the productivity differences during the unbalanced, extensively raw material-exploiting phase were determined in large part by raw material concentration and accessibility, of which the first factor is given by Nature while the second factor is influenced by the society's technical level and degree of infrastructure development. When the economic structure was developed step by step in a more balanced direction, the Nature-given factor declined in significance and the productivity differences came to be determined more and more by the relative development of the infrastructure.

Historical data on productivity at the republic or other regional level are of very sparse occurrence. At all events Table 1.7 shows the ratio of value added per head and industrial fixed capital per head, and how the 18 economic regions ranked according to this criterion in 1975. The Far East and East Siberia are the regions which have the highest capital stock per inhabitant, but only Central Asia and Kazakhstan show lower capital productivity than theirs. It is unclear whether physical infrastructure is included in fixed capital in the table, but to the extent that this is so, there is no doubt that, because of indivisibilities, the infrastructure becomes considerable dearer per inhabitant in sparsely populated regions compared with densely populated ones. Investment in peripheral regions such as the Far East and East Siberia accordingly give low returns per inhabitant on capital, and it has therefore been confined mainly to branches enjoying comparative advantages compared with other regions: wood processing, ferrous metallurgical and chemical/petrochemical activities; that is, 'extractive activity which necessitates large initial investments in productive fixed assets and infrastructure' (Schiffer, 1989, p. 177). In like manner the diversification of the economy ought to have developed furthest where the infrastructure has been most developed. The results in Table 1.7 thus support the hypothesis that the swing from imbalance to balance in the economy aggravated disparities between the regions.

Table 1.7   Ratio of value added per head to industrial fixed capital per head, and fixed capital per head by region, 1975

Region	Ratio value added/ fixed capital	Rank	Fixed capital per head
Northwest Russia	0.21	7	3947
Central Russia	0.31	2	3102
Volga–Vyatka	0.40	1	2401
Central Black Earth	0.18	9	2304
Volga	0.14	13	3478
North Caucasus	0.16	12	2354
Urals	0.24	6	3187
West Siberia	0.16	12	3981
East Siberia	0.11	15	4560
Far East	0.10	16	5145
Donets–Dnepr	0.18	8	3270
Southwestern Ukraine	0.30	3	1577
Southern Ukraine	0.17	10	2537
Baltic republics	0.25	5	2734
Transcaucasus	0.12	14	1958
Central Asia	0.09	17	1690
Kazakhstan	0.07	18	3308
Belarus	0.27	4	2314

Source: Lydolph (1979, pp. 208, 212, 470 and 473).

The regions with both the lowest and the highest capital productivity of the whole USSR are parts of the Russian Republic, which means that the great regional disparities are equalised at republic level. In other words, the high aggregated values for the Russian Republic conceal a productivity in the Asiatic part of the republic which, relatively speaking, is very low. Table 1.7 may thus help to explain the problem of why the disparities in industrial production and national income start to increase at republic level from as early as the beginning of the 1950s, whereas at regional level a corresponding process does not start until the closing years of the 1960s. Properly speaking, the large-scale investment in Asiatic Russia gave low returns compared with the capital committed, but it still increased production per head in those areas. A factor which in all probability signified reduced growth for the Russian Republic as a whole still helped in the direction of continued equalisation between the regions. Why the disparities between the regions nevertheless began to widen around 1970 cannot be fully explained without more detailed study, but if the low capital productivity of the whole Asiatic part of the Soviet Union was not compensated by increasing investment, sooner or later it must of course have resulted in a slackening, relatively speaking, of progress in production per head and thus in growing disparities. In other words, the explanation could be that investment in the Asiatic regions could not in the long run match and compensate for the disparities in productivity.

As was observed earlier in this chapter, the regional disparities in the USSR can also be evaluated, for example, on the basis of various measures of living standards. Scholars who have tackled these questions have ascertained that, as far as the available source material extends (from about 1960), disparities in wages and educational facilities have lain at a considerably lower level than production disparities, and that the disparities in wages and educational facilities were *declining* right up to the 1980s (cf., for example, Spechler, 1979; Liebowitz, 1991). The variations in infant mortality, housing outlays, retail trade and saving accounts, however, show greater disparities between the republics than in production, and in most cases these disparities increased after 1960 (Liebowitz, 1991). It is unclear how long a tradition the transfers of resources from more to less developed republics and regions have, but it is probable that their importance to the Union's solidarity was enhanced when the disparities of production within the Union began to rise. It seems as though Soviet leaders after Stalin increasingly sought to alleviate the interregional socioeconomic tensions within the Union by employing the guidance mechanisms directly under their control; that is consumption possibilities rather than production opportunities (cf. Schiffer, 1989, pp. 234–5 and 238). Other aspects of living standards, however, did not form the subject of the same equalisation policy.

Objections and Conclusions

Before summing up this section it is advisable to refer again to one of the problems discussed in the previous section, the extent to which non-market pricing and Soviet methods of indexation may be considered to have influenced the results. Because this study did not include time series but was based mainly on prices at the respective points in time, the indexation problems have been avoided for the most part. But there remains the question of non-market pricing and whether changes in relative price levels between, for example, production goods and consumption goods industries are reflected as changes in the regional production values. In short, can the shift from diminishing to increasing regional disparities be caused by price changes and thus be merely illusory?

Earlier literature has scarcely touched on the question. But there are two circumstances associated with the problem which ought to be emphasised. On the one hand it can be asserted that the Soviet method of estimating the net material product (NMP) of the regions gives a certain degree of upward bias, for example to regions with a higher than average proportion of light industry (Schiffer, 1989, p. 232). This helps to exaggerate the regional disparities, in the same way as the absence of data on the service sector understates the disparities, but ought not of itself to have any effect on the changes in regional disparities over time *unless the regional distribution of light and heavy industry is changed*. On the other hand it must be observed that the price reform of 1967 clearly favoured regions with a large proportion of heavy industrial activities. The effects of this are not entirely easy to judge, however. The interregional production disparities ought to diminish in the short term as a result of relative price changes, but in the longer term the cost-raising effects of the price reform must also carry weight. Dearer bulk goods may have had a moderating effect on the desire of ministries to invest in manufacturing industries in peripheral raw material-exploiting regions (ibid., pp. 96–9).

Altogether, then, we can say that the methods of calculating NMP and relative changes in administrative prices may well have had some effect on regional production disparities as they have been measured in this study, sometimes reinforcing and sometimes moderating them, but that there are no indications of these factors having caused the break in trend from diminishing to increasing regional disparities or of their having been the chief driving force during the period when regional disparities were rising.

The conclusion reached in this chapter is that, because of a time perspective which was too short, earlier studies have interpreted the changes in regional production disparities in the Soviet Union erroneously in terms of Williamson's U-curve. The unique aspect of the Soviet Union's regional development is missed entirely, namely the fact that *the regional disparities diminished during the earliest phase of industrialisation and that they began to increase when the economy moved into a, structurally speaking, 'balanced' phase.*[3]

What happened in the Soviet Union may therefore be characterised as paradoxical when it is compared with both the neoclassical theory's equalisation, which Williamson takes as his theoretical foundation, and Myrdal's self-reinforcing polarisation. *Imbalance of economic structure went hand in hand with regional equalisation, while the shift towards a balanced economic structure brought increased regional disparities.*

THE SOVIET PARADOX IN AN INTERNATIONAL COMPARISON

As we have found above, Williamson had no misgivings about also applying his theory to a command economy such as that of the Soviet Union since he took it for granted that the goal of growth received priority there, too. Consequently, the U-curve would stand 'above' the issue of social system. There is no lack of arguments against such an approach. During the harshest decades of the command economy it seems as though strong economic growth and regional convergence actually went hand in hand – wholly contrary to both theory and practice in other countries – and that *this was not the result of a deliberate regional policy* but an incidental effect of the unbalanced industrialisation strategy. This could only indicate that the Soviet Union was a very special case.

On the other hand the development pattern in the USSR from the 1950s and onwards indicates that even the command economy failed to decrease the regional production gaps when the economy turned more diversified. As in the West, the Soviet Union adopted means for levelling the standard of living between the regions, when the new 'production forces' were concentrated in certain regions.

The results in this chapter probably show with all the clarity one could wish the great methodological problems entailed in comparing regional disparities between countries when even the disparities within the USSR are on quite different levels depending on the regional division used. However, the question is how this conclusion stands up in face of the arguments for 'the Soviet paradox'. If the Soviet Union was too big and had regions which were too big for the coefficient of variation to be capable of direct comparison with those of other European countries, what real grounds are there for holding the Soviet paradox to be a result raised above criticism? The statement on a Soviet paradox may partly be examined in a comparative way. Even though it is impossible to compare coefficients of variation between countries at a given point in time without making corrections for the effects of a number of different variables, it is considerably less problematical to compare long-term developmental *tendencies*, that is whether the coefficients of variation increase or decrease over time, regardless of their level, which of course is determined by, for example, the regional division and the size of the nation.

One question which Williamson did not touch on in detail was whether the U-curve was to be regarded as a phenomenon only within *individual nations* or whether it might also be applicable to studies of the development of national differences within a *group of nations*. In principle there ought to be no objections to employing Williamson's theory in the latter case as well. The industrialisation process has evolved unevenly between nations just as it has within nations, and trade and factor mobility have assisted equalisation between countries in the same way as they have gradually begun to even out the regional disparities within a country. Protectionism and other frontier obstacles obviously may have retarded the processes at international level, but they have definitely not prevented them.

Since the Soviet Union, because of its size and extreme regional disparities when it came into existence, does not lend itself to comparison with any other single country, there should be no impediments in principle to comparing the course of events in the Soviet Union command economy with a grouping of market economy countries which *to some extent* is comparable to the USSR in terms of size and differences of developmental level at the start of the 20th century. The British Empire and Commonwealth has been selected to this end, partly because no important frontier barriers existed within the Empire and Commonwealth.

However, it is important to stress the reservation 'to some extent', since it is possible without detailed study to point a finger at two important differences between the two empires, beside the social systems. First, the Russian Empire and later Soviet Union consisted of a connected landmass whereas the British Empire's possessions and dependencies were separated by the oceans of the world. Second, Great Britain at the turn of the century was an old-established industrial nation with high production per head. Russia at that time had only a few large industrial centres, while agriculture continued to dominate the economy. Because Great Britain had reached a higher industrial level than Russia's key areas while the developmental level of the respective empires' possessions are comparable in their broad features, the disparities within the British Empire ought to be larger than within the Russian (if a measurement based on an equivalent regional division were possible). Moreover, according to the theory on which the U-curve is based, the fact that Great Britain was already a 'mature' industrial nation at the turn of the century ought to mean that the disparities within the British Empire diminish as industrialism is diffused within the Empire (and over the world). In Russia/the Soviet Union, on the other hand, the disparities ought to increase before the key areas have 'matured' and a spatial diffusion of industrialisation has taken place.

As has been shown earlier, developments in Russia/the Soviet Union differed from those expected by the theory. How, then, did the disparities in the British Empire and Commonwealth develop during the 20th century? Figure 1.5 shows weighted and unweighted coefficients of variation for GNP per capita in 15 countries of the Empire between 1900 and 1990. The coefficients of variation lie at a considerably higher level than for the Soviet Union, but, as has been pointed out, this cannot in itself be taken as evidence that the disparities were really so much greater in the British Empire and Commonwealth. This being so, what is more interesting is that the disparities within the Empire and Commonwealth were increasing all the time. The sole exception is that the weighted value levels off and actually diminishes somewhat during the 1980s. It is possible that this will show itself to be the historical turning point for the disparities within this 'empire'. However, this possible change of direction was preceded by a long period of growing disparities, which shows that equalisation within an 'empire' is a considerably more protracted and complex process than it is within a country. This latter conclusion makes developments within the Soviet Union even more remarkable.

Many have played with thoughts of what would have happened if the October revolution had failed and how the history of the 20th century would have turned out in that case. How would Russia and other parts of the former Soviet Union have looked today if they had continued on the capitalist road even after 1917? Of course it is impossible to give conclusive answers to such questions. As regards the question under consideration in the present study, however, it seems more or less beyond doubt that the regional disparities would have developed differently from the way they actually did. All the indications are that there would have been increased polarisation in the same way as happened in the British Empire. It is not improbable that the western parts would have been at an average European economic level, while the level of the less developed parts of the former Soviet Union would have been considerably lower than it actually is today. When all is said and done, in 1992 the least developed republics of the former Soviet Union, the central

Asiatic republics, on average had a higher GNP per head than Albania and Egypt, twice that of Pakistan and nearly three times that of India, to cite some examples (*Encyclopaedia Britannica*, 1995).

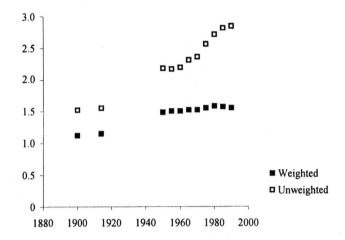

Source: Maddison (1995). The 15 states are UK, Ireland, Canada, Australia, New Zealand, Egypt, Nigeria, Kenya, South Africa, Tanzania, Ghana, Pakistan, Bangladesh, Burma and India.

Figure 1.5   Coefficients of variation for GNP per capita in 15 countries of the British Empire/Commonwealth, 1900–90

CONCLUDING REMARKS

In the long run, the uneven spatial distribution of the 'productive forces' became a factor weightier than the strongest planning apparatus the world has ever seen. In the light of the results presented in this chapter, however, there is cause to emphasise the importance of 'the strongest planning apparatus the world has ever seen'. During the harshest decades of the command economy it seems as though strong economic growth and regional convergence actually went hand in hand – wholly contrary to both theory and practice in other countries – and that this was not the result of a deliberate regional policy but an incidental effect of the unbalanced industrialisation strategy.

In this respect the economic events of the Stalin epoch are still an almost unresearched field, and there is no doubt that future studies will be able to shed a clearer light on the various phases and developmental features of the Soviet paradox, and probably to modify some of the conclusions drawn here.

We know that Soviet policy had an extremely high price: liquidation of the kulaks, not just as a class but in the downright physical sense, a backward agriculture and an unbalanced economy in general, the Gulag archipelago and other forms of persecution of political opponents, unimaginable environmental devastation in some places, and so on and so forth. The socialist system having collapsed and class and regional disparities now apparently running amok, naturally the questions crowd forward, demanding answers. Was this high price paid for nothing? Were all the sacrifices in vain? Must that long polarisation process on the social and spatial planes, which the command economy prevented during the first half of the 20th century, now be suffered to the full? Or has the policy which lifted the poorly developed Asiatic regions to levels of production and education clearly higher than those of their Asiatic neighbours at any rate laid the groundwork for continued economic growth under the market economy?

If, over and above these questions, we set the realisation that the U-curve and, in truth, all other theories of social and spatial convergence and divergence were formulated in the industrial society which for the last couple of decades has been in course of rapid transformation through developments in data and information technology and construction of new networks, it is obvious that the study of both the historical and the current regional developmental processes of the former Soviet Union have many interesting and burning questions to answer.

NOTES

1. For a more detailed account of how the figures in the two tables are produced, see Holubnychy (1982, p. 203) and Wagener (1972, pp. 93f).
2. The regions are those presented in Tables 1.3 and 1.4, with the exception of the Baltic States and Kaliningrad in the latter table.
3. It should be added that, after the presentation of the first version of this chapter (February 1996), Dmitrieva (1996) has published results for the republic level, supporting this conclusion. However, she does not discuss the results in the context used here and does not seek explanations for the trend shift.

2. Soviet regional policy

Boris Shtoulberg, Aleko Adamesku, V.V. Khistanov and Murat Albegov

MAIN STAGES OF REGIONAL POLICY

The vastness of the Soviet Union's territories and the diversity of its natural and climatic conditions invest regional policy with a special importance. So also do its disparities of natural resources and the contrasts to be found between the national and sociohistorical characteristics of the various regions. Four main problems addressed by the official regional policy of the USSR throughout its history may be specified. A general task in the economic sphere was to develop the rich resources of the eastern regions. A major problem in this was the spatial gap between the raw materials and energy resources, which were concentrated mainly in Siberia and Kazakhstan, and the processing industries centred historically in the Urals, St Petersburg and Moscow regions.

The main task in the political sphere was deemed to be the fostering of industrial development in agricultural regions and the establishment of an adequate proletarian sub-class. From the standpoint of nation building, the main concern was to strengthen the centralised state on the basis of a national and territorial structure. The central government was to play the key role in this. And finally, defence doctrine was predicated on a military posture that included the dispersal of industrial potential and the duplication of basic industries in regions located at a sufficient distance from the frontiers with potential enemies.

The whole 70-year period of the USSR's existence may be divided, somewhat tentatively, into six stages differing quite significantly in terms of regional policy. What is striking about these stages (excluding the period of war and postwar reconstruction of the economy, 1941–50) is the successive contrasts they present in favouring first a regional economic and political approach (1920s), then a strengthening of centralisation and sectoral management (1930s and 1940s), next a further attempt to invigorate the regional management principle (1957–65) and again a reversion to the centralisation-sectoral principle (1966–80). The1980s were characterised by a general weakening of the socialist system along with a gradual loosening of centralised management and a democratisation of society, processes which have greatly increased the emphasis on the regional aspect of policy and precipitated disintegration of the unitary state. Different objectives of regional policy cited above received priority at different stages of development.

During the economic reconstruction phase following the civil war, the period when the GOELRO (electrification) plan was being drafted and implemented, the economy of the Soviet Union was in dire straits. Power and industrial raw materials were in short supply and the transport system was barely functioning. The material and financial resources available to the state were insufficient to accomplish the overall reconstruction of the economy. For these reasons the maximum possible mobilisation and concentration of local resources at crucial points was of cardinal importance to the industrial development which alone could restore the nation's economy.

An extremely urgent problem on the political front was that of promoting unity between proletariat and peasantry. This could only be solved by creating an economic linkage between industry and agriculture. Economically weak provinces could not furnish solutions to these problems. Many of them did not have any large-scale industry at all or else specialised in one industry only. This made it impossible either to organise rational coordination between industrial enterprises or to supply the peasantry of the province with industrial goods. Relatively small territorial divisions did not fit in with the requirements of the scheme of national electrification laid down in the GOELRO plan, which envisaged the creation of regional electric power systems, not coinciding with provincial boundaries but based on modern technology.

This situation made rezoning imperative. A system of large economic regions was devised which facilitated the merging of certain national and regional enterprises into 'fairly large production units ... obtaining raw material supplies jointly and exploiting their own resources independently' (Alampiev, 1959, p. 146). This in turn made it possible 'not only to reconstruct and operate existing industrial enterprises but also to initiate the construction of new ones, large in size and with the benefit of more advanced equipment' (ibid.). Each region was considered on the one hand to form a part of the state but on the other hand to constitute a self-sufficient entity capable of functioning and developing independently in future, thus enabling industrial growth to be achieved even without adequate improvements in transport. The strengthening of regional ties had important social and political functions to fulfil inasmuch as the core of each region consisted of a large industrial centre, and it was this, in the opinion of those directing the reforms, that would link the villages to the economic system and thus establish political control over the peasantry. This line of reasoning influenced not only the shaping of the economic regions but also the organisation of individual local management bodies.

Thus, in the first stage of socialist construction (1922–30), economic regions[1] were established as independent components of the national economy, with important policy functions to perform at regional level. This was clearly reflected in the way planning was organised. It was the regions that compiled the GOELRO plan. The regional aspects were elaborated in detail in the Soviet Union's first five-year plan.

However, the policy's practical results were far from those expected. Relative success was achieved only in the production sphere. In 1927 total industrial output increased by 18 per cent compared with 1913 (Verg, 1994, p. 177). Overall livestock herds were restored, and the total volume of agricultural production increased by 10 per cent compared with 1909–13 (ibid.). Even so the difficulties of supplying industrial centres with foodstuffs were magnified by two falls in the amount of grain for sale on the domestic market. This may be explained by a sharp decline in the number of large farms operating commercially, by shortages of manufactured goods and by understated purchase prices. The situation was such that state purchases of grain decreased year by year. By the late 1920s the policy of industrialisation on a broad front with accelerated development of heavy industry had found favour in ruling circles. Agriculture was the only practicable source of funds for large-scale investment. The result of this was that the market economy was replaced by a more widespread application of administrative coercion as a method of dealing with the peasantry. This wrecked the whole political idea of the unity of proletariat and peasantry.

From the mid-1930s onwards the territorial approach gradually lost ground. By now large changes were going on in the nation's economy. Large-scale heavy industries were being created. Power stations and mines, metallurgical, engineering and chemical plants by the dozen were coming into operation. Large material and financial resources were being accumulated. In agriculture there were radical changes. The class of well-to-do peasants (kulaks) was purged and collectivisation enforced by political action. By 1932 collective farms were predominant, accounting for over 60 per cent of the total producing area. These changes enabled compulsory grain purchases to be increased, so tightening the grip of centralised economic management.

While these events were going on, Josef Stalin was consolidating his personal political dictatorship, crushing all opposition whether of 'right' or 'left' and establishing a single system of administrative control. In such a situation the existence of large independent regions headed by powerful political figures necessarily conflicted with the interests of the 'leader'.

Consequently, the 1930s were a period when both democratic regional policy and centralisation of national economic management on sectoral lines were rejected. Narkomtyazhprom (the People's Commissariat for Heavy Industry) was established in 1932, and the territorial bodies composing the former VSNH (All-Union Council for the National Economy) of the USSR were liquidated.

The establishment of Union republics as the main territorial representative bodies was a new feature of regional policy. The status of the republics was enshrined in the Constitution of the USSR of 1936. In practice, however, the powers of the republics in the economic sphere were significantly reduced compared with those which the large regions had enjoyed at the beginning of the 1930s. The economic centre of gravity was shifting to the individual branches of industry. As regards control over regional development, the primacy of the republics was manifested only in a single task assigned to them, that of equalising economic development and creating modern industries in the individual peripheral national territories.

Major defence undertakings of this period were limited to the construction of duplicate plants in the main branches of the national economy and the creation of a number of large heavy industry complexes supplying adjacent regions with their main requirements of metal, power, machinery and other equipment. Forced prison-camp labour was employed on a large scale in this period to exploit raw materials and forest resources and to construct industrial communications in regions hampered by remoteness and unfavourable climatic conditions. It was extremely important to enhance the country's defence potential by creating a new complex of electric power and metallurgical industries in the east (the Urals–Kuznetsk enterprise). This would provide a basis on which to develop engineering and chemical industries in these regions. The proportion of industrial production accounted for by the eastern regions reached 16 per cent in the years immediately preceding the Great Patriotic War (we use the Russian term for the Second World War, and the Russian dating, that is 1941–45) compared with 6–7 per cent in 1928. However, industrial development was lopsided in the new regions: that is to say, the construction of production facilities took priority while the development of infrastructure lagged behind. Inasmuch as the construction of new industrial plants took place mainly in the eastern regions of the Russian Soviet Federated Socialist Republic (RSFSR), the breakdown into republics for planning purposes revealed itself to be inappropriate, and Russia was subdivided into nine economic regions in the 1940 plan. The planning relating to the rest of the republics was carried out independently, without changing them into regions. It should be noted that economic regions lost their powers of independent management, being considered merely as groups of autonomous republics, krais and oblasts brought together for planning purposes.

The volume of industrial production in the economic regions rose by varying amounts over the ten-year period 1928–37: in Azerbaijan by a factor of 4.5, in the Ukraine and Uzbekistan by 5.7, Turkmenia 6.5, Belarus 8.5, Kazakhstan and Armenia 12, Georgia 12.5, Kyrgizia 14 and Tadzhikistan 26 (*Planning of the USSR Productive Forces Location*, 1985, p. 26). In spite of a degree of exaggeration in the official statistics, a real acceleration of the pace of industrial development did occur in the national republics. In the early years after the Soviet assumption of power, industrial enterprises were few and small in Kazakhstan, Uzbekistan and Turkmenia. By the end of the second five-year period, 3500 large-scale enterprises were in operation, providing year-round employment for an average of nearly 300 000 workers (ibid.). This may serve as a typical example.

Collectivisation of agriculture required strong administrative management. A tier of subordinate administrative regions was formed in the early 1930s, with managerial bodies exercising day-to-day control over collective farms. Oblasts and krais were called into being for the purpose of providing subordinate regional management. The total number of large oblasts (economic regions) reached 24 in the first five-year period. By 1936 the number had increased to 39, by 1938 to 66 and by 1940 to 96 (Alampiev, 1959, pp. 164, 167, 169, 170). This process of proliferation continued in the years that followed.

During the period of the Great Patriotic War the planning objective when determining the siting of production was to shift industry eastwards. Over 1500 large plants were removed from the western regions in the summer and autumn of 1941 alone, being relocated in Volga (Povolzje), the Urals, Siberia and Kazakhstan. This enabled a large military–industrial base to be established in the east as early as 1942–43. The creation of this base was the main task of regional policy in these years.

A total of 3590 large industrial plants were established in the rear regions during the war years. The result was that in the first half-year of 1945 total industrial output in the east was twice as large, and that of the defence industries 5.6 times as large, as in the first half of 1941. As occupied areas were liberated from the enemy their economic reconstruction became a priority task. A total of about 7500 large plants were rebuilt in these regions during the wartime years.

In the postwar period attention was focused mainly on the reconstruction of manufacturing plant and rationalisation of its locational pattern. Mass deportations of entire nationalities considered by the Soviet leadership to have been lacking in patriotism during the war became a new feature of regional policy in this period. Barbaric methods were employed to resettle Germans from Volga (Povolzje), Tartars from the Crimea, Chechens and Balkars, mainly in Kazakhstan and Central Asia. These actions were of a political rather than an economic character.

After Stalin's dictatorship came to an end, Khrushchev attempted to strengthen the role of regional policy and territorial management. In this endeavour he obviously had political purposes in mind: the need to replace the upper tier of management which, in a totalitarian state, determined not only the thrust of but also the scope for socioeconomic development of the country. By the end of the 1950s, 54 'Councils of the national economy' ranging in coverage from one to several oblasts had been established to replace the dozens of sectoral ministries and departments. Over a period of eight years (1957–65) the number (over a hundred in the 1960s) and boundaries of these councils (sovnarkhozes) were revised several times: thus no stable structure was ever established. In the early 1960s the role of the Union republics, with more than nine-tenths of industry at their disposal, including the three-quarters of industry managed by sovnarkhozes, increased substantially in importance. Experience of the working of these sovnarkhozes has shown the advantages they offer in solving the problems entailed in developing production and a social infrastructure, and encouraging housing construction everywhere. At the same time decentralisation of the economy into over a hundred territorial economic units under conditions of command management diminished the opportunities for intrasectoral coordination, slowed the pace of scientific and technical progress, and reduced the state's ability to implement large-scale programmes. The key factor was that strengthening the role of republics and regions undermined the principles of the centralised administrative-command system and reduced the scope for imposing political and economic dictatorship. This is why, once Khrushchev had retired, the sectoral management system was restored and continued to function until the end of the 1980s, enabling vast material and financial resources, and therefore power, to be concentrated in the hands of central management bodies.

During the whole of this period the tasks of speeding the development of the eastern regions of the country and equalising levels of economic development in the Union republics continued to occupy a prominent place in regional policy. In 1926 production of industrial goods per head in the regions of the USSR was 28 times greater than in the republics, but by the mid-1960s the ratio had diminished to 3.4 times. Economic growth was rapid in the republics of Central Asia and Transcaucasus. Industrial production in the USSR as a whole grew tenfold during the period 1940–70, whereas in Kazakhstan this index figure was over 16, in Armenia 17 and in Kyrgizia

15.5.[2] Faster growth in the eastern regions[3] brought a significant increase of their role in the national economy (see Table 2.1).

Large-scale industries were being created in the republics of Central Asia and Kazakhstan, throughout these years, and the industrial potential of Siberia and the Far East grew sharply. Thus, in Kazakhstan there were plants representing 30 industrial branches in the mid-1930s (15 branches prior to the Revolution) but over 200 by the end of the 1970s, including more than 60 branches of mechanical engineering and metalworking. The eastward shift of the resource base of many industries was going on during the same period, however. The small mineral deposits in the European part of the country were becoming rapidly depleted at the same time, while intensive geological surveys in Siberia, Kazakhstan and some of the republics of Central Asia were disclosing the presence of huge industrial reserves of oil, gas, coal, non-ferrous metals and other valuable minerals. The consequence is that, although the mismatch between the location patterns of production facilities and natural resources is still fairly considerable, it has diminished to some extent over the past 20–30 years.

Table 2.1   Eastern regions' share in production of individual products, as percentage of the USSR total, 1940, 1960 and 1965

	1940	1960	1965
Electric power	9.2	21.6	29.4
Natural gas	0.5	2.4	78.8
Coal	28.7	35.9	58.8
Iron ore	1.7	11.1	16.3
Mineral fertilisers	6.9	15.9	13.7
Timber	23.4	26.2	37.3
Cellulose	–	9.3	29.6
Cement	13.5	21.4	26.0

Grave errors occurred in spite of a measure of success in speeding up the development of the eastern regions. These arose largely from underestimating the importance of the local idiosyncrasies and traditions of indigenous peoples. The result was that many large industrial plants built in Central Asia with the intention of providing job opportunities for surplus local labour were forced to import labour from the European regions of Russia because the local people were untrained in industrial work. Prisoners were widely used as labour at many constructional sites and in some branches of industry in the northern and eastern regions. These were employed chiefly in tree-felling and mining, the latter mainly in branches with a high fatality risk (uranium, lead, asbestos, gold, diamond extraction). Many hundreds of prisoners participated in the building of the Baikal–Amur, Salekhard–Igarka railway (not yet completed) as well as in the construction of large dams (Ust–Kamenogorsk, Bratsk) and a number of sizeable towns. The widespread use of prisoner labour obviously went hand in hand with a neglect of human needs, with the result that the social infrastructure was poorly developed almost everywhere in the eastern regions.

The biggest of the large-scale regional programmes was implemented in agriculture. Virgin tracts of Kazakhstan, the South Urals and Siberia were brought under cultivation (37 million hectares during the 1950s, representing about 30 per cent of the total cultivated area of the USSR at that time), mainly at the cost of having to attract labour from the Ukraine and European regions of Russia.

The problems of industrial location tackled during the 1970s included such projects as the establishment of large territorial production complexes in regions of Siberia. Others included limiting the growth of large towns while encouraging that of small and medium-sized ones, taking account of the ecological effects flowing from industrial locational decisions, and the need to maximise efficient, and at the same time more complex, use of resources.

This was the time when the plants forming the largest production complexes were being built: oil-gas in the north of Western Siberia, Kansk–Achinsk, South Yakutia, Ekibastuz (coal mining and processing), Kursk Magnetic Anomaly, Sayany (iron ore extraction and processing) and so on. The main objective in establishing these complexes was to facilitate coordinated industrial development based on abundant power resources and multiple utilisation of raw minerals. All the complexes included in the ninth and tenth five-year plans were established, but none was completed to the advanced scientific level which had been envisaged.

Other state programmes which were likewise not implemented were those for developing the Non-Chernozem zone, building small towns and solving environmental problems. The resources assigned for these purposes seem to have been insufficient. Increased production volumes, primarily at the expense of new construction, still remained the main objective under the administrative-command system. Ministries, Union republics and oblast authorities regarded it as their principal task to cajole investment capital from the USSR Gosplan (the main distributor of funds) for financing new construction The cost estimates for such construction would often be lowered several times. The important thing was to be included in the plan, for if this happened the financial tap would not be turned off even if the estimated cost of construction was exceeded. The siting of major heavy industries, to which central government gave priority until recent years, was considered to confer prestige. Because of this, industrial plants were often sited without due regard being paid to regional idiosyncrasies and contrary to scientific recommendations (metallurgical works in Moldova, a nuclear power station in Armenia, and so on).

In the late 1980s the problems associated with regional policy became more intractable. In the majority of regions the factors favourable to economic growth were becoming exhausted. There was a need everywhere to improve the quality of life of the people. Many of the USSR's component nationalities were making unprecedented demands for economic and political independence. The USSR's economic and political systems, however, failed to devise and implement appropriate regional policies in time, and this was one of the reasons for the Soviet Union's disintegration.

ORGANISATION OF TERRITORIAL MANAGEMENT

The transformation of administrative units during the 1920s and 1930s is shown in Table 2.2. The territorial management structure was unstable during the earliest stage of peacetime reconstruction in the 1920s. The administrative–territorial structure of Russia was reorganised at this time. The former gubernias (counties) were replaced by a union of autonomous republics. New economic regions, krais and oblasts were formed. The economic weakness of the central managerial bodies resulted in a considerable degree of independence being permitted for the newly established territorial structures. However, the powers and responsibilities of the various territorial units were not defined precisely, and their relations with the central managerial bodies were not established in legal form. Moreover, the territorial structure of the state was in constant flux. It may suffice to remark that the number of basic territorial sub-units changed almost every year. In 1921 the Soviet Union's entire territory was subdivided into 21 economic regions, but the first five-year plan was based on 24 regions and the second on 32. The administrative–territorial structure changed even more, and by the mid-1930s it had been radically altered, for the pre-revolution gubernias, uyezdy and volosts (districts) no longer existed.

The role of territorial units in the system of management was revised in the 1930s for the economic and political reasons considered above. All-Union people's commissariats (narkomaty) became the linchpin of this system, while the key position in the territorial structure was occupied by the Union republics.

The USSR Constitution of 1936 consolidated the established structure of the economy and its management. The system of management was rigid and centralised, giving no significant powers to the regions of the Union and even less to the autonomous republics, krais, and oblasts.

Table 2.2   Administrative territorial units, 1922, 1929 and 1937

	1922	1929	1937
Union republics	3	6	11
Autonomous republics	9	15	22
Autonomous oblasts	10	16	9
Krais and oblasts	–	8	47
Districts (including national)	–	176	35
Administrative regions	–	2426	5567
Gubernias (counties)	84	16	–
Uyezdys (districts)	759	298	–
Volosts (districts)	15072	1595	–

Union narkomats controlled heavy industry, construction and transport. Union republics were invested with control of agriculture and social welfare. Sectoral economic bodies in the republics were represented by the narkomats of local government economy. At the level of autonomous republics, krais and oblasts, the narkomats and departments were subordinated to the appropriate soviet of people's commissars, executive committee of krai, oblast soviets and to the republic ministry. The Union republics were wholly responsible for controlling these sectors and there was no all-Union coordination (see Figure 2.1).

During the Great Patriotic War the state had to centralise economic management even more rigidly, so that practically all managerial functions became concentrated at the centre. Even the local industries supposedly under Union republic control were assigned tasks directly by central managerial bodies of the USSR.

The transition to peacetime reconstruction disclosed a need to strengthen the regional managerial element. This is reflected in the territorial approach which was taken to the reorganisation of the existing system of narkomats. A narkomat appeared for the coal industry of the eastern regions of the USSR, another for the coal industry of the western regions of the USSR, one for the oil industry of the eastern regions of the USSR, one for the oil industry of the western regions of the USSR, and so forth. This regionalisation was strongly centralised in character and did not result in any kind of enlargement of the powers of republics and local bodies.

The process of enlarging the powers of Union republics started in the 1950s. Over 15 000 enterprises were transferred into their jurisdiction. For this reason a number of Union ministries were changed to Union–republic ministries, and this resulted in the establishment of corresponding ministries in the Union republics. We may cite as examples the ministries of coal, oil industries, the building materials industry and others. In some cases similar sectoral bodies were established at the level of autonomous republics, krais and oblasts. In particular, such regional managerial structures were established in the building materials industry, light industries and food-processing industries. The Union–republic system of management functioned in conformity with the principle of double subordination (see Figure 2.2).

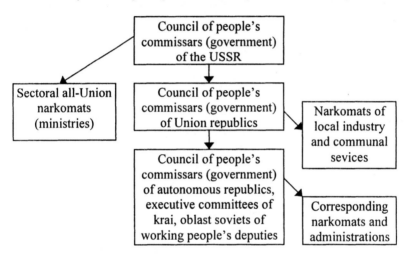

Figure 2.1   Organisation of territorial management in the USSR in the 1930s and 1940s

By 1957, 23 Union and 27 Union–republic ministries controlled sectors of the national economy. A number of resolutions were adopted with the aim of enlarging the powers of Union republics and local bodies in the planning field. However, these did not radically improve the management of the national economy. In 1957 the main responsibility for managing manufacturing industry and building construction was shifted to the economic regions. Councils of national economy established for the economic regions became the main organisational forms of public management of these sectors. Sovnarkhozes (Councils of national economy) were given broad powers of control over subordinate enterprises in the fields of planning, capital construction works, raw materials and technical supplies, finance and credit, labour and wages. Their activities were subordinate to the Council of Ministers of Union republics.

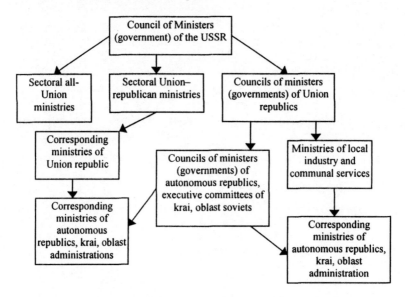

Figure 2.2   Organisation of territorial management in the USSR in the 1950s

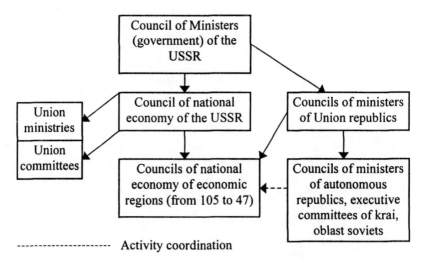

Figure 2.3   Organisation of territorial management in the 1960s

Simultaneously with the abolition of most of the Union and Union–republic ministries, a number of committees were established for the purpose of pursuing common financial and technical policies. The Sovnarkhoz of the USSR was established in order to achieve general coordination of sovnarkhoz activity (see Figure 2.3). Local councils found themselves deprived of their control over the economy of the regions. Control over local industries, formerly under their authority, was delegated to the territorial sovnarkhozes instead. In this way the sovnarkhozes became independent of both central and local authorities.

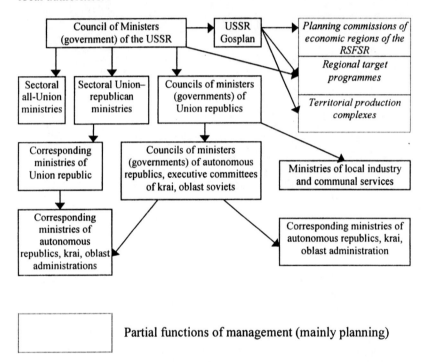

Partial functions of management (mainly planning)

Figure 2.4 Organisation of territorial management in the 1970s and 1980s

A gradual centralisation of management began in 1962. State committees (in fact ministries) for the various branches of industry were established and a considerable number of plants were brought under their authority. In 1963 the Supreme Council of the National Economy of the USSR was established for the purpose of coordinating the activities of Gosplan, Sovnarkhoz and Gosstroy (the State Construction Committee). The Council was subsequently changed into the Union–republic body. The organisational framework for a

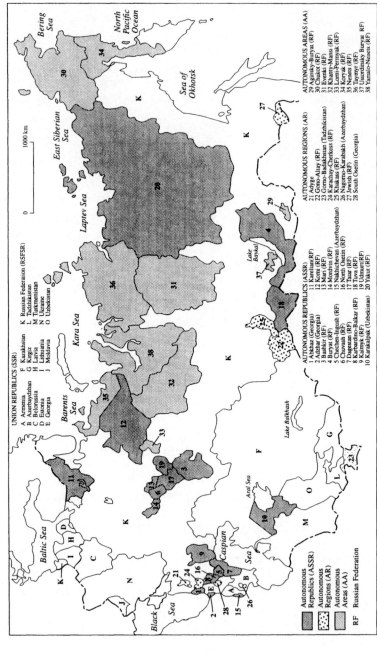

Source: Brown, Kaser and Smith (eds) (1992), pp. 306–7.

Figure 2.5 Political administrative regions of the USSR

reversion to the sectoral approach to management was created. The reversion took place in 1965. An organisational management system was established on lines broadly similar to the system of the 1950s and repeated almost all the latter's faults.

Over the next 20 years decisions were regularly adopted favouring both joint sectoral and territorial management and enlargement of the powers of Union republics and autonomous republics, krais and oblasts. In practical terms, however, these remained paper decisions which were not implemented. The planning of territorial-production complexes and development of regional target programmes (Zone of Nechernozemye, BAM) represented an attempt to regionalise the centralised approach. Planning commissions for ten economic regions in the territory of the RSFSR (see Figure 2.4) were established simultaneously, each of these regions comprising five to ten oblasts, krais and autonomous republics.

In the 1980s the system of administrative and economic division of the USSR included 15 Union republics and 19 economic regions along with 20 autonomous republics, eight autonomous oblasts and ten autonomous districts, 128 oblasts and krais, over 3000 subordinate administrative regions and over 2000 towns. Figure 2.5 shows the Union republics, and the autonomous republics, oblast and districts (okrugs). Along with the territorial units mentioned, which enjoyed legally established economic powers, the following units were defined for planning purposes: Zone of Nechernozemye (29 oblasts of the European part of the RSFSR), Zone of economic development of the Baikal–Amur trunk railway line (part of the territory of Eastern Siberia and Far East) and eight large territorial-production complexes. If we bear in mind that the managerial bodies of each of the types of territorial unit cited possessed partial and patently inadequate powers, the extremely low efficiency of such a structure of territorial management becomes evident. In the long run the problem of establishing efficient regional management structures in the USSR was not solved, and this was one of the factors which led to the USSR's disintegration.

SOVIET PHILOSOPHY OF TERRITORIAL PLANNING

Regional policy is implemented through the medium of the overall system of national economic management. During the Soviet epoch, under a rigidly centralised and authoritarian system, territorial planning played the most important role in this management process. It had to perform two functions: first, to secure efficient participation by the regions in the conduct of the nation's affairs, and second, to promote each region's economic and social development in all its complexity. In the former case the regions were considered, from the standpoint of the state, to be components of a single economic complex. The function of territorial planning was to distribute production targets and centralised resources rationally between the regions. Society as a whole was to benefit from the maximum possible exploitation of regional conditions favourable to the kinds of production whose development within the region concerned would enable the efficiency of the whole national economy to be increased.

In the latter case, each region was regarded as a relatively independent sub-system within the national economy. The task of planning was to secure balanced and well-proportioned development of all components of the region's economy and the most expedient use of regional resources, thus creating further economic benefits not only for the region itself but for the nation as a whole. The problem of achieving rational specialisation between regions was directly bound up with the division of labour, and the intricately interwoven strands of economic development mirrored the processes of labour integration.

Territorial planning was an integral feature of the overall planned system of management throughout the Soviet epoch, fulfilling a variety of functions at different stages of history. The main objective of planning prior to the 1960s was to enhance production levels generally, meaning simply to accelerate the rates of industrial growth. Planning in its territorial aspect consequently concentrated on the achievement of this goal. The foremost concerns of territorial planning were the production targets set for the main kinds of products and the bringing into operation of additional productive capacity.

From the 1960s onwards a broader range of issues connected with population increase began to be brought within the scope of territorial planning. These issues related to the development of the social infrastructure, meaning primarily housing and the training and retraining of personnel, and the use made of labour resources. In the 1970s issues connected with increased use of natural resources and management of the environment gravitated into the planning orbit. Along with traditional indices of mineral reserves and targets for geological investigation of the most important resources, indices showing the nature and scale of exploitation of forest and water resources, land reclamation and the protection of atmospheric air were introduced into territorial planning.

Thus, the topic of territorial planning was gradually being enlarged in step with changes in the character of planning generally. The focus was shifting from individual indices of industrial and agricultural production to regulation of the most important aspects of the social and demographic environment, the standard of living, use of natural resources and environmental protection. It should be observed that there were objective reasons why planning should assume a more comprehensive character. Under the command system of management, the lion's share of public resources went into solving the problems specified in the state plan. The resultant lag in other spheres of activity eventually started to impede progress in the so-called strategic directions. This exposed to view the need to plan not only production capacity but infrastructure, not only numbers of workers but also their training, not only production of raw materials but conservation of natural resources. However, the enlargement of the range of issues to be planned complicated the planning process to an extreme degree. The number of planned targets grew from several dozen in the first five-year period to tens of thousands in the tenth five-year period. It is manifestly a practical impossibility to match these masses of indices and coordinate their timings with the diverse resources of a vast country. This was one of the reasons for the decreasing accuracy and efficiency of planning, and it contributed to the collapse of the entire Soviet system.

The role of territorial planning in the management of the national economy was changing as its substance changed. During the period 1922–32, while the economy was reviving and a centralised command system for managing it was being developed after almost ten years of destructive internal and external wars, territorial planning had a crucial role to play. Territorial plans secured the harnessing of Russia's regional resources to the revival of industry and realisation of the first stage of electrification of the economy. Targets were set for state grain procurements. Fleets of tractors and machinery were produced. V.V. Kuibyshev, chairman of the USSR Gosplan, remarked on the importance of the territorial approach to planning at this time:

> Only consideration of the complex development of the entire economy of a given oblast produces a competent, economically viable ... plan ... for a given oblast, and then a plan for the overall national economy of our Union ... The territorial aspect in a regional context should be introduced as a principle from the very beginning. (Kuibyshev, 1937, pp. 102–3)

In the early 1930s the priorities in the system of planning changed under the influence of economic, political and organisational factors. The economic role of large-scale state-owned industries grew dramatically. Collective farms occupied a vital position in agriculture. Transport was restored. The central government amassed resources of hard currency by exporting large volumes of grain (often at the cost of considerable hardship for the people). And, finally, the continued quarrelling between the various factions of the

Bolshevik Party was resolved once and for all in favour of authoritarian government.

All these factors encouraged the transition to sectoral planning, which was more suited to the nature of a centralised command system of management. By the mid-1930s territorial plans had lost their paramount importance and become subordinate. The majority of targets for increased production and public resources were distributed by sectors. The function of the regional plan, according to one of the USSR Gosplan leaders of that time, 'was to represent rational coordination of branches of the economy of local and interregional importance' (Korobov, 1939). The secondary and auxiliary character of territorial plans was emphasised in another of Korobov's remarks: 'A sectoral plan can be most effectively worked out only when it is incorporated into the complex plans of regions' (ibid.). It should be noted that in and after the late 1930s territorial plans started to lose their complex character: they no longer embraced the entire economy of the territory in question but were reduced to the planning of specific enterprises under the authority of the appropriate republics or local Soviets. In 1953 they accounted for 31 per cent of the USSR's total industrial output and only 5 per cent of public capital investment (Urinson, 1963, pp. 60 and 84).

Extreme concentration and the prevailing sectoral approach resulted in a serious imbalance of the national economy with a negative effect on the allocation of productive resources. Glaring disparities in levels of industrial and social development revealed themselves practically everywhere. Because most investment in social infrastructure was associated with construction projects, towns tended to be built around the sites of industrial undertakings, and this often interfered with the layout of large cities. The achievement of sectoral objectives in the exploitation of natural resources has had damaging effects on ecological conditions in industrial regions, through the creation of systems of gigantic water reservoirs and irrigation canals, for example, and the total clearance of vast expanses of forest, none of which is helpful to the functioning of natural ecosystems.

Measures to decentralise management and planning were introduced from the end of 1953 onwards, and by 1957 these had brought about a transition to the territorial approach. In 1957–58 the control of industry and building construction was radically reformed: Union ministries were liquidated and councils of national economy were established in Union and autonomous republics, krais and oblasts, with authority to control industry and construction on their territories. In 1961 the proportion of industry under the authority of Union republics reached 93 per cent, 73 per cent being controlled by sovnarkhozes. Union republics controlled 80 per cent of construction organisations and their share of capital investment was similar (77 per cent).

This redistribution of managerial functions yielded certain positive results, primarily in the sphere of housing construction and other forms of social infrastructure. It should be noted that complex territorial planning covering all aspects of economic development was practised mainly at the level of Union republics during this period. As long as such large sectors as agriculture, transport and the non-production sphere were excluded from the jurisdiction of sovnarkhozes, the latter were unable to plan the overall economies existing within the territories of krais, oblasts and cities. In the 1950s and 1960s, therefore, Union republics became the chief units for territorial planning purposes. However, this by no means met the needs of such large republics as RSFSR, Ukraine, Kazakhstan and Uzbekistan.

Further redistribution of functions between sectoral and territorial planning took place at subsequent stages of regional policy (after 1967), after the proportion of enterprises subordinated to Union ministries and departments had increased sharply, reaching 55 per cent by 1983. The share of economic activity controlled by Union bodies expressed as a proportion of the total volume of state capital investment was almost the same (Pavlenko, 1984).

Along with the elaboration of plans for the economic activities under their jurisdiction, Union republics were charged with drawing up master plans for the entire economies contained within their territories, along with proposals for the development of enterprises under Union jurisdiction. After the mid-1970s this planning procedure was extended to krais and oblasts, first in the RSFSR and then in other republics. It is important to observe that questions of production, use of local natural and labour resources, development of non-manufacturing activities, increased living standards, infrastructure development and environmental activity were considered in coordinated form in master territorial plans. For the first time territorial planning actually did become complex in character. The summary analytical character of complex plans should be regarded as their drawback, for targets in these plans were not obligatory for enterprises under Union and republic jurisdiction, and these enterprises provided the major share of industrial and constructional potential in the majority of oblasts. At the same time the balancing and intersectoral calculations forming part of the process of developing a complex plan made it possible to formulate recommendations for developing the economy as a whole, and these were used by local managerial bodies.

The appearance of other planning papers, of complex character and aimed at solving specific large-scale regional problems, is typical of this period. These are programmes for development of territorial-production complexes and for developing the Non-Chernozem zone of the RSFSR and the zone of the Baikal–Amur railway. Unlike complex territorial plans, these programmes were approved by the Union government and were mandatory in character. However, the sectoral mechanism for their realisation resulted as a rule in serious failures to coordinate the introduction of programme measures in the correct order. In consequence, the efficacy of these programmes was seriously impaired, scientifically necessary technological and economic linkages between the various plants were badly timed, and the benefits expected from the complex preplanned exploitation of natural resources were nullified. Thus, in the 70-year period of the USSR's existence, territorial planning has travelled a road leading from paramountcy to almost complete extinction and thence to a fairly high but still subordinate position in the management system.

Throughout this period the combining of sectoral and territorial planning presented incessant philosophical problems. The issue was especially acute in the last decade of the Soviet Union, when the powers of Union ministries on the one hand and Union republics on the other became almost equal. The councils of ministers of Union republics exercised almost complete control over the branches of agriculture and industry, trade, geological exploration, municipal housing construction and inland water transport. Local industries, consumer services, health care, education, the arts and other branches of the service sector were fully under the jurisdiction of republic bodies. The exceptions were housing services and preschool institutions, which were only partly subordinated to territorial bodies because the majority of them were owned by the undertakings they served. A considerable proportion of enterprises and organisations in such branches as light, power and building materials industries was subordinated to republic bodies.

In 1980 the proportion of total industrial output represented by industry under the jurisdiction of the Councils of Ministers of Union republics was 46 per cent for the USSR as a whole and ranged from 82 per cent in the Moldavskaya SSR to 47 per cent in the Belarusan SSR and even less in the RSFSR. About three-fifths of the overall national income was produced by economic activity under the authority of Union republics (Pavlenko, 1984, p. 211). This did not mean, however, that the scope for sectoral and territorial planning was comparable at all levels of management. The fact is that economic activity under Union republic authority was also planned in accordance with the sectoral approach. It was a matter almost of indifference to the individual oblast whether the enterprises located on its territory were under Union or republic jurisdiction, since plans for their development were approved 'over its head' by Union or republic ministry.

Some local industrial enterprises, all collective and state farms, some housebuilding and road construction were under the jurisdiction of the main agency of territorial planning, the autonomous republics, krais and oblasts.

Local soviets owned a significant proportion of housing resources, water supply and sewage facilities, systems of heating and power supply, municipal transport, trade and public catering. Welfare, leisure and cultural institutions were under their jurisdiction.

The general scheme for drawing up the territorial plans of republics, krais and oblasts and other administrative–territorial units may be described as follows. Every territory was set targets for the enterprises falling under superior jurisdiction. Territorial planning bodies summarised these tasks and worked out territorial estimates of the requirements of labour and natural resources (land, water). These figures also included the money incomes and expenditure of the population, industrial and agricultural production capacities, fuel and power estimates for the territory, training requirements, utilisation of skilled labour and sundry other estimates. Territorial managerial bodies worked out their own proposals for adjusting sectoral plans at the different levels by analysing and assessing the congruence between plans for new construction and development of functioning enterprises and the potential and needs of the regions.

Because of its extreme complexity and the manifestly unequal powers of the planning authorities participating in the process, this theoretical scheme did not reflect territorial interests. The fact is that local proposals could not be taken fully into account, since enterprises were allotted production targets and resources by the ministries concerned and as a rule had no power to change them. Neither did ministries and departments give serious consideration to proposals made by krais and oblasts, since they had no actual responsibility for dealing with them. In addition, the large number of territorial units (over 100) and the extremely short space of time in which plans had to be developed made it impossible to amend draft plans to take account of comments made by the regions.

Alongside the combining of sectoral and territorial plans, the principle of continuity of planning played an important role in Soviet planning philosophy. The essential feature of this principle was a scheme of pre-plan studies with varying perspectives. Long-term (15–20 years), medium-term (five years) and current (one year) studies were developed for territorial units. All documents had to be coordinated with each other. These pre-plan studies determined development and allocated productive resources by economic region, Union republic and territorial-production complex while also establishing target programmes for economic zones. The role of pre-plan studies for oblasts, cities and administrative districts was played by schemes for housing and associated facilities, for district layouts and for overall town planning, all this being more in the nature of physical planning. Both economic and physical planning perspectives were updated every five years to enable pre-plan studies to take account of empirical events and thus furnish a basis on which plans could be formulated. This system functioned from 1970 to 1990.

Hundreds of research and planning organisations were involved in devising schemes of development and resource allocation. The 'General scheme of development and location of productive forces of the USSR', synthesising both sectoral and territorial pre-plan studies, was the major pre-plan document. In fact it was the only document in which any attempt was made to coordinate sectoral and regional aspects of the development of the national economy on an iterative basis.[4]

The studies turned out to be an insufficiently effective instrument in the event, despite their ambitious scale. Firstly, they failed to coordinate fully the interests and proposals of sectors and regions. Secondly, even those recommendations for rational regional economic development which were accepted were often not brought to fruition at the five-year plan stage because priority was given to the pressing need to develop the production branches. This was one of the major reasons for inadequacy of social welfare provision, severe ecological mishaps and backwardness of infrastructure in many regions of the country.

Thirdly, many decisions on new construction projects were adopted on the basis not of technical justification but of resolutions. Efforts were made to change this situation: for example, a Resolution of the Council of Ministers was adopted in the mid-1970s to the effect that financial provision for new construction projects could only be made if such projects were envisaged under the schemes of development and location of productive resources. However, this resolution was not observed. Only one-third of the construction projects implemented during these and subsequent years was started up in accordance with pre-plan studies. The fact that centrally determined capital investments were allocated 'free of charge' had a severe negative effect, in that it encouraged this unsystematic mode of construction. This being so, the essential thing was to be included, by hook or by crook, in the plan of capital construction, for, once a project had secured a place in the plan, it was financed almost automatically, though only partially. This situation has given birth to a massive proliferation of unfinished construction works. Thus the standard duration of construction in 1987 was exceeded 2.7 times, while 79 per cent of the total volume of capital investment consisted of unfinished projects (73 per cent in 1970) (*Financy i statistika*, 1988, pp. 68–9).

Table 2.3 System of territorial plans

Objects of territorial planning		Types of plans			Periodicity of development		
		Directive or based on the approved plans	Target programmes	Summary-analytical	Year	Medium-term (5-year)	Long-term
Administrative economic regions	Union republic	+	–	–	+	+	+
	Autonomous republic, krai, oblast	+	–	–	+	+	–
	City, town	+	–	–	+	+	–
	Administrative district	+	–	–	+	+	–
Economic regions	Enlarged economic region	–	–	+	–	+*	+
	Zone	As an exception	+	–	As an exception	+*	+
	Economic region of the USSR	As an exception	–	+	As an exception	+	+
	Territorial production complex	–	+	–	+	+	+

Note: * Within long-term plan.

59

The system for territorial planning projects changed in accordance with developments in state regional policy and in the general methodology of economic planning. As we have already remarked, in the initial stages of the USSR's development large oblasts or economic regions were the main planning units. After the Second World War, and especially during the reform period 1957–65, Union republics and councils of national economy became the main territorial planning units. In the 1970s it was the autonomous republics, krais and oblasts, along with territorial production complexes, that came to the fore. By the 1980s an extensive system of territorial planning had taken shape. This covered both administrative–territorial units, which had their own bodies of power and management, and economic regions, which were selected mainly for the purposes of planning and analysis (see Table 2.3).

One of the most important principles for improving the territorial organisation of the economy and the siting of production plants was the principle of paramountcy of the economic criterion of efficiency. This principle came into its own when various aspects of territorial development were under consideration in the course of pre-plan studies. Throughout the entire period of the USSR's existence, much attention was devoted to the problem of equalising the development levels of different regions of the country. The problem remained acute at least until 1980, when it was announced that it had been largely solved.[5] When attempting to solve this problem it was customary to compare various macroeconomic and per capita indices of Union republics and economic regions with the average Union indices. The objective was gradually to reduce the gap between the values of these indices. Insufficient account was taken of the social and historical idiosyncrasies of the regions, and the problem itself was simplified and frequently reduced to purely mathematical methods.

The second sphere in which mainly national criteria were applied comprised the problems of economic assessment of natural resources. The main task here was not to estimate the potential of the territories for increasing revenues from the exploitation of resources but to determine which of them to include in the economic turnover. The final costs estimate method was employed for this purpose, in which the costs mean the value of allowable economic costs per unit of increase of the given product over a certain period of time.

Verification of the economic efficiency with which enterprises were allocated was one of the main aspects of study. Maximisation of social labour efficiency, expressed in terms of achieving the lowest possible discounted unit costs, was taken as the principal criterion. For this purpose unit capital investment and manufacturing costs were calculated for all possible variants of the allocation of new enterprises. The total allowable economic costs were calculated. These included not only the data for individual enterprises but also incremental costs, including the services infrastructure and delivery of goods to consumers. Such matters as rationalisation of the territorial balance and improvement of interregional economic linkages over the country as a whole were considered in the course of development of the General Scheme.

It was typical of the economic approach to assessing the efficacy of the allocation of productive forces that insufficient account was taken of the interests of the populations of regions, the production potential of the territories and the local natural conditions. The result was that many regions became narrowly specialised in particular kinds of activity which were profitable from the standpoint of the national economy as a whole but did not furnish normal conditions of life in the territory. These problems of territorial organisation were smoothed over to a certain extent as long as the national economy was functioning, and the defects of hyper-specialisation were offset by centralised distribution of resources. However, by the late 1980s the crisis of extreme territorial specialisation had become more acute, and this aggravated the growth of regional economic disparities.

In the conditions presented by the USSR's disintegration and transition to a market economy this failure of regional policy acquired huge destructive force. The rupture of economic linkages in a situation of extreme specialisation was largely responsible for precipitating a deep crisis of production in all regions of the former USSR.

THE ROLE OF ECONOMIC SCIENCE IN INDUSTRIAL AND TERRITORIAL POLICY

Activities in the Early Soviet Period

The territorial planning system of the Soviet period has involved a number of actors in different ministries and agencies associated with the central government. In the planned economy the forecasting and planning activities become intimately connected with the actual commodity and service production. The role of planning is not only to indicate directions for private enterprises, households and public organisations to adjust to but to determine production plans. The Soviet planning system contained strong institutions for territorial planning. The importance of economic science in the planning activities was not necessarily equally strong. The present section provides an overview of the major connections between economic science and industrial and territorial policy during the period from the 1920s to the 1990s. The presentation focuses on the issues treated and the tools used, rather than on the institutional aspects.

The level of economic research and scientific substantiation of the most important economic decisions in the first years of the Soviet period was rather high for that time. This was due to the advanced level of economic thinking in the pre-revolutionary period and the possibility of free statement of scientific positions, absence of suppressing ideological control and access to the world literature. Among mathematical economists of pre-revolutionary Russia we should mention first of all V. Dimitriev (1868–1913) and E. Sloutsky (1880–1948).

The first known work of Dimitriev was devoted to an attempt to apply the theory of labour cost and the theory of marginal utility (Dimitriev, 1904). In the process of his research work Dimitriev developed a model of total costs and balanced prices in the form of a system of linear equations with technological coefficients. For several decades a formula proposed by him for the calculation of total costs found wide application in the modelling of inter-branch linkages. Dimitriev also made a significant contribution to the resolution of the problem of the formation of socially necessary costs. Thus he discussed problems which became topical for Soviet economists in the 1960s and 1980s many decades before a wide discussion of them started.

Sloutsky occupies a special position in the history of the development of economic thought in Russia. In 1915 he published in Italy an article (Sloutsky, 1915) devoted to the balancing of consumers' budgets. In 20 years this article received worldwide acknowledgement. The Nobel Prize laureate D. Hicks wrote that Sloutsky was the first economist to make a significant step forward in comparison with the classics of the mathematical school. Sloutsky is one of the founders of the discipline of praxeology, dealing with the principles of rational activity of people. The most distinguished Polish mathematical economist O. Lange considers that it is a great merit of Sloutsky that he introduced praxeology into economic science. Sloutsky also wrote a number of works on the cyclic variations in economic life (see the reprinted texts of Sloutsky, 1960).

A high level of research in the pre-revolutionary period created the basis for further intellectual development. As the first country in the world the USSR developed a flow balance of the national economy for 1923–24 (see Gosplan, 1926). This work, carried out under the supervisorship of P. Popov, was several years ahead of studies both on master balance tables (national accounts) and on inter-branch balances, carried out later in the United States under the supervision of V. Leontiev.

Among the most distinguished names of the beginning of the Soviet period we should also mention D. Kondratiev and A. Chayanov. The former formulated in 1922 the idea of the existence of long cycles of economic development, the so-called 'Kondratiev waves' (Kondratiev, 1922). Processing of time series (prices, interest rates, capital stocks, wages) and plotting of trends, the deviations from which were smoothed with the help of moving averages, formed the basis. Kondratiev's approach to the revealing of long cycles prompted a number of critical remarks. The interest in his works outside the USSR has never died, however, and in the last two decades it has sharply increased. Chayanov was another distinguished scientist of that period, who gave his main attention to the efficiency problems of the national economy and its individual sectors (agriculture, water). Along with undoubtedly novel approaches to the assessment of the efficiency of economic management under socialism, as to the choice of the optimal size of the enterprise, he also tried to substantiate a system of accounts based on in kind values and estimates in spatial points (see Chayanov, 1921). At this time books by the widely known German economists Weber (1957) and von Thünen (1966) were published in Russia. Von Thünen, studying the influence of the allocation of land plots (distance from the market) on farms' incomes, prices and wages, came to the conclusion that the organisation of agricultural production will be most efficient when its intensity varies with the closeness to the market. These works influenced the economic thinking during a large part of the Soviet period.

In the period of Stalin's repressions, after the beginning of collectivisation and the rejection of market methods of economic management, economic planning approaches not based on calculations were widely spread. Formulation of principles of production allocation, and the identification of factors influencing these principles, classifications and even decisions, became the main task. The practice of the application of mathematical and statistical methods in economic research, accumulated over many years, was forgotten for a long time. For a quarter of a century (1928–53) development of economic thought was practically stopped, and contacts with foreign scientists were lost. Excellent scientific studies such as those made by Nobel Prize laureate L. Kantorovich, and by V. Novozhilov, appeared as exceptions.

Serious calculations were often replaced by slogans, for example about the realisation of 'great construction projects of communism'. Such principles were used when constructing the hydroelectric power stations on the Volga and supported the hypertrophied attention given to the construction of canals and the plantation of forest belts. It should be mentioned that some of these slogan-based initiatives turned out to be useful: for example, the necessity of developing the resource-rich eastern regions of the country and the necessity of the equalisation of the level of economic development among the USSR regions. The first was proved to be correct politically by the outcome of the Second World War, and economically it was proved in the works of Siberian scientists many decades later (Academia Nauk, 1980b). The economic expediency of the realisation of the second slogan has never been calculated in figures, though examples of such estimates on the basis of econometric models exist, for example, in Japan.

Methods of Economic Substantiation before 1970

The level of degradation of the official political economy by the early 1950s was terrifying. Stalin's purges ensured that, by the postwar period, Soviet economic science had lost much of its potential of the earlier period. It took until the end of the 1960s for the problems created to be partially remedied. For example, the possibility of comparing capital investments and maintenance costs accruing in different time periods was not acknowledged and there were no approaches to the assessment of goods quality. The exchange value of products in agriculture was liquidated partly because so-called machine and tractor stations took a part of the harvest from peasants at fixed norms in kind, implying that there was no necessity for value indices. Practitioners were supposed to choose as the best alternatives those which simultaneously provided minimum unit capital investments and maintenance costs and provided maximum labour productivity. When there was no best variant by all indices applied it was recommended to further estimate the values using additionally involved indices.

This uncertainty of the procedure of the choice of the best decision inevitably led to voluntarism in the economic practice. Four groups of Soviet economic and regional scientists over time managed to break this theoretical stalemate and practical impotence:

1.   specialists in individual branches (power engineering, transport);
2.   participants in special commissions of the USSR Academy of Science;
3.   specialists in economic–mathematical modelling at different regional levels;
4.   individual economists working on the allocation of productive forces and regional development policy.

Among those who in the postwar period started work in the field of development of common rules for the calculation of the efficiency of capital investments were power engineering specialists (Metallurgizdat, 1959, 1966; Energia, 1973). It was recommended in that sector to use the formula of discounted costs for the static case and in the more complicated case, when capital investments, operation costs and output are changing in time, the formula of average discounted costs. It was also recommended to use in all calculations uniform standard efficiency coefficients. This approach in fact was the first step on the way to the creation of an officially adopted document for the choice of the most efficient power engineering technologies.

As in the practice of power engineering, practice of economic–mathematical modelling stimulated the development of sets of rules for the choice of the best alternative. By the early 1960s, studies on the optimisation of sectoral and territorial planning became rather intensive. For instance, already in 1961–62 the basic scheme of the system of models of territorial-sectoral planning was developed in Novosibirsk, and since 1965 a dynamic inter-branch model covering 29 branches has been applied for pre-plan calculations (see Shemetov, 1978). However, dynamic models cannot be implemented in practice if the problem of comparison of costs and benefits in time is not solved. Also, if product substitution is included, it is impossible to use norms of capital investment efficiency using recommended standard methods.

Different norms of capital investment efficiency may exist for one and the same product. Thus developers of economic–mathematical models had to promote theoretical studies in the field. Finally, this work resulted in principal methodical provisions for the optimisation of the development and allocation of production (Academia Nauk, 1978). The main methodical provisions included in this publication had been published several times earlier (Academia Nauk, 1967, 1969). We should mention the following provisions fixed in these documents:

- methods for the location of the system under consideration;
- methods for the assessment of resources and products used in related production;
- choice of planning period and methods for comparing costs and benefits over time;
- choice of efficiency criteria;
- uniformity of sectoral and territorial economic efficiency standards;
- methods for the estimation of transport costs.

The practice of the application of mathematical methods in sectoral and territorial planning forced the developers of such methods to carry out analysis of problems, unsolved in classical Soviet political economy from the point of view of a systems approach. The first widely disseminated publication of standard methods for the estimation of economic efficiency of capital investments (Academia Nauk, 1966c), was published at about the same time as methods of technical–economic calculations in power engineering and the first drafts of the principal methodical provisions for the optimisation of the development and allocation of production (Gosplan, 1969; Academia Nauk, 1969). In spite of this, a number of provisions adopted in documents already published by sectoral institutions were not acknowledged as standard methods. There was no uniformity in the choice of criteria for the estimation of capital investments efficiency. The uniformity of coefficients of comparative economic efficiency was not acknowledged and every branch could require changing the coefficients (in practice to make them lower), referring to the specific character of the branch. There was no strict recommendation on the discount factor for costs and benefits over time; there were no formulated terms for making output composition, product quality and production technology comparable across sectors.

Supervisors of the development of these standard methods were constantly criticised for their retrograde positions. Adjustments to the officially published documents were made with large delays. During the period under consideration, in 1966 a volume of common methods for the development of a general scheme of the allocation of productive forces of the USSR for 1971–80 was published (see Energia, 1973). It was stated in this version of the guidelines for general planning methods that calculations at the national level were to be made on the basis of scenarios (first of all variants of national income distribution). The necessity of balance calculations by branches and regions was acknowledged as well as the possibility of choosing the best alternative of production allocation with minimum discounted costs. It was also acknowledged that some specific tasks should be solved with the use of simplified models.

By this time inter-branch balances of the country were already being regularly developed at the Research Economic Institute of the USSR Gosplan. In some organisations, including the territorial planning agency SOPS, sectoral optimisation calculations were carried out. In spite of this, the authors of the general methical guidelines did not consider it necessary to take into account the interrelations among networked branches, and adjacent regions in the schemes. The rejection of a profound use of mathematical modelling methods made it impossible for the authors of the general methods to consider optimality criteria and the comparison of costs accruing over time. In this fashion the level of scientific substantiation of recommendations was significantly decreased. It could be said that the theoretical level of the general methical guidelines of production allocation was not higher than that of earlier standard methods.

Methods of Economic Substantiation after 1970

The group of power engineers (Academia Nauk, 1977), was again one of the first to develop a new stage in Soviet economic analysis. In their work a system of estimates of life-cycle costs was calculated for the first time in planning practice. Such estimates were made for different kinds of fuel (bituminous coal, pit coal, fuel oil, gas), for electric and heat power, for all main regions of the country and for two periods of perspective planning (1981–85 and 1986–90). The work considered the use of fuel-power resources only for power production, but it was clear from the analysis that life-cycle costs were to be recommended also for other individual cases. The demand of an individual enterprise will be negligible in comparison with the total output in the processing of power resources and will not influence the total level or the interregional trade.

The principle of estimating the benefits of activities of related production in accordance with the estimates of optimal life-cycle costs obtained a formal character and qualitative estimates were performed. In 1977 methods for the assessment of new machinery efficiency were prepared and published by two institutes of the USSR Academy of Science, the CEMI and the Institute of Economics, with the participation of representatives of the USSR Gosplan (see Academia Nauk, 1977). This document proposed methods which differed greatly from the earlier standard methods. However, it did not contain all the methodological achievements of the work published earlier:

The necessity to compare capital investments, operation costs and output varying in time was not mentioned since these were not considered important for new machinery. The full statement of the necessity to use life-cycle costs of the output of related production was not adopted. Specialists in the field of optimal planning published in 1978 a final variant of the main provisions document.

What was the methodological progress in the field of allocation of productive forces and regional economic development? A draft programme of methods for the development of a general scheme of allocation of productive forces of the USSR for the planning year 1990 is the most representative work in this field (SOPS and Gosplan, 1972). It was proposed in this draft to classify all branches according to the most important factor determining their allocation (branches which shift towards regions where labour resources or raw materials are concentrated, branches which shift towards regions of product consumption) in order to estimate the economic efficiency of production allocation. It was necessary to develop for these branches a system of comparable technical–economic indices for the consumption of fuel, raw materials, electric power and water per unit of finished product as well as specific labour costs and specific capital investments. Then the main task was reduced to determining the specific costs per worker. Since the task being solved was complex and the choice of the best alternative using other methods was difficult or impossible, it was recommended to apply economic–mathematical methods. It was not explained in the document how the proposed methods correlate with the earlier recommended main factor method for employment productivity calculations.

By the end of the 1970s another exceptional document was published. At that time in the USSR and abroad the application of systems methods became more common (Academia Nauk, 1980a). The document emphasised the necessity to take into account all kinds of internal and external interrelations, a multitude of input resources and social, environmental and other consequences of adopted decisions in the substantiation of production allocation. A group of researchers of SOPS recommended that the allocation of an individual production unit be made on the basis of an index measuring the minimum of discounted costs. However, in retrospect it seems that the authors of this document had never solved dynamic, multi-product economic models with product substitution, come across the problem of measurement of costs and benefits or applied methods of expenditure accounts to intermediary input branches. In its theoretical part this work had not made much progress in comparison with the location theory of Veber, popular at the beginning of the century. The conclusion is that in the 1970s the methodological principles underpinning the general schemes of allocation lagged behind in comparison with the most advanced theoretical and methodological studies, carried out internationally and by economic research scholars in Moscow, Novosibirsk and other research centres of Russia.

The development in the 1980s and 1990s was characterised by the improvement of earlier studies and, more recently, the narrowing of the gap between domestic developments and generally accepted international standards. Thus the methodological recommendations on the efficiency evaluation of investment projects and their selection for financing (published in Academia Nauk, 1994), are now rather close to the international standards oriented to market relations. On the whole, calculations made in the period of transition to new economic conditions are characterised by approaches similar to international standards.

What, then, is the actual state of methodological developments of the transition period in the field of allocation of productive forces? We will consider as an example the methodological recommendations on the development of sectoral schemes of development and allocation of productive forces elaborated by SOPS of the USSR Gosplan (SOPS and

Gosplan, 1992). It is said in this document that the profitability of fixed capital, growth of labour productivity, reduction of costs and materials consumption, and other indices are to be compared for operating enterprises of the branch. How these indices are to compare in practice remains unknown. Furthermore, it is stated that, when evaluating the efficiency of allocation among branch enterprises, indices of discounted costs may be applied with the use of capital profit rates, calculated with discount rates differentiated in the territorial aspect. It remains unknown where the authors found the idea of the necessity to differentiate profit rates in the territorial context, and who precisely will calculate these indices. Thus the general conclusion is that present-day regional economic policy in Russia still partially repeats the background of the Soviet classical economic school of the 1950s and has not yet found the way to the high road of international regional economic methods.

The Development and Use of Input–Output Tables

In 1957 Nemchinov proposed using the input–output scheme, popular at that time in the market economies, for making five-year plans of development of the national economy. The necessity of applying this method was determined by the need not only to balance production and consumption, but also to find ways to reduce the very high intermediate consumption (about 60 percent of the production cost) and to increase the value-added share (see the account given in Nemchinov, 1962).

Studies on input–output tables were started in two directions: construction of tables for the country and construction of tables for economic regions. The main efforts of the researchers were concentrated on the USSR input–output tables. Its indices of gross outputs would be the basis for solving the task of production allocation over the territory of the country. The first special developments on the basis of data for 1955 and 1957 were carried out by the Research Economic Institute of the USSR Gosplan. As a result, an experimental commodity balance of inter-branch linkages for 1957 was constructed covering 24 products and branches of industry. Then, on the initiative of the USSR Gosplan, construction of input–output tables of the national economy of the USSR for 1959 was started. The Central Statistical Bureau of the USSR organised a selective data collection of approximately 20 per cent of industrial enterprises and construction sites. Direct technological coefficients were obtained as the result of this data collection exercise.

The problem of the application of mathematical methods in planning practice including methods and results of input–output table construction was discussed at a Moscow meeting in 1960. The work carried out before was criticised at this meeting for the first time. Drawbacks of the method itself were noted, and inadequate results of economic experience were mentioned. Examples were the static formulation of the task, the fixed final consumption, the fixed technological labour input coefficients and the use of net branches in calculations instead of economic branches. In spite of these drawbacks, some of which were later removed, results of input–output calculations (first of all, production volumes) were widely used later in the 1970s in solving the tasks of production development and allocation. For many years there existed an alliance between the Research Economic Institute and SOPS of the USSR Gosplan, where the former was responsible for the estimation of production volumes and the latter for the rational allocation of productive forces.

In parallel with input–output table construction work was carried out on tables for individual regions. In the early 1960s input–output models for 1958 and 1959 were built at the Gosplan laboratory of economic–mathematical methods headed by Nemchinov for Mordovskaya ASSR and for Kaliningrad oblast. At the same time staff of research and planning institutions of Tatarskaya ASSR constructed input–output tables of their region for 1959 (Dadayan and Kossov, 1962). Some time later construction of tables of individual republics started in the Baltic region (Latvia) and Transcaucasus (Georgia, Azerbaijan). The situation changed radically when the USSR Central Statistics Bureau started construction of input–output tables not only for the whole country but also for all Union republics. National and republic tables were constructed for 1966, 1972, 1977, 1982 and 1987. By the second half of the 1960s attempts had been made to construct input–output tables for individual towns, for instance, Kineshma in Ivanovo oblast and Kizel in Perm oblast.

The input–output tables of individual regions and towns failed to become an instrument for the elaboration of plans of national economic development for the perspective period. The researchers did not succeed in the simultaneous development of models of the choice of specialisation of the region and models of production allocation and population settlement. Such linkages would have been necessary to analyse the balance of production and consumption in the region. Nevertheless, models of upper-level planning were significantly developed, both in the sense of regular practical use and in the sense of their empirical validity.

Studies carried out at the Research Economic Institute of the USSR Gosplan and at the Novosibirsk Institute of Economics and Organisation of Industrial Production of the Siberian branch of the USSR Academy of Science promoted practical use of input–output tables of the country most of all. These institutes, together with the Central Economic–Mathematical

Institute (CEMI) in Moscow also carried out work on further improvement of input–output models to include the dependence between costs and output, to include consumption functions and income generation, to provide reflections of the interaction between the economy and the environment. An attempt was also made to account for the institutional framework of the national economy (see Yaremenko *et al.*, 1975).

The problem of input–output table construction significantly depends on whether branches are modelled in net or real economic terms. For a correct application it is important to reflect the interdependence between net and real economic branches. This is especially important for a planned economy where market prices do not exist. Models using detailed input–output tables in kind and in value were developed at the Research Economic Institute of the USSR Gosplan. They included three groups of conditions: equations of production and distribution of output in kind, structure of goods production in kind by branches, ministries and departments, and equations of goods production by branches in value. These models were applied at the stage of development of main planning directions and for draft economic plans. For example, for the period 1976–90, tables have been constructed, including 136 kinds of products and 20 branches embracing 26 ministries and departments.

From the early 1970s a boom in economic modelling with the use of input–output models started in the USSR. The works of the Nobel Prize laureate V. Leontiev served as its source (see also Leontiev and Ford, 1972). As seen from the summary exposition above, significant achievements were made in this direction during the later Soviet period. However, it is true to say that with the beginning of the economic crisis in Russia in the 1990s, the practical interest in the development of economic models of the input–output type sharply decreased.

Modelling of Production Development and Allocation

It is beyond question that in the USSR the classical work of Kantorovich on the economic calculations of the best use of resources (Kantorovich, 1960) started studies in the field of modelling of production development and allocation. The first models of individual production units were developed in the early 1960s. Gradually, development of sectoral models came to cover about 70 sectors of the economy and the main products. All this work was officially submitted to corresponding departments of the USSR Gosplan, which included necessary recommendations on the development of sectoral models in the methodological instructions for the development of state plans of the national economy (Academia Nauk, 1974). Among the most large-scale studies the following should be mentioned.

- Fuel-power complexes of the country (Siberian Energy Institute, Energosetproekt and other organisations).
- Development and allocation of the coal industry (CNIEIugol: Central Research Institute of Economic Studies in Coal Industry, CEMI).
- Development and allocation of ferrous metals production (Institute of Economics and Organisation of Industrial Production (IEOIP), Novosibirsk).
- Development and allocation of branches of the forestry complex (IEOIP, Novosibirsk).
- Development and allocation of agriculture (SOPS of the USSR Gosplan, IEOIP).

The development and implementation of sectoral models required uniform methodological approaches in the preparation of initial information, evaluation of results obtained and preparation of recommendations. This work has been carried out within the Gosplan system and the results were published as main methodological principles of optimisation of production development and allocation, first in 1969 and later in 1978 (see Academia Nauk, 1969, 1978). The methods employed officially fixed a number of provisions for which there was no common point of view among the Soviet economists. They concerned the methods for qualitative comparison of inputs and benefits over time, the methods for estimation of created capital and production capacities, and the methods for estimation of transport costs in optimisation calculations.

A set of guideline principles of economic formulation of the planning tasks was given in Academia Nauk (1969). They concerned fundamental properties of scientific economic analyses as rules of location of individual sub-systems, choice of the planning period, methods for governing sub-systems functioning beyond the period under consideration, choice of efficiency criteria, choice of the most relevant model formulation and choice of the specification of the structure of the economic models including resource restrictions. Rules common to all sectors of the economy and non-conflicting rules for the preparation of initial information were also formulated (cost accounts, expenditures on transport, costs in intermediary industries, discount rates).

We shall discuss the experience of the practical use of sectoral models of production development and allocation using the example of the chemical industry. The planning tasks reported were initiated at CEMI in 1964–66. The task of optimisation of the development of the chemical industry was enacted for the period 1971–75. Sub-branches of plastics, chemical fibres and mineral fertiliser production were considered as specific objects for analysis.

Conditions of replacement of less efficient kinds of products by efficient chemical materials within the fixed technological limits were introduced. As a result of increases in the demand for chemical production the sector grew by 10–12 per cent on average, while capital investments declined by 8–10 per cent and saving of operation costs decreased by 5–8 per cent. The integrated profit of the branch due to optimisation of the plan for plastics production and use in 1971–75 alone amounted to 150 million roubles. The results of the optimisation of production in the chemical branches of industry were significantly lower, and calculated savings turned out to be approximately 2–3 per cent of the costs.

In the process of accumulation of experience in the use of models of production development and allocation, negative attitudes grew among the leaders of sectoral ministries and departments towards the application of mathematical methods. This was explained by the fact that the essence of all planning practice under socialism consisted in the concealment of production potentials. Plans were understated in order to receive increased capital investment. Also the practice of voluntaristic decisions according to their own interests concerning the allocation of new industrial enterprises was rather typical among the leaders of corresponding ministries and departments. It is obvious that, under such conditions, results of objective calculations with the use of computers became a means of revealing reserves as a control over the arbitrary rule of sectoral authorities. As a consequence, in the early 1980s the role of arbitrary sectoral calculations in the elaboration of plans of development of the national economy started to decrease. The main provisions documents now formulated means of maximum possible coordination of sectoral development and allocation of production. Only within the framework of inter-branch models was it possible to solve these new coordination tasks in a scientifically appropriate way.

One system of models of industrial production allocation was developed at SOPS of the USSR Gosplan in the early 1970s (Albegov, 1975). This system of models was included in the general scheme of allocation of productive forces for the period up to 1990. It allowed coordination of sectoral and regional decisions. The essence of the idea of the proposed method of sectoral and regional plan coordination was as follows. Calculations according to optimisation of development and allocation of individual production sectors resulted not only in finding the optimum plan. The optimum decision was supplemented by a series of parametrical decisions for which the level of use of local resources in the region under consideration varied within a range from zero to a maximum possible value. For single-product establishments outputs could serve as response function parameters, and for multi-product establishments labour and capital resources could be used. When such response functions are constructed the allocation of individual production units and complexes reduced to the minimisation of a complex goal expression. The target function of the task is the sum of three cost components: at specialised enterprises, in complex production units and of local resources. Balances account for regional limitations for labour resources and capital investments.

Results of calculations according to the models presented were used many times as pre-plan calculations for the substantiation of allocation of productive forces for the future. The shift from the analysis of separately considered branches to simultaneous consideration of the aggregate of branches made it possible to find coordinated decisions from the point of view of national economic interests.

Modelling of Regional Economic Development

Concerning the two known patterns of regional analysis, top-down and bottom-up, the former was more popular in the USSR from the start. This was explained by the high level of centralisation of planning and the need for regular forecasting of the indices of social–economic development of the country, and the directions of specialisation of individual regions (republics of the former USSR). Work of such institutes of the USSR Gosplan as the Research Economic Institute and SOPS, and the Institute of Complex Transport Problems, created necessary prerequisites for the elaboration of forecasts of economic and social development of individual regions.

Since the late 1960s studies according to the bottom-up pattern developed, where the local development potentials of the region were the starting point instead of the above-mentioned indices of sectoral specialisation (Danilov-Danilyan and Zavelsky, 1975). Regional studies according to the bottom-up pattern were most successful in the Baltic republics and in the Ukraine. The essence of these works is considered below, using the example of Lithuania (see also Rayatskas, 1982).

The general scheme of the model system was oriented to the detailed forecasting of the economic development of the republic corresponding to the existing scheme of planning. Calculation started from the modelling of demographic processes. Key indices were selected for each region as birth rates for females at the age of maximum fertility and mortality. Problems of formation and movement of labour resources as well as personnel training were considered in the second stage of the model. The model of labour resources and personnel training described not only the structure of labour and its use in the national economy but also the future impact of labour resource formation. Demand in the branch was the main regulator of sectoral movement of labour. The need for labour in a certain year produces an impact on the availability of labour resources in the same branch in the ensuing years. The model could be used to follow the annual redistribution of labour resources between sectors. Estimation of the volume and structure of money incomes and consumption of the population was carried out with the help of differential wage balances. The idea of this balance construction was to obtain differentiated data on incomes and expenses, grouped by households with different levels of material well-being. It made it possible to plan the living standards of households at different levels of material security.

In order to estimate personal consumption a complex model was built, which consists of applications of trend functions and methods of regression analysis to determine solvent demand. Models were built on the basis of forecast population grouped by per capita income and structure of personal consumption expenditures. The model helped to make calculations both for the medium-term period and for the long-term perspective. Thus practical realisation of the model was oriented towards determining physiological and rational norms of personal consumption.

Precise calculations of the volumes of public consumption, as well as the volume and structure of the final use of material production, depended on a correct determination of the regularities in the formation of the cost structure in the non-production sphere. Normative methods of determination of the structure of inputs in this sphere were not sufficiently elaborated by the time the study was carried out. Instead, results of selected observations were used which were made in the process of input–output table construction for production and consumption of republican output. Estimation of real incomes of the population is a logical completion of the calculation of income as well as personal and public consumption.

The model presented forms a closed system allowing detailed analysis of the development of economy in the Lithuanian republic. Results of such calculations were used in the 1970s and 1980s as pre-plan materials. In these studies, carried out in the Latvian SSR (Adirim *et al.*, 1975), the focus was on the use of econometric models. Dynamic single-sector models, developed in Latvia, were used for growth projections on the basis of production functions with exogenous technical progression. The economic basis of these models was the relationship between the physical volume of production, national income and production factors as the number of employed in the material production sphere and the value of capital production funds. The first model of this type covered only production; the second one covered the sphere of services. In the second econometric model the balance of money incomes and expenditures of the population were taken into account as well as the balance of capital funds. A further model was developed using a lower level of aggregation, intended for working out summary indices of the sectors of the economy. An iterative regime of the use of models of different levels was envisaged. The ambition was to provide tools for combined short- and medium-term analyses.

Models of Territorial Production Complexes

Two directions prevail in the Soviet economic studies which are connected with the optimisation of intraregional allocation of production. The first one is the optimisation of production mix and spatial structure of territorial production complexes (TPCs). These studies were carried out for many years at the Institute of Economics and Organisation of Industrial Production of the Siberian Branch of the USSR Academy of Science (Albegov *et al.*, 1975; Academia Nauk, 1976; Bandman, 1980). The second direction which is connected to the TPC assessment work is the optimisation of the intraregional allocation of production (Albegov *et al.*, 1975). Work in this direction was concentrated at SOPS of the USSR Gosplan.

The practice of TPC formation revealed a number of faults, typical of all complexes: the failure in keeping to planned terms and of placing main objects into operation, unforeseen changes in their composition and sometimes of their specialisation, backward development of investment programmes and production infrastructure. There was a constant non-fulfilment of construction plans for elements of social infrastructure. The rule was deferred plans for improving living conditions for the population.

The major part of these faults is explained by non-observance of terms and changes in the volume of financing by individual ministries and departments, and by the unilateral refusal of some ministries and departments to build establishments on which agreement had been reached. This caused changes in the TPC structure and in the conditions for the creation of establishments serving the whole complex, in the sense of shared participation of ministries and departments, and lack of long-term feasible construction and financing plans. These factors made it impossible to carry out the planning for the construction teams, including the deliveries from the construction industry. The result was an uneven load and a less rational use of the financing and building organisations.

The faults are also explained by the poor level of infrastructure financing through ministries leading to forestalled infrastructural preparation of the territory. This implied an overall backward development of those elements of TPC and resulted in losses and decreases in the reliability of carrying out transport operations, the organisation of power supply and the formation of work teams. Another reason was the departmental approach to the resolution of individual questions on TPC formation and the lack of uniform technical–economic design documents. As regards the TPC coordination it would often lead to difficulties in the use of multi-purpose resources as capital investments, land, water and labour resources, and to an inadmissible load placed on the environment. It was also typical of the TPC projects that local bodies were removed from the resolution of the problems of social infrastructure from the very beginning, the argument being that they were not provided with resources since the assignments were carried out through industrial ministries. This made them dependent on ministries in Moscow and decreased their local influence on the process of TPC formation.

One of the major reasons for such a situation was that there was not an approved comprehensive action programme for any of the complexes. In spite of the importance of TPCs in the planned economy there were thus no binding comprehensive plan documents. As a result, authors of studies on TPC practice (Bandman *et al.*, 1990) proposed the following list of activities, corresponding to stages of TPC formation over a 15–20 year period:

- hypotheses on TPC formation via initial forecasts,
- scheme of TPC formation via analyses of variants of production structure and spatial organisation,
- general design of TPC via engineering–economic pre-plans,
- a programme of TPC development to plan the process of TPC formation.

With the help of this programme coordination would be carried out to comply with final objectives and development goals for the given object. Pre-plan and plan documents on the TPC would be developed with similar documents for ministries, departments and construction firms. This task could be solved comprehensively only with the help of detailed economic–mathematical model tools. The task of such a model (see Academia Nauk, 1976) is to determine the specialisation in the region, the complex-forming production and the appropriate elements of production infrastructure of interregional and intraregional significance. This would be done under conditions of minimisation of aggregate costs of the formation and the functioning of the economy of the region with account taken of the planned living standard.

Resolution of the task required taking into account the place of the region in the territorial division of labour, the specific features of individual production establishments, the natural conditions and resources of individual areas of the region as well as the level of economic development of the territory, and the availability and conditions of labour resources. The proposed formulation of the task was formalised in an economic–

mathematical model system. The selection criterion of this grand model of TPC formation was that the aggregate costs of creation and functioning of all production establishments under consideration, transport of products from outside and within the region, development of sections of mainline inter-area transport networks, creation and functioning of power stations, creation of power lines, creation and functioning of construction bases, settling of local and attracted population, development of the territory for industrial and civil construction and water supply for productions and populations should be as low as possible while fulfilling the production plan requirements.

This model would allow the analyst to obtain initial data for the next stage, to forecast the main specialisation of the TPC and to determine its spatial structure. Two problems were solved in the task of determining the intraregional allocation of production and the spatial structure. First, on the basis of response functions, the problem of the choice of direction of the regional specialisation was solved. Then target volumes of production were distributed across the territory of the region with account taken of costs of resources and effects of joint allocation of enterprises within the production units of the complex. The model presented was used to solve the task of optimisation of industrial specialisation in Kyrgizia. Territorial allocation of production volumes in the republic and the specific composition of production units were obtained. The calculated results provided cost savings of approximately 5–6 per cent in comparison with proposals put forward by local organisations.

Interregional and Inter-branch Models and their Application

The most grounded recommendations on the development of individual regions of the country could be obtained within a system of models of economic development covering all branches and all regions. There were two such systems developed in the former USSR, at CEMI (Baranov *et al.*, 1971) and at the Institute of Economics and Organisation of Industrial Production of the Siberian Branch (Granberg, 1988). The latter work is still used in scientific assessments of Russian regional economic development. The general structure of this interregional inter-branch model (GIIM) is given below.

The main orientation of the interregional inter-branch model is central planning calculations of territorial proportions within the national economy. Under conditions where Union republics and economic regions develop their own models, information from these models will be included in GIIM. The significance of GIIM increases in relation to the coordination of regional economic activities and the correction of summary indices of the national economy as a result of the introduction of spatially varying production factors and economic conditions.

Regional sub-models in GIIM are linked by conditions characterising necessary elements of regional living standards, conditions of balancing interregional exchange and development of transport networks, and limitations on common economic resources. Each regional sub-model represents the region with open entries and exits; that is, there exist systems of balances of production and distribution of branch output, use of labour, investment allocation, use of natural resources, and transport activity. The model includes balances of net capital investments for the planning period. Capital investments in transport development are assumed to be known as well as balances of production and distribution of the output. All variables and parameters are related to a final year of a planning period.

When the model is used at the upper level of territorial planning of Russia it is possible to identify up to 24 regions (14 Union republics and ten economic regions of the Russian Federation). If we take as a base classification already constructed regional input–output tables (involving approximately 105 branches), the total number of equations of the model for only one region will exceed 2500 in number. Therefore the problem of the level of aggregation is important. In particular, it does not seem possible for the present moment to use efficiently dynamics in the model system with an annual breakdown of the long-term forecasts.

In GIIM all kinds of transport are unified among sectors and transport costs are averaged. Costs of transport between adjacent regions are related to the sending region. Export and import of produce is carried out through the points of frontier regions of the country, with only one point chosen in each region. Local resources are fixed by regions and special conditions of labour resource mobility are not specified. On the other hand migration flows are accounted for in the substantiation of labour supply limits. GIIM is an optimisation model where the room for consumption is employed as the central criterion for the comparison of development alternatives. The level of consumption of the population of the country is optimised under fixed structures of regional levels of consumption and rules for determination of intraregional consumption structures.

Experimental calculations of optimum variants of territorial proportions of the USSR national economy using GIIM were made at the Institute of Economics and Organisation of Industrial Production for the ten-year period 1966–75 for 16 branches of material production and ten economic regions of the USSR. Significant attention was given to the interpretation of the results obtained, assessment of impacts of errors in the initial information, and possible changes of results arising from the model structure and data specifications.

A detailed analysis of the main variants of territorial proportions of the USSR national economy for 1966–75, calculated according to GIIM, is given in Granberg (1973). A number of stable qualitative characteristic features of optimum decisions have been revealed. In particular, significant differentiation of growth rates of the majority of branches by zones was found. On the whole the forecasts of economic development until 1975 turned out to be optimistic. Forecasts of structural shifts in the system of territorial proportions of the national economy proved to be true to a significantly larger extent.

Some results of the optimisation calculations, considered at first as invalid or occasional, were later acknowledged. For instance, this could be said about the recommendations on the optimum interval of growth rates of Siberia and the Far East in comparison with average Union rates, expediency of more narrow specialisation of a number of regions, potentials for advanced development of the mining industry in Siberia, and the necessity to limit the growth rates of the light industry. There were discovered a number of effects of inter-branch and interregional interactions, for example expediency of reducing capital investments in some regions while increasing capital investments in the national economy as a whole.

In the process of accumulation of experience of working with GIIM, the conviction grew that at least at the stage of pre-planning studies the model should be oriented mainly to the understanding of the mechanisms of inter-branch and interregional interactions, quantitative assessment of mutual impacts of main factors and illustration of stable dynamic and structural regularities of the system of economic proportions. Already at the first stage of GIIM applications multivariant calculations were made with some conditions changed. Attempts were made to use optimum assessment of products and resources and other structural indices in the analysis of possible directions of improvement of territorial proportions.

With the help of GIIM, studies on the problems of territorial development of the USSR for the future were carried out. In contrast to the first stage of calculations an improved model was used, including the optimisation of parameters of capital investments. Experimental fulfilment of the task with a larger number of branches was also carried out. Work was started on the inclusion of GIIM in the automated system of plan calculations in the territorial planning system of the USSR Gosplan. The model system was also implemented in the Main Computer Centre of the USSR Gosplan.

When modelling territorial proportions for the future, most attention was given to the problems of the interdependence of national economic and regional factors in the USSR economy. The focus was on the use of scenario methods. Calculations according to GIIM have allowed researchers to determine main indices of development of all large regions of the country. At the same time the model system offers the possibility of deeper studies of intraregional problems. Siberia is one such region for which detailed studies were carried out with the help of GIIM. The main result of the analysis of many variants with changing conditions revealed the following dynamic regularity: the average annual rate of increase of national income generation of Siberia should be 1.2–1.4 times higher than the average union rate; on the other hand the rates of increase of the gross regional product should be approximately the same. This excess in consumption for Siberia is optimal in the sense that it corresponds to the maximum achievable consumption level meeting all-Union needs.

The methods of study for Siberia could be used for accentuated study of other large regions. Addition of corresponding regional sections to the database and mathematical apparatus of GIIM allows organisations concerned to make multivariant calculations of development of any region within the Russian national economy.

The concept of systems modelling of sectoral and regional development gradually underwent significant development in the USSR. By the mid-1970s the main direction of applied developments on the system modelling of the economy had been determined. The focus was on the introduction of individual models and sets of models in the automated system of plan calculations (ASPC) of the USSR Gosplan and Gosplans of Union republics. Four alternative projects of system modelling were included in the draft ASPC of the USSR Gosplan, approved in 1977. It was expected that, after scientific elaboration and experimental application, one or two variants would be included in the second generation of ASPC. But this development did not materialise. None of the proposed experimental systems of models of economic planning was realised to the full extent. Intensified work on the introduction of models in the actual planning process gave new understanding of the requirements of individual models and sets of models, and revealed a number of unacceptable methodological, organisational and other features of the initial projects of systems modelling. Let us consider some typical faults.

First, the iterative process of obtaining coordinated decisions for the whole national economy and its sub-system in particular did not work in practice. The second problem which hampered development was the too global character of the model systems. The fact of the matter is that, in accordance with the design level of preparation of the system, the level of preparation of the last constructive element limited the applicability of the work. For example, when modelling a branch or a region the system of models would function, as a rule, only on the condition that all elements were present, including the corresponding empirical information, mathematical provision and computer software. The scientific situation in the field of development of different economic–mathematical models is quite variable, a fact that strongly restrains the possibilities for complex modelling of interlinked elements, and delays approbation of any accomplished model system. Third, introduction of complex, multi-level and multi-aspect model sets was restrained by the low interest of planning and managerial bodies and their functional divisions. Even in the USSR Gosplan there was no department which was competent to apply a system of models at large.

From the second half of the 1970s new conceptualisations of the immediate tasks of systems modelling of the national economy were gradually developed. The most significant achievements were connected with the development of specialised models, the accounting systems of planning and pre-plan studies, new potentials of empirical information, mathematical and technical provisions with the emergence of distributed computer technology, and professional skills of users. One such model complex was the project SIRENA–SONAR (synthesis of regional and economic decisions and coordination of sectoral and economic decisions). This system has a common methodological, informational and technical base, through which different problems can be treated. The model is used during development of multivariant forecasts in preparing the complex programmes of scientific and technical progress, assessment of economic consequences of the implementation of large-scale production, and social and sociotechnical programmes.

The model complexes forming the methodological basis of the project SIRENA–SONAR have common basic economic models at the national level. More detailed study of the problems of large regions and multi-branch complexes is carried out with the help of special optimisation interregional inter-branch models such as GIIM, where the object of main interest is characterised in more detail. For instance, the special GIIM model for the Ukraine includes a more detailed section for the Ukrainian SSR, and the special GIIM for the chemical sector includes a detailed analysis of the chemical industry. Devising scenario calculations is a typical form of the use of the SIRENA–SONAR model.

On the basis of national economic scenarios, studies have been carried out on changes occurring at the regional level. These changes are now much more prone to influence from the global economic level than earlier. In the perspective of both the international connections of the Russian economy and the new interregional relationships within the Russian Federation, model systems for the prevision of medium- and long-term changes will become more and more important. It seems that Russian regional economic modelling will be facing unprecedented challenges in the next century. The problem is to strike a balance between the scientific ambitions of the regional economic research necessary to understand the development forces in the transition economy, and the policy ambitions to provide decision support on economic development issues in the emerging Russia of regions.

NOTES

1. It should be noted that large territorial units, considered as economic regions, were referred to by various names at that time: oblast, krai, district.
2. The rates at which production grew are given in accordance with the official statistics, but it is obvious that economic development was fastest in the republics mentioned.
3. Siberia and the Far East of the RSFSR, Kazakhstan and republics of Central Asia.
4. From the first years of its existence SOPS (then the 'Council for Location of Productive Forces') was responsible for developing the General Scheme for Location of Productive Forces of the USSR Gosplan. For further details of the history and methodology of the development of the General Scheme, see SOPS (1988).
5. Evidently this was a hasty announcement, since the problem of large regional disparities in levels of development is still acute in Russia.

3. Regional development and regional policy in the Gorbachev period

Alexander Granberg

TERRITORIAL ORGANISATION OF THE ECONOMY: MAIN PROBLEMS

By the time *perestroika* began, a highly integrated economy based on state ownership and centralised management had taken shape in the USSR. The term 'single complex of the national economy', widely used in the Soviet literature, had both pragmatic and ideological connotations. On the one hand it reflected a high level of internal integration of the national economy and was of special significance in a country of vast territories and extreme regional diversity, relatively isolated from the disciplines of the global economy and expending much wealth on supporting its status as a superpower. On the other hand this term was utilised to affirm the Soviet Union's alleged success in integrating the interests of all its economic components, and especially of Union republics.

Granting the high integration of the Soviet economy and even the numerous successes of Soviet practice in the allocation of productive forces, no conclusions should be drawn concerning the *efficiency* and *fairness* of the system of territorial economic organisation created in the USSR (including the territorial division of labour, allocation of productive forces and regional development), particularly as regards reconciliation of the interests of different regions. A critical analysis of this system is of practical topical importance in assessing its ability to adapt itself (broadly speaking and in its major elements) to the post-Soviet model of political and economic development.

We believe that an accumulation of distortions and contradictions within the 'single complex of the national economy' have accelerated and intensified the general crisis of the USSR's political and economic system while also creating severe transitional difficulties as the republics and regions of the former USSR move towards an open market economy. Interethnic relations constitute another problem, closely associated with the Soviet practices of centralised planning of production and employment, development of new regions and forced resettlement of whole peoples.

The territorial organisation of the Soviet Union's economy as it had evolved by the middle of the 1980s had a number of specific features. We shall mention but not repeat the analysis made and the conclusions formed in earlier chapters concerning the main problems distinguishing the Soviet Union from other countries, whether with market or planned economies.

1. *Concentration of the population and production potential (mainly secondary and tertiary branches) in the European territories of the USSR (comprising one quarter of the whole).* The mining industry shows a similar concentration in Siberia and the Far East (together accounting for 57 per cent of the Soviet Union's territory and 10 per cent of the population) and in sparsely populated northern regions of European Russia and Kazakhstan. This was the main characteristic feature of the all-Union territorial division of labour along the west–east (or west–east, north) axis.

Long-distance shipments of bulk cargoes are the consequence of this kind of specialisation of production in macro regions. In the second half of the 1980s over a billion tonnes per year of fuel alone were transported from east to west over distances of up to 5000 km, as also were vast quantities of industrial raw materials, machinery, various industrial finished products and consumer goods from west to east. The economic incentive to transport mass cargoes over such long distances was sustained artificially by means of both low transport tariffs and low prices for fuels and industrial raw materials. Thus economical utilisation of resources was discouraged while long-distance shipments were stimulated. At the same time the centralisation of external economic activity prevented the peripheral regions (especially in the Far East) from compensating for their remoteness from the European part of the country by developing trade with adjacent countries. In Siberia and the Far East various planning directives were adopted with a view to developing industries processing locally produced fuel and raw materials along with the requisite industrial and social infrastructure. These efforts failed. The conditions required to stabilise the population attracted to the eastern and northern regions over a period of several decades in order to develop the natural resources there simply did not materialise.

2. *Increasing backwardness of the southern Union republics (especially those of Central Asia) in terms of level of economic development and standards of living,* given the growing able-bodied population surplus and the rapidly rising share of the USSR's demographic potential accounted for by these republics. Rates of population growth and therefore of labour resources (up to 2.5–3 per cent per annum) still remained high in these republics. Unsuccessful attempts were made to diversify the economy and so provide jobs for the rural and urban populations. The agriculture of the Central Asian

republics specialised to an extreme degree in the cultivation of cotton, resulting in an excessive consumption of water. This precipitated an environmental crisis in these vast territories, notably in the basin of the Aral Sea. Local political leaders proposed a solution to this crisis in the form of a superproject for transferring water from the rivers Ob and Irtysh, which provoked objections from the Russian regions.

Large plants erected in towns were unable to make use of local labour because of lack of skill and low social mobility (especially in the case of the rural population). They therefore had to attract labour from other regions of the country, mainly from regions of Russia where labour was already in short supply: thus the potential for interethnic conflict gradually accumulated. The relative backwardness of the Central Asian republics' economic base was increasing, growth of the industrial national income per head having ceased since the end of the 1970s. This necessitated the redistribution to these republics of ever-increasing quantities of material and financial resources. The result was a growing resistance on the part of the more developed republics and a gradual reinforcement of the negative sociopsychological background to inter-republic relations.

3. *Extreme specialisation and concentration of industrial production resulting from the economic policy of all-powerful sectoral ministries and supported by ideological 'gigantomania' in state planning.* A single branch of production, not necessarily having anything to do with the exploitation of local natural resources, dominated the industrial structure of a number of regions and many towns. Examples are the textile industry in Ivanovo oblast and the defence industry in Udmurtia and towns of Siberia. In mechanical engineering, chemistry and metallurgy the tendency towards monopolisation of production was growing. By the early 1990s there were about a thousand enterprises in the USSR with a monopoly of the manufacture of certain kinds of product. There are other aspects of hyperspecialisation and hyperconcentration of production which are not rational: these include the long-distance shipment of semi-finished products, components and so on between plants subordinate to the same ministry (intra-ministry turnover).

4. *Organisational and economic subordination of the social life of towns to the functioning of manufacturing enterprises.* Many towns in the USSR are designed to serve the needs of a single gigantic enterprise. Examples are Magnitogorsk with its metallurgical works, Tolyatti and Naberezhnye Chelny with the Volzhsky (VAZ) and Kamsky (Kamaz) motorcar plants, and so on. This made such towns completely dependent on economic conditions in a single branch and the policy of a single ministry. Extreme cases of this kind of town planning are the dozens of 'closed' towns servicing secret enterprises, facilities and research institutes (such as Arzamas-16, the largest

centre of atomic science and industry). The actual government of such towns was in the hands of ministries, and local authorities had no financial powers. Organisational and economic coalescence of production enterprises and social services became a typical phenomenon in the USSR. Not only in the group just cited but in the majority of towns, a considerable proportion of residential accommodation, child welfare and medical services, shops, heating supply, public transport and other such facilities became subordinated to large production enterprises which provided them with material resources and finance.

These idiosyncrasies of territorial economic organisation, all greatly strengthened by the late 1980s, exercised much influence over political and economic change in the USSR and, subsequently, in its former territories.

INTER-REPUBLIC ECONOMIC INTERDEPENDENCE

In the USSR – nominally a federation, but in fact a unitary state – the role of Union republics as economic *actors* or *subjects* was significantly limited (the effect of this being most palpable in the case of the Russian Federation). The Union republics could not create independent national economies developing along stable lines. Hence their main role was to be passive *objects*, regions of the upper (state) rank in the all-Union system of territorial economic organisation. It is obvious that the common features permeating this system (in particular, hyperspecialisation, hyperconcentration and the resultant large flows of products) made heavy economic interdependence of Union republics inevitable.

Several methodological approaches are employed in order to analyse this economic interdependence empirically and assess the consequences of the collapse of the system of economic linkages between republics. Attention is focused chiefly on the analysis of inter-republic exchanges of goods, since this form of economic linkage was dominant in the USSR. Inter-republic mobility of population (including labour resources) was not high in the 1980s. Financial transfers played a subordinate role compared with material flows, and no inter-republic market existed at all. The system of republic intersectoral balances (input–output tables) and tables of inter-republic exchanges of goods devised by the Central Statistical Bureau (CSB) of the USSR furnish the groundwork for the analysis.

Intensity of Inter-republic Exchanges of Goods

On the whole the intensity of inter-republic exchanges of goods in the USSR in the 1980s was significantly greater in relation to GDP than that of inter-state trade within the present European Union (USSR approximately 20.5 per cent, EU approximately 16 per cent). Up to 1987 the volume of such inter-republic exchanges was increasing more rapidly than the USSR's gross product (at comparable prices) and this is one of the signs of an increasing territorial division of labour and greater economic integration of the USSR republics. Naturally, the republics which were largest in terms of economic potential and territory (Russia, Ukraine, Kazakhstan) had economies of a more closed type. In the remaining 12 republics the coefficients of exports and imports lie within the ranges 18–27 per cent and 21–31 per cent, respectively.

Dependence of the coefficient of inter-republic turnover (K_{it}) on the scale of the economy output (Q) is approximated by the regression equation:

$$K_{it} = 74.38 - 27.61Q^{0.19} \qquad (3.1)$$

the correlation coefficient for which is equal to 93.8 per cent.

The intensity of inter-republic turnover is less dependent on the size of the republic's territory than on the influence of Russia. If Russia is excluded from the reckoning, all correlation coefficients are negligible. The coefficients employed give a preliminary idea of the importance of inter-republic linkages to the economies of every republic of the USSR. If we apply the simplest macroeconomic multiplier (ratio of gross product to gross and final product, the latter consisting of exports and – with a minus sign – imports), which in the USSR is approximately 2.5, then we find that in the majority of republics considerably more than half of the gross product either went to other republics as exports or was saved in the form of products imported from other republics; that is to say, most of the goods produced participated directly or indirectly (via material expenditure on production) in inter-republic trade.

The Problems of Equivalence of Inter-republic Linkages

As long as Union republics of the USSR were not economic actors in the full sense, measurement of the results of inter-republic intercourse was not a necessary condition of the economic system's functioning. The problem of balanced inter-republic linkages (equivalence) was regarded initially as purely academic and, since the early 1980s, as an aspect of ideological preparation for the reform of economic relations between Union centre, republics and regions.

In 1987–88 the idea of 'territorial self-financing' became popular, its rational basis being the establishment of direct dependence (but not necessarily equality) between what the region gives to the national economy and what it gets from the all-Union funding pool.[1] The immediate result was that the trade and payments balances of the regions were calculated and the concept of equivalence (economic balance) was applied to relations between the centre and the regions (primarily the Union republics).

Table 3.1   *Balance of inter-republic exchanges of goods in 1986–90 in current domestic prices of final consumption (billion roubles)*

Republic	1986	1987	1988	1989	1990
Russia	+6.89	+3.65	+0.26	+4.40	+7.75
Ukraine	−1.03	+1.56	+3.62	+0.49	−1.03
Kazakhstan	−5.93	−5.43	−5.35	−6.37	−7.26
Belarus	+2.17	+3.15	+4.05	+3.47	+2.72
Uzbekistan	−2.94	−3.92	−1.67	−3.51	−3.12
Azerbaijan	+1.94	+2.04	+2.10	+2.88	+1.86
Lithuania	−0.45	−0.40	−0.81	+0.06	−0.57
Georgia	+0.39	+3.65	+0.29	+0.83	+0.71
Moldova	+0.08	+1.56	−0.19	0.00	+0.77
Latvia	+0.23	−5.43	−0.12	+0.52	+0.18
Armenia	+0.54	+0.59	−0.33	−0.24	+0.04
Kyrgizia	−0.39	−0.52	−0.44	−0.81	−0.57
Estonia	−0.10	−0.24	−0.33	−0.33	−0.25
Tadzhikistan	−0.90	−1.11	−1.00	−1.07	−0.81
Turkmenia	−0.47	−0.27	−0.10	−0.32	−0.42
Sum with the same sign*	12.24	12.19	10.32	12.65	14.03

Note: * The sum of all plus and minus quantities in each column should be zero. Discrepancies are explained by rounding-off errors. The last line of each column shows the sum of its plus quantities.

The problem of the efficiency and fairness of existing economic relations between centre and Union republics, and finally between Union republics, occupied the leading place in political discussions. Each republic put forward its own arguments demonstrating how its economic interests had been infringed, but infractions of the market principle of *equivalence* in inter-republic trade and economic relations were cited more frequently. This is why reliable assessments of the equivalence of these linkages should be arrived at as a first step towards analysing objectively the problem of the efficiency and fairness of inter-republic linkages. Turning our attention away for the moment from the influence of the USSR's external economic linkages on the balance of inter-republic trade (which will be discussed below), *the criterion of equivalence (or balance) of inter-republic trade would be a zero export–import balance for each republic.*[2] The dynamics of the balance of inter-republic exchanges of goods are shown in Table 3.1.

One of the paradoxes of the economic system of the USSR was that every republic benefited from an unfavourable trade balance (a surplus of imports over exports), since flows of goods between republics did not create equivalent indebtedness for the republics. The incentive to incur an unfavourable trade balance was reinforced by shortages of goods and suppressed inflation. During the five years analysed, four republics had a favourable trade balance, namely Russia, Belarus, Azerbaijan and Georgia. Six republics had an unfavourable balance: all Central Asian republics and Estonia. In the remaining five republics the balances alternated between favourable and unfavourable. The annual trade imbalances (sums of favourable and unfavourable balances respectively) for all republics amounted to between 10.3 and 14.0 billion roubles.

The data in Table 3.1 do not furnish sufficient ground for any conclusions as to which republics were goods donors or recipients. Even less do they indicate the winners and losers in inter-republic trade. These data have to be interpreted in the light of the characteristic features of statistics and of the economic mechanisms existing at the time. The following are the chief factors of which account must be taken:

- arbitrariness of the prices applied,
- influence of external economic linkages (exports and imports) on the balance of inter-republic trade,
- incompleteness of figures for inter-republic exchanges of goods,
- dependence of a part of inter-republic linkages on all-Union (federal) expenditures.

Changes in Inter-republic Exchanges of Goods at More Realistic Prices

Volumes of inter-republic exchanges of goods were calculated in terms of the domestic prices at the point of final consumption, which reflected the special nature of Soviet pricing and the methodological peculiarities involved in striking intersectoral balances. It is known that plan prices were heavily understated in the USSR in relation to both total costs of production and world market prices for the output of raw material-producing sectors, while prices of the majority of consumer goods were heavily overstated as well. The uneven distribution of turnover tax and state subsidies between sectors, along with compensation from the Soviet Union budget for the difference between purchasing and retail prices of foodstuffs (amounting to 100 billion roubles per year) had a very considerable effect on the real final prices as distinct from nominal prices. Under the surrealistic pricing system which prevailed, the most 'profitable' economic sectors for republics were oil refining, the clothing industry and the manufacture of alcoholic beverages (maximum turnover tax), while the most unprofitable were the coal industry (subsidies), meat production and dairying (retail prices lower than purchase prices). As a result, naturally, the balance of exchanges of goods was understated for the republics exporting mainly raw materials, fuel and power and overstated for those exporting mainly goods subject to turnover tax.

Conversion of the volumes of inter-republic exchanges of goods to more realistic domestic prices (in which turnover tax, subsidies, compensation for price disparities and so on are included) gives significantly different values for republic trade balances (see Table 3.2).

Table 3.2   *Balance of inter-republic exchanges of goods in 1987–89, in 'adjusted' domestic prices (billion roubles)*

Republic	1987	1988	1989
Russia	+7.25	+2.25	+6.88
Ukraine	+0.08	+4.42	+2.65
Kazakhstan	−7.00	−6.37	−7.40
Belarus	+2.97	+3.88	+3.34
Uzbekistan	−2.28	−0.21	−2.04
Azerbaijan	+1.74	+1.57	+2.47
Lithuania	−0.63	−0.97	−0.46
Georgia	+0.05	−0.17	+0.05
Moldova	−0.24	−0.75	−0.83
Latvia	−0.47	−0.29	−0.17
Armenia	−0.06	−1.01	−1.09
Kyrgizia	−1.11	−1.09	−1.63
Estonia	−0.44	−0.48	−0.43
Tadzhikistan	−0.86	−0.78	−0.98
Turkmenia	−0.34	−0.02	−0.38
Sum with the same sign	12.09	12.12	15.39

As a result of the 'improvement' of domestic prices, the quantities of goods redistributed increase to a certain extent; the signs of the republic balances become more stable (the sign of the balance changes only in Georgia during the years observed). Ukraine is added to the group of republics with a stable plus balance, and the number of republics with a stable minus balance is ten. The maximum trade imbalances increase (favourable in Russia, unfavourable in Kazakhstan).

Thus a popular hypothesis is proved to be wrong in saying that non-equivalence of inter-republic exchange is of artificial character and explicable chiefly in terms of the defects of domestic pricing. The overall effect of conversion to 'improved' domestic prices would be to increase the imbalance of inter-republic trade and would move only Ukraine from the goods-recipient to the goods-donor category.

World prices are another alternative system for measuring inter-republic exchanges of goods. Of course, under the centralised economy of the USSR any conversion to prices in world trade would be impossible. It became practicable only after the USSR's disintegration. However, to assess the consequences of a hypothetical conversion to world prices was valuable not merely in theoretical analytical terms. Such calculations were interesting from the standpoint of assessing the economic expediency of entering the world market independently, including the scope for reducing inter-republic trade.

Results of the conversion of the balance of inter-republic exchanges of goods into world prices according to the practice of the USSR CSB are given in Table 3.3. The most significant increases of world prices compared with domestic prices at the point of final consumption were observed in the following sectors: oil industry (more than 3), gas industry (2) and other mechanical engineering: armaments production to a large extent (coefficient is more than 2). Sectors at the opposite extreme, that is with the lowest conversion coefficients, included distilling (0.06), wine making (0.15), livestock rearing (0.2) and dairying (0.3). It is obvious that conversion to world prices benefits those republics specialising in the production of fuel and power and armaments, and worsens the position of those specialising in branches associated with agriculture.

Only Russia and Turkmenia would have a favourable balance if calculations were made in world prices (23.88 and 0.10 billion roubles respectively). For the remaining 13 republics, the balance would not only be unfavourable but would be worse compared with the calculations in domestic prices at the point of final consumption.

Results of the conversion of the balance of inter-republic exchanges of goods into world prices according to the practice of the USSR CSB are given in Table 3.3. The most significant increases of world prices compared with domestic prices at the point of final consumption were observed in the following sectors: oil industry (more than 3), gas industry (2) and other mechanical engineering: armaments production to a large extent (coefficient is more than 2). Sectors at the opposite extreme, that is with the lowest conversion coefficients, included distilling (0.06), wine making (0.15), livestock rearing (0.2) and dairying (0.3). It is obvious that conversion to world prices benefits those republics specialising in the production of fuel and power and armaments, and worsens the position of those specialising in branches associated with agriculture.

Only Russia and Turkmenia would have a favourable balance if calculations were made in world prices (23.88 and 0.10 billion roubles respectively). For the remaining 13 republics, the balance would not only be unfavourable but would be worse compared with the calculations in domestic prices at the point of final consumption.

Table 3.3   Balance of inter-republic exchanges of goods in 1988, at world prices (billion roubles)

Republic	1988
Russia	+23.88
Ukraine	−1.57
Kazakhstan	−5.94
Belarus	−1.59
Uzbekistan	−2.63
Azerbaijan	−0.24
Lithuania	−3.33
Georgia	−1.61
Moldova	−2.22
Latvia	−0.99
Armenia	−1.06
Kyrgizia	−0.54
Estonia	−1.06
Tadzhikistan	−1.20
Turkmenia	+0.10
Sum with the same sign	23.98

The fact is that Russia's extremely high favourable balance was often cited by Russian politicians as evidence of the inefficiency, as far as Russia was concerned, of the established system of inter-republic linkages (including prices). They likewise cited the necessity of economic sovereignty and a changeover to the terms of world trade in relations with the other republics. Politicians of other republics preferred to ignore these results in favour of other data and sources of information.

Combined Analyses of Inter-republic and External Economic Linkages

A more general approach to the problem of equivalence of inter-republic linkages ought to take account of the part played by the republics in the USSR's external trade, since domestic inter-republic and external flows of economic goods are to a considerable extent interchangeable. For example, when republic A imports grain from other republics and republic B imports the same quantity of grain from abroad, the position of both republics in relation to the country's grain balance is the same.

If the external trade of the USSR was in balance (total exports equal to total imports), the criterion of equivalence of inter-republic trade would be a zero balance of exports (including exports to foreign countries) and imports (including imports from abroad) for each republic. But imbalance in the USSR's external trade (and heavy dependence of the external trade balance on the prices used) creates certain methodological difficulties when assessing the influence of external trade on the inter-republic linkages. In 1988 the Soviet Union's balance of external trade turnover at actual external trade prices was positive (+ 2 billion roubles), but if measured in prices at the point of final consumption it was negative (– 50.4 billion roubles). The reason is that on the domestic market the prices of imported goods were dramatically increased by turnover tax, customs dues, supplementary trade transport charges and so on. Up to the moment during the second half of the 1980s when a special incentive to stimulate exports was introduced by allotting a proportion of the hard currency earned to exporters, the republics were not interested, from the economic standpoint, in increasing exports but simply tried to get more imported goods. Even after the mechanism for stimulating exporters (whether individual enterprises, republics or regions) had been introduced, republics still wanted import quotas to be increased, since no additional indebtedness would be incurred by themselves and they were not responsible for the USSR's external economic obligations.

While refraining from entering into details of all aspects of the problem of equivalence of external economic linkages for individual republics, we shall now turn our attention to two problems: the establishment of 'fair' import quotas conforming to the export revenues of republics and the corresponding adjustment of the balance of inter-republic and external economic exchanges, and calculation of the total balance of inter-republic and external economic exchanges at world prices. When calculations are made in terms of domestic prices at the point of final consumption (see Table 3.4), Russia, Ukraine, Uzbekistan, Tadzhikistan and Turkmenia account for a higher share of exports than of imports. The converse is the case with the remaining ten republics.

Table 3.4   *Exports and imports of Union republics in 1988, in domestic prices (billion roubles)*

Republic	Billions of roubles		As % of total	
	exports	imports	exports	imports
Russia	33.31	66.90	70.60	68.53
Ukraine	6.88	13.43	14.58	13.75
Kazakhstan	0.80	2.70	1.70	2.77
Belarus	1.70	3.67	3.60	3.76
Uzbekistan	1.53	1.70	3.24	1.74
Azerbaijan	0.40	1.40	0.85	1.43
Lithuania	0.53	1.25	1.12	1.28
Georgia	0.40	1.27	0.85	1.30
Moldova	0.26	1.10	0.55	1.13
Latvia	0.40	1.00	0.85	1.02
Armenia	0.08	0.86	0.17	0.88
Kyrgizia	0.06	0.77	0.13	0.79
Estonia	0.30	0.70	0.64	0.72
Tadzhikistan	0.33	0.47	0.70	0.48
Turkmenia	0.20	0.40	0.42	0.41
USSR	47.18	97.62	100	100

If we assume that a republic's share of imports ought to correspond to its share of exports (formula 1), then Russia's quota of imports will be higher by 2.02 billion roubles, the Ukraine's by 0.80 billion and Uzbekistan's by 1.46 billion. Kazakhstan's decreases by 1.04 billion roubles, and so on (see Table 3.5). The total quantity of imports redistributed represents a value of 4.5 billion roubles. The adjustment of import redistribution according to formula 1 has a serious drawback inasmuch as the domestic prices of exported goods do not reflect hard currency revenues from exports. As a rule, external trade prices (in exchange roubles) were considerably higher than domestic prices (especially for fuels and raw materials).[3]

Table 3.5   Different import measures for the Union republics and their shares of exports and currency reserves, 1988

Republic	Imports, calculated by formula 1 (in proportion to the share of exports in domestic prices)		Imports, calculated by formula 2 (in proportion to the share of currency revenues)		Difference between estimated and actual imports	
	Share of exports (%)	Estimated imports 1	Share of currency revenues (%)	Estimated imports 2	By formula 1	By formula 2
Russia	70.60	68.92	79.18	77.30	+2.02	+10.40
Ukraine	14.58	14.23	11.37	11.10	+0.80	-2.33
Kazakhstan	1.70	1.66	1.46	1.43	-1.04	-1.27
Belarus	3.60	3.51	2.87	2.80	-0.16	-0.87
Uzbekistan	3.24	3.16	1.28	1.25	+1.46	-0.45
Azerbaijan	0.85	0.83	0.85	0.83	-0.57	-0.57
Lithuania	1.12	1.09	0.75	0.73	-0.16	-0.52
Georgia	0.85	0.83	0.52	0.51	-0.44	-0.76
Moldova	0.55	0.54	0.34	0.33	-0.56	-0.77
Latvia	0.85	0.83	0.45	0.44	-0.17	-0.56
Armenia	0.17	0.17	0.06	0.06	-0.69	-0.80
Kyrgizia	0.13	0.12	0.06	0.06	-0.65	-0.71
Estonia	0.64	0.62	0.22	0.21	-0.04	-0.48
Tadzhikistan	0.70	0.68	0.42	0.41	+0.21	-0.06
Turkmenia	0.42	0.41	0.16	0.16	+0.01	-0.24
USSR	100	97.62	100	97.62	0	0

Table 3.6 Balance of inter-republic exchanges of goods taking account of external trade of republics, 1988 (billion roubles in domestic prices)

Republic	Balance of inter-republic exchanges of goods	Adjustments		Adjusted balance of inter-republic exchanges of goods	
		Formula 1	Formula 2	Formula 1	Formula 2
Russia	+0.26	+2.02	+10.40	+2.28	+10.66
Ukraine	+3.62	+0.80	-2.33	+4.44	+1.29
Kazakhstan	-5.35	-1.04	-1.27	-6.39	-6.62
Belarus	+4.05	-0.16	-0.87	+3.89	+3.18
Uzbekistan	-1.67	+1.46	-0.45	-0.21	-2.12
Azerbaijan	+2.10	-0.57	-0.57	+1.53	+1.53
Lithuania	-0.81	-0.16	-0.52	-0.97	-1.33
Georgia	+0.29	-0.44	-0.76	-0.15	-0.47
Moldova	-0.19	-0.56	-0.77	-0.75	-0.96
Latvia	-0.12	-0.17	-0.56	-0.29	-0.68
Armenia	-0.33	-0.69	-0.80	-1.02	-1.13
Kyrgizia	-0.44	-0.65	-0.71	-1.09	-1.15
Estonia	-0.33	-0.04	-0.48	-0.37	-0.81
Tadzhikistan	-1.00	+0.21	-0.06	-0.79	-1.06
Turkmenia	-0.10	+0.01	-0.24	-0.09	-0.34
USSR	0	0	0	0	0

If we define a republic's quota of imports as directly variable according to the hard currency revenues the republic earns (formula 2), then we will get significantly different results. Russia's quota is the only one that increases(by 10.4 billion roubles). This is explained by the high proportion of fuels, raw materials and heavy industrial plant and equipment in its exports, which are the USSR's highest earners of hard currency. According to formula 2, the import quotas of all other republics should be reduced (by 10.4 billion roubles in total). The disparities between estimated and actual imports of the republic could be interpreted as adjustments of the balance of inter-republic exchanges of goods (Table 3.1), taking account of the participation of republics in external trade and a 'fair' distribution of the effects of external trade. The number of republics enjoying a favourable balance of exchange of goods falls as a result of the adjustments (see Table 3.6): Russia, Ukraine, Belarus and Azerbaijan. If formula 2 is applied, this brings out more clearly the role of Russia as the main donor in the inter-republic system of intercourse. It should be observed that these results were obtained by applying domestic prices.

Table 3.7   Balance of inter-republic and external economic exchanges of goods at world prices, 1988 (billion roubles)

Republic	Inter-republic exchange	External economic exchange	Total
Russia	+23.88	+6.96	+30.84
Ukraine	−1.57	−1.32	−2.89
Kazakhstan	−5.94	−0.64	−6.58
Belarus	−1.59	−0.46	−2.05
Uzbekistan	−2.63	+0.09	−2.54
Azerbaijan	−0.24	−0.21	−0.45
Lithuania	−3.33	−0.36	−3.69
Georgia	−1.61	−0.30	−1.91
Moldova	−2.22	−0.41	−2.63
Latvia	−0.99	−0.32	−1.31
Armenia	−1.06	−0.31	−1.37
Kyrgizia	−0.54	−0.52	−1.06
Estonia	−1.06	−0.24	−1.30
Tadzhikistan	−1.20	+0.08	−1.12
Turkmenia	+0.10	−0.06	+0.04
USSR	0	+1.98	+1.98

If we change over to world prices, then, Russia benefits most of all, as we have already observed. Turkmenia benefits slightly as well; but for all other republics the inter-republic balance becomes worse. Conversion of external economic exchanges into world prices increases the favourable balance of Russia even more (see Table 3.7).

Official Soviet statistics did not take account of inter-republic exchanges of goods or movements of goods carried out by physical persons. These invisible exchanges of goods may be estimated indirectly by the difference between the incomes received and spent by the inhabitants of the territory of the republic (after allowing for cash savings deposited in banks and kept at home). This makes it possible to estimate the volume of physical movement of the population's cash used to pay for these movements of goods and services by physical persons. According to the estimates made by the Central Statistical Bureau of the USSR in 1988, exports of consumer goods exceeded imports in Lithuania and Latvia by 500 million roubles, in Moldova by 600 million and in Estonia by 300 million. This adjustment to the data of Table 1.2 changes by itself the sign of the Latvian and Moldovan trade balances. In addition, account should be taken of the tourism and recreational services furnished by the Ukraine, Baltic republics and Georgia to the population of the USSR as a whole.

Impact of All-Union Expenditures

Statistics of inter-republic exchanges of goods create the illusion of 'republics without a centre', meaning that the Union centre as an agency of inter-republic relations is missing. But a considerable part of inter-republic turnover was determined by the functioning of the all-Union (federal) structures: supplies of *matériel* for the army, capital city functions of Moscow, activities of territorial organisations of Union management. These structures function only as consumers (in a material sense). Their concentration in a particular republic meant that some proportion of imported goods were fulfilling not republic but all-Union needs.

For example, it is known that, in accordance with USSR military doctrine, a substantial concentration of military units, installations and equipment was located in the Ukraine, Belarus and the Baltic and Transcaucasian republics. It is obvious that by excluding the military element from the balances of inter-republic exchanges of goods the trade-balance figures for the republics involved would be substantially improved. It is equally obvious that to eliminate its 'capital city' costs would improve the trade balance of Russia, and so on. But really precise quantitative estimates of the impact of 'non-territorial' exchanges of goods would require labour-intensive retrospective statistical studies.

Analysis of inter-republic exchanges of goods from the standpoint of equivalence reveals the heavy dependence of the results on the methods of analysis and the completeness of the statistics. But at least one conclusion is clear. The systems of inter-republic exchange which existed were of least benefit to Russia. Most other republics were *objectively* interested in the maintenance of the mechanism of inter-republic intercourse by whose operation considerable flows of goods were redistributed in their favour. The figures we have examined yield no more than an indication of the general trend as regards equivalent or balanced exchanges of goods. To ascertain the true facts of equivalence is not a simple bookkeeping operation but requires the reconstitution not only of inter-republic linkages but of the economic structure of every republic as well. More complex analytical instruments would therefore have to be employed in order to analyse the consequences of changes in inter-republic exchange.

EFFECTS OF INTER-REPUBLIC TRADE LINKAGES ON THE ECONOMY OF REPUBLICS

The effects of changes and breakages of linkages have been measured by means of experiments with the models based on a process of elimination of the respective linkages. The effect of republic interaction is defined as the difference between the actual level of final product and the level which could have been achieved, had trade linkages been broken. Special methods are applied for choosing the order in which individual linkages are eliminated and the results averaged.

The results of the calculations are given in Table 3.8. The final product used in the republic (region) is expressed as a sum of the 'contributions' received from each republic and from external trade linkages (see columns 'Russia', 'Ukraine' and so on). The 'Total' column shows the combined contribution of republics (regions) and external linkages to the total final product of all 15 republics. The diagonal of Table 3.8 shows the possibilities for autarchic development of the republics. In this hypothetical situation, Russia provides 64.6 per cent of its own actual final product, Kazakhstan 27.1 per cent, Central Asia 26.4 per cent and the Ukraine only 14.8 per cent. The economies of the Baltic republics, Belarus and Moldova were absolutely incapable of autarchic development within the Soviet Union. It is clear that links with Russia, the largest trade partner, make the largest contribution to the final product of each republic (60 per cent overall). But Russia also benefits from its trade with every republic, and the aggregate contribution of

Table 3.8   Effects of inter-republic trade linkages, 1987 (percentage of the final product of republics)

	Russia	Ukraine	Belarus	Kazakhstan	Central Asia	Moldova	Transcaucasia	Baltic republics	Total
Russia	64.6	67.3	55.5	42.5	36.3	31.7	35.8	65.0	60.2
Ukraine	1.2	14.8	16.6	4.9	18.0	52.1	7.4	8.1	6.3
Belarus	2.3	4.0	3.8	3.5	2.1	4.2	3.3	3.7	2.8
Kazakhstan	1.7	0.6	-1.4	27.1	3.8	-0.6	6.7	-0.6	3.0
Central Asia	3.7	1.1	15.4	0.5	26.4	1.7	0	2.8	4.8
Moldova	0.8	-2.7	-0.3	0.7	0.3	0	0.6	1.0	0.1
Transcaucasia	2.6	1.7	0.5	4.5	3.9	0.2	25.7	0.7	3.4
Baltic republics	1.9	1.5	4.3	3.3	2.5	1.9	2.7	8.0	2.2
External linkages	21.3	11.8	5.7	13.0	36.3	8.8	17.8	11.1	17.2
Total	100.0	100.0	100.0	100.0	18.0	100.0	100.0	100.0	100.0

the 14 republics to the final product of Russia amounts to 14 per cent.

Most of the effects of pair interactions of republics are positive (81 per cent of pairs). Negative signs (for example, Kazakhstan for Baltic republics, Moldova for the Ukraine) show the inefficiency of the currently existing linkage for one of the partners. But the aggregate value of these 'damages' amounts to only 2 per cent of the total benefit from trade interaction. The main conclusion is that breaking trade linkages turns out to be a very painful and even destructive matter for all republics. However, little attention was paid to this factor in the period of political manoeuvrings which resulted, first, in the Soviet Union's disintegration and subsequently in a disastrous decline in exchanges of goods between the successor states.

Just the same, the high values obtained for the effects of inter-republic linkages in the closing years of the Soviet Union's existence do not justify retrospective euphoria over the rational system of 'the single complex of the national economy of the USSR'. The interdependence of the economies of the republics was largely the consequence of their hyperspecialisation and low ability to adapt to external circumstances.

The quantitative estimates given in Table 3.8 should be interpreted only as short-term ('shock') consequences of the cutting of inter-republic and external economic linkages. The adaptability of republic economies has not yet manifested itself (for example by changing the structure of production costs and consumption, respecialising production facilities, reorienting towards external markets, and so forth). However, to accomplish adaptation requires time and means. Of course, a total rupture of linkages is hardly realistic even between individual pairs of republics. And the main purpose of the method used is not so much to analyse marginal situations as to assess the consequences of actual changes in the structure and geography of inter-republic trade.[4]

Economic Expediency of Cooperation between Republics (Coalition Analysis)

Determining the conditions in which the regions may show interest in economic cooperation, that is the economic prerequisites for the formation and functioning of coalitions of regions, ought to be a logically important aspect of the analysis of multiregional systems (at the national and international levels). At first sight the Soviet Union, with its federal state structure uniting republics of diverse characters and interests, seems to have represented an ideal field for coalition analysis. But up to the very last years of the USSR's existence even to pose academically the question of the efficacy or otherwise of coalitions of republics was regarded as practically useless and ideologically harmful. By the time the importance of analysing this problem was acknowledged it was too late to have an impact on practical policy. The process of collapse of the economic Union of republics and regions of the USSR had become irreversible, rendering it necessary to create new mechanisms for economic interaction between the republics of what had already become the former USSR.

Analysis of the efficiency of different coalitions of republics of the USSR was accomplished by means of an inter-republic intersectoral optimisation model with a variable number of republics (from one to 15). A complete succession of coalitions was plotted for each republic. The first coalition in this succession is the one consisting solely of the republic in question (coalition ranking 1), and the last is the entire system of 15 republics plus foreign countries (coalition ranking 16). The term 'plotting of the coalition' means determining its main economic characteristics as disclosed by the optimisation process and comparing them with the characteristics of other coalitions. The discussion below will be confined to the main results, which in our opinion consist of the *identification of the core and economic equilibrium of the system of USSR republics.*

Study of the efficiency of inter-republic interaction in its most complete manifestation (including identification of the core and states of equilibrium) was conducted via the most aggregated inter-republican model, in which 15 republics are united into seven macro regions: (1) Russia, (2) Ukraine and Moldova, (3) Belarus, (4) Kazakhstan, (5) Central Asia, (6) Transcaucasian republics and (7) Baltic republics. Optimisation was effected in accordance with the criterion of maximisation of consumption by population and state. Linkages with third countries (exports and imports) were postulated at their actual level (1987); that is to say, complete centralisation of external trade was assumed. (Individual republics cannot make a choice between inter-republic and external linkages.) Generalised results appear in Table 3.9 and Figure 3.1.

Identification of the core of the system of seven macro regions was carried out by optimisation of parameters (according to the inter-republic model) for seven changes of direction of the territorial pattern of consumption. At each change the share of one of the macro regions increases (or decreases) while the shares of other macro regions decrease (or increase) proportionately. The actual territorial pattern of consumption in 1987 is given in the first column of Table 3.9. The upper and lower limits of the core for the seven changes of direction are given in the second and fourth columns.

The zone of the core identified is rather small. It occupies less than 1 per cent of the potential distribution of the total volume of consumption. Only the share of Russia within the limits of the core manages to change significantly (by 33.4 percentage points), reaching 89.6 per cent of the total Union consumption. This results from the almost monopolistic Russian ownership of many kinds of primary raw materials and from the development of associated branches of production. For all other republics (macro regions), the difference between the upper and lower limits of the core is considerably less than one percentage point. Only Russia's actual share of consumption lies within the core. The actual shares of consumption accounted for by the Ukraine and Moldova, Belarus, the Transcaucasian republics and Baltic republics are lower than these, while the shares of Kazakhstan and Central Asia are higher, when a mutually beneficial exchange is achieved for all republics.

Table 3.9   Territorial pattern of consumption of population and state in the USSR, 1987 (%)

	Actual state	Lower limit of the core	Economic equilibrium	Upper limit of the core
Russia	58.06	56.25	56.37	89.62
Ukraine and Moldova	18.50	19.21	19.42	19.82
Belarus	3.79	4.76	5.01	5.08
Kazakhstan	5.07	3.91	4.36	4.41
Central Asia	6.71	5.05	5.54	5.59
Transcaucasian republics	4.24	4.92	5.47	5.52
Baltic republics	3.55	3.56	3.81	3.89
Total	100.0	–	100.0	–

The point of economic equilibrium lies inside the core of the system. It represents the condition of equivalence (balance) of trade for each region when calculations are made at equilibrium prices, uniform throughout the USSR. During the transition to the equilibrium, the shares of all-Union consumption are decreasing for Russia (which may seem paradoxical), Kazakhstan and Central Asia (which is quite obvious since they had large unfavourable trade balances). The shares of a further four macro regions in Union consumption are increasing.

A provisional graphic representation of the core appears in Figure 3.1. The lower (dotted line) and upper (continuous line) limits of the core are shown relative to the point of equilibrium. Lengths are given in percentage points (see Table 3.9). The part of the core studied is shaped like a needle, and is located inside the area of regional target indices (consumption volumes), almost parallel to the axis of Russia. The 'length' of this needle is approximately 50 times larger than its 'width'. The condition of equivalent exchange lies at that end of the needle where Russia's share of Union consumption is almost minimal. It should be remembered here that the given results of the analysis of the efficiency of economic interactions of the USSR republics represent a condition of complete centralisation of the external trade of the USSR. (The Union centre distributes quotas of exports and imports between republics; these quotas are exogenous values in model calculations.) It is known that the Union centre's monopoly was disliked by the majority of republics, whose politicians and economists were sure (at least during political discussions) that liberalisation of trade with third countries would yield the republics large benefits. This was one of the main irritants provoking centrifugal tendencies in the USSR as the republics struggled for state sovereignty.

The study of inter-republic interaction under liberalisation of external trade has a dual importance, firstly as an analysis of hypothetical opportunities which existed with the USSR and were associated with liberalisation (and decentralisation) of external trade, and secondly as an analysis of the possible consequences of the external trade policy of republics after the Soviet Union's disintegration. Modified models were used for the studies in which the linkages of republics with the outer world (that is, beyond the USSR) were assumed to be endogenous, and some additional restrictions such as external trade balances in world prices, terms of protectionist policy and so on were introduced. The main results of the study carried out are as follows.

Only four republics benefit significantly from the liberalisation of external trade within the USSR: Russia, Kazakhstan, Azerbaijan and Turkmenia. These are able to export raw materials and fuel both within the USSR and abroad. As the liberalisation of external trade proceeds, the size of the core of the system is sharply reduced. The core is approaching the point of economic equilibrium. This means that the differences between scenarios of mutually beneficial distribution of coalition effect and scenarios with equivalent exchange are narrowing. A geometric illustration is given for the system 'Russia–other republics' in Figure 3.2 (p. 110).

Thus the external trade monopoly of the Union centre is the main factor governing the close economic interdependence of Union republics. The delegation to all republics of the power to trade independently with third countries and to choose freely between trade partners within and without the USSR severely undermines the economic interdependence of republics and narrows the sphere within which their cooperation solely within the framework of the USSR is mutually beneficial. But the only republics which can benefit appreciably from the liberalisation of external trade are those which have universal export potential.

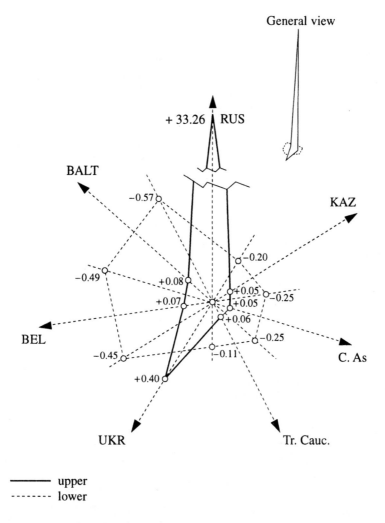

——————— upper
- - - - - - - lower

Note: Lengths in percentage points (consumption structures) from equilibrium point to the limit.

Figure 3.1   Projections of the limits of the core of the USSR's system of macro regions on the horizontal plane

THE PLACE OF RUSSIA IN THE ECONOMY OF THE USSR

Russia occupied a special position in the USSR. Three characteristic features of Russia were of the utmost importance to the functioning of the USSR as a federal state:

1. the highest natural, demographic, economic, scientific and technical potential, exceeding the potential of the other 14 republics combined;
2. a relatively closed and self-sufficient economy (see, for example, Table 3.9);
3. the subordination of republic institutions to all-Union ones in the most important economic and political spheres (heavy industry, transport and communication, defence industry, institutional framework of the Communist Party), that is a severe limitation of state sovereignty compared with other republics.

Russia's share of most of the USSR's volumetric (extensive) economic indices was considerably in excess of 50 per cent (see Table 3.10). Because of this, the values of intensive indices for Russia and the USSR (for example, labour productivity, capital efficiency and consumption per head) differ only insignificantly as a rule. Therefore, in order to bring in to view the characteristic features of the republics, we need to introduce comparisons not between Russia and the USSR but between Russia and the remainder of the USSR, that is, to use a two-zone economic analysis[5] in which the economy of Russia (zone I) is analysed not only in comparison but also in interaction with the other 14 Union republics combined (zone II).

Analysis of economic dynamics in the context of zones of the USSR carried out since the 1960s has shown a number of stable trends. Russia's growth rates of national income, industrial production and fixed capital were a little ahead of the rates of the other republics combined. The growth rates of some intensive indices were substantially higher: labour productivity, production per head of national income and so on. Other republics had higher rates of population growth (especially rural) and agricultural production. The zones under consideration differed significantly in terms of economic growth factors. The share of intensive factors in Russia was 2.5 times higher than in the other republics (analysis was carried out for macroeconomic production functions).

Heavy industry (especially mining and defence *matériel*), construction and transport took up a larger share of Russia's production structure compared with zone II. The exchange of goods between Russia and zone II was patterned accordingly. Russia exported considerable volumes of power resources, industrial raw materials and semi-finished products, machinery and equipment. Agricultural produce and foodstuffs accounted for a considerable proportion of the consumer goods imported. Such patterns of exchanges of goods established functional differences in the economic linkages: Russia provided much of the capital investment in the other republics, and the republics in aggregate contributed actively to meeting Russia's requirement of non-production consumption.

Table 3.10   Weight of Russia in the USSR, 1990 (%)

Territory	76
Population	52
National income produced	61
National income consumed	59
Number of employees and workers	57
Value of fixed capital	62
Production of the most important products	
Oil	90
Natural gas	79
Coal	56
Rolled ferrous metals	57
Motor cars	87
Workable wood	92
Consumer goods	56
Meat	51
Volume of goods shipment	54

All calculation methods show Russia to have had a stable favourable balance in its economic intercourse with other republics (see Table 3.11). Because of imbalance of trade and dissimilarities of labour-intensity and capital consumption between the products exported and imported there, were indirect flows of labour and capital between the two zones of the USSR. Figures derived from a two-zone input–output table (method of matrices inversion) allow us to estimate that in 1989, for example, production capital in the amount of 27 billion roubles was exported indirectly along with the labour of two million people (annually employed workers) from Russia.

Exchanges of goods with Russia were a very important factor in the functioning of the economies of all the republics of the USSR. As may be seen from Table 3.12 (which includes the 'Russia' row and column from

Table 3.8), Russia's trade (including its own non-exported final products) furnished 60.2 per cent of the USSR's final product, including that of Ukraine (67.3 per cent), the Baltic republics (65 per cent) and Belarus (55.5 per cent). The total contribution by republics to Russia's final product is a more modest figure, 14.2 per cent, which includes that of Central Asia (3.7 per cent), Transcaucusus (2.6 per cent), Belarus (2.3 per cent) and Ukraine (1.2 per cent only). Nevertheless, it is important that the contribution of all republics is positive in principle in spite of the non-equivalence of exchange.

Table 3.11   Balance of Russia's exchange of goods with other USSR
republics according to different methods, 1988 (billion roubles)

In current domestic prices at point of final consumption (Table 3.1)	+0.26
In corrected domestic prices (Table 3.2)	+2.25
With external trade taken into account (import correction, Table 3.6)	
according to formula 1	+2.28
according to formula 2	+10.66
In world prices (Table 3.7)	
inter-republic exchange	+23.88
external economic exchange	+6.96
Total	+30.84

Table 3.12   Effects of Russia's trade with other republics of the USSR, 1987
(as percentages of the final product)

Russia's share of the republics' final product		Republics' share of Russia's final product
Ukraine	67.3	1.2
Belarus	55.5	2.3
Kazakhstan	42.5	1.7
Central Asia	36.3	3.7
Transcaucasus	35.8	2.6
Baltic republics	65.0	1.9
Moldova	31.7	0.8
Total	60.2*	14.2

Note: * Including Russia's own non-exported final product.

The results of the analysis of the efficiency of trade cooperation and economic equilibrium within the system of two partners – Russia and the other republics combined – can be interpreted graphically. Figure 3.2 shows the Pareto boundary, core and equilibrium for a maximised index of non-production consumption under conditions of centralisation of the external trade of the USSR. As can be seen, the size of the core is quite large: 139 billion roubles (378 – 239) for Russia and for 142.2 billion roubles (186 – 43.8) for the other republics. The equilibrium point is near the lower limit of the core for Russia and the upper limit for the other republics.[6] The lower limit of the core and equilibrium point show values for Russia's final consumption slightly in excess (by 3 billion and 3.8 billion roubles, respectively) of those under autarchic conditions. But for the other republics 'entry into the core' produces a very substantial effect.

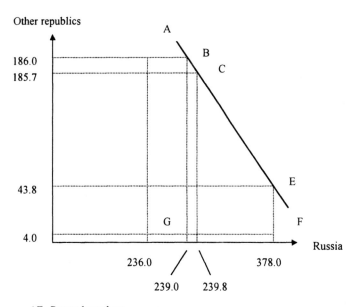

AF - Pareto boundary
B   - Lower limit of core for Russia
C   - Equilibrium
E   - Upper limit of core for Russia
G   - Isolated development

Note: Blocking coalitions for B: Russia, Ukraine, Belarus, Baltic republics; for E Kazakhstan.

Figure 3.2   Pareto border, core and economic equilibrium of the system, Russia–combined other republics of the USSR, 1987 (billion roubles of final consumption)

Figure 3.3 compares the shift of the Pareto boundary, core and equilibrium resulting from three variants of liberalisation of the external trade of the USSR: (a) exogenous external trade, (b) maintenance of import controls (in the form of customs dues and import quotas) and (c) complete liberalisation of external trade. Liberalisation of external trade results in a considerable increase in the economic system's efficiency. The Pareto boundary moves away – in Russia's case a considerable distance – from the starting point of the coordinates. The size of the core diminishes rapidly as liberalisation proceeds. The equilibrium point moves to the upper limit of the core for Russia. Russia's share of Union final consumption in the core and equilibrium point grows as liberalisation proceeds, becoming larger than that shown by line 4 in the figure.

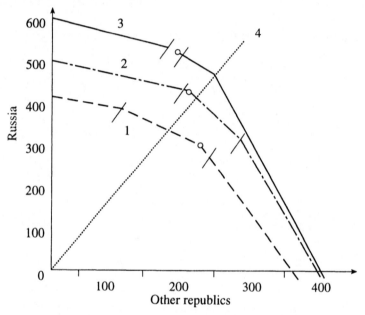

Notes:
1 = exogenous external trade.
2 = partial liberalisation of external trade.
3 = complete liberalisation of external trade.
4 = line of actual inter-republic structure of final consumption.
/ = core limit.
o = economic equilibrium.

Figure 3.3   *Pareto boundary, core and equilibrium under different variants*
               of regulation and liberalisation of external trade (billion roubles
               of final consumption)

The analysis carried out leads to the conclusion that, by virtue of its production structure, available natural resources and trade opportunities, Russia in the late 1980s was objectively well prepared for a transition to the rules and conditions of international trade in its intercourse with the other republics. Objectively the prerequisites were in place for Russia to enjoy more profitable trade cooperation with the republics in the event of the Soviet Union's disintegration.

DISINTEGRATION OF THE UNION ECONOMY

The crisis in the Union and regional markets for goods became especially apparent after 1988. Volumes of inter-regional exchange of many kinds of products were decreasing, while the total volume of inter-republic trade grew over a period of a year but by an amount (3 per cent) less than that of the total volume of production (4 per cent). The erosion of the inter-republic market gathered pace in 1989, when the absolute value of the total volume of imports declined in three Union republics, as did the total volume of exports in five republics.

In 1990 a general fall in production occurred for the first time in all the years of the Soviet Union's existence. The volume of GDP shrank by another 10 per cent in the first half of 1991, and the volume of generated national income by 12 per cent. This naturally reduced the potential physical capacity of the Union market and thus the disintegration of interrepublican linkages speeded up dramatically.

The turnover of external trade decreased by 6.5 per cent in 1990, despite various liberalising measures (export promotion, direct access to the external market, initiation of joint ventures and partial internal convertibility of currency). By the first half of 1991 the decline had already reached 37 per cent (23 per cent in exports, 48 per cent in imports) compared with the first half of 1990. Comecon was collapsing (trade with the former Comecon members halved in a year) and trade conditions were deteriorating. Shrinking export opportunities (notably as a result of reduced oil production), the state's growing external debt and the insolvency of Soviet commercial partners were all reasons for contraction of the volume of external trade. For the first time since the Second World War, increases in state wholesale and retail prices by two to three times at the beginning of 1991 failed to bring equilibrium to the markets in goods. Black market prices remained much higher than prices in state trade (three to five times for foodstuffs, clothes and footwear, more than four times for motor cars and 14 times for medicines). Stocks of most goods in trade and industry fell to a minimum.

Reasons for Economic Disintegration

A combination of several processes aggravated the chronic failings and progressive disintegration of the market in goods during the period 1988–91. A crisis of money circulation arose. There was always too much money in circulation. There was also a constant excess of consumer demand over goods supply, along with rising prices, depreciation of savings, a catastrophically falling rouble rate on the domestic currency market (40–60 times lower than the official rate) and confiscatory fiscal measures by the Union government. All these factors in combination ultimately undermined the confidence in the rouble of both public and private sectors. The consequences were a frenzy of consumer demand which bought up all the goods for sale at state prices and the emergence of cashless exchanges in kind; that is, barter.

The changeover from a command to a market economy proceeded slowly and with lengthy, asynchronous and selective pauses. Thus abolition and reduction of state targets and liberalisation of state prices were accomplished in uneven stages by the various sectors and products. Some enterprises had opportunities to choose new trade partners and produce goods of their own choice, while others continued to work within the rigid confines of state-determined planning and prices. As a result, old economic linkages were severed while the establishment of new and mutually beneficial linkages was delayed.

Decontrol of prices in a situation of producer monopoly and shortage of goods leads inevitably to fitful price rises, but this failed to stimulate any increase in production. Those producers who sold their products at fixed prices and purchased the means of production at contract prices found themselves in a difficult financial situation and had to reduce output.

Other reasons for falling output were the destabilisation of the political system and revolutionary changes in the power and management structure. After 1988 the movement for economic and political independence of Union and autonomous republics gathered momentum. After the Baltic republics, the Russian Federation joined this movement, which then penetrated to the intrarepublican level. In the meantime, the political system of the USSR was undergoing a transformation which included liquidation of the monopoly of the Communist Party, the establishment of new elective power bodies and the democratisation of the body politic. There was a redistribution of central managerial functions to republic and regional bodies. These multifaceted political developments created additional tension in the economy and encouraged its fragmentation.

Republic and regional authorities began to promulgate their own laws, conflicting with the decisions of superior authorities ('the war of the laws'). The supreme soviets of six Union republics adopted resolutions to secede from the USSR, as a result of which many Union statutes, including economic ones, became invalid in their territories. Mass strikes of miners and ethnic conflicts became a new factor in economic destabilisation.

Disintegration Phenomena

Restrictions were imposed on the movement of goods. In their attempts to protect regional markets in a situation of general shortage of goods and excessive money supply, republic and local authorities introduced bans on the export of goods produced in the republic or available in trade. Official actions of this sort had populist motives and found support among local populations. In some republics the authorities tried to establish general control of exports of all products by means of licences and quotas. Thus intermediary administrative links were created between enterprises in different republics operating direct linkages, since there was no such administrative control even before perestroika.

Some republics introduced special taxes (duties) instead of, or in addition to, direct bans on export. For example, duties on exports of agricultural products (July–September, 20 per cent of average annual price; October–December, 80 per cent) were introduced in Uzbekistan in 1991. In other republics duties were introduced on exports of goods exceeding the established quotas (as in Moldova). Some republics started to organise their own customs services in order to control goods and population movements (for example, Estonia, Latvia, Lithuania, Belarus and Ukraine). In 1990–91 laws were adopted establishing republic economic borders. Their partners in economic intercourse naturally took retaliatory measures, and inter-republic tariff wars began.

The prior and absolute right of local bodies to purchase a proportion of the goods produced in the territory (usually between 5 and 15 per cent; though territories of the Far East were allowed to purchase 30 per cent) came to constitute a novel form of demonstration of the 'sovereignty' of regions. Products were used for intraregional consumption as well as for barter transactions with other regions. But this measure narrowed the scope for free interregional trade even more.

Prices were distorted. Pricing in the Soviet Union was always isolated from the market, being almost a complete monopoly of the state. It did not exercise any significant influence over the structure and dynamics of production, or on the movement of capital. The destructive force of price distortions was made manifest as public enterprises were privatised, controls over the operations of individual industrial sectors lifted, cooperative and private sectors allowed to grow, and the independence of republics and regions in economic policy extended. New pricing phenomena appeared which dissolved the Union spatial market.

Previously, when the majority of prices were fixed by the Union government, differences in prices between republics (regions) were negligible and did not much influence the movement of goods. This situation changed after the autumn of 1990, when the republics began to increase food prices unilaterally. Russia started the process by raising cattle prices, and subsequently Estonia, Latvia and Lithuania independently increased their food prices (over three times on average) while simultaneously increasing wages of state employees (two to two and a half times) and paying compensation to the population. The purchasing power of the rouble decreased sharply in the Baltic republics compared with other republics, to which additional consumer demand has shifted (especially for foodstuffs in frontier regions). This triggered retaliatory protective measures: a foodstuffs embargo, a strengthening of the system of rationed distribution and a subsequent general increase in prices in all republics and the start of a new cycle.

The gap between the state and market prices of means of production widened. Under conditions of shortage and producer monopoly, liberalisation of prices for some kinds of product inevitably triggered spasmodic rises. Uneven liberalisation of prices by different economic sectors led to a situation in which the products of some regions were sold mostly at free prices and those of other regions (primarily raw materials) mostly at fixed state prices. As a result, the financial and social disparities already existing between 'manufacturing' and 'mining' regions increased considerably: regions of the second group raised questions about transition to free prices in categorical terms. The government explained its caution by reference to its fear that immediate decontrol of fuel and power prices might lead to the bankruptcy of thousands of enterprises and depress production levels.

It was oil prices that offered the most dramatic spectacle. The state price of a ton of Tyumen oil was 60 roubles. In mid-1991 it was selling on the commodity exchange at 350–400 roubles, six to seven times the cost, and when resold for export (including oil sold by producers themselves) the price jumped to $150. One dollar could be sold for 30–35 roubles at a hard currency auction. Thus, after selling the dollars, a producer would have earned 4.5–5.2 thousand roubles on one ton of oil, which is equivalent to having sold 75–87 tons at the state price. It is obvious that with such colossal differentials between state price, market price and the domestic exchange rate of the dollar, it was not the process of oil production itself that the producer was concerned with. It was much more profitable for him to secure the right to sell freely as a dealer.

A particular feature of this period was the great disparity of prices between local food markets because of impediments to the movement of goods, including the blockading of markets in the largest cities (Moscow, Leningrad) by mafia groups. Barter developed. Widespread exchanges in kind are an inevitable consequence of the collapse of the system of material and technical supply and of the rouble's loss of the attribute of real money. Barter transactions were made first by producing enterprises, then municipal and public authorities joined in such operations. Some kind of scarce good such as meat, cigarettes or motor cars became 'money' on various local markets. For example, at the agroindustrial fair held in Omsk in March 1991, meat acted as money, and rates of exchange for other goods were determined by reference to it: one ton of meat was equal to ten colour TV sets or 50 washing machines, and so on.

Both the president of the USSR and the Union government attempted to prohibit barter by means of decrees and resolutions, but such official bans were systematically broken. Moral censure of barter as a regression to mediaeval times was of no avail, of course. In the end the government realised the uselessness of fighting against the consequence without eliminating the causes. Barter was then sanctioned. Moreover, the government itself began to use barter (under the euphemism of 'counter-sale') in order to implement the most important programme of the autumn of 1991 – the purchase of grain. One 'Kamaz' truck could be exchanged for 400–500 tons of grain, one 'Lada' passenger car for 250–300 tons, one refrigerator for 8–10 tons and one sewing machine for 5–10 tons, and so forth.

Rationed Trade and Substitute Money

To switch from free trade to target-limited distribution of rationed consumer goods would be to revert to the methods of the war and early postwar period. The qualitative difference would consist firstly in the variety of distributional forms used and secondly in the fact that the mechanism of distribution would be controlled only by republic and municipal authorities. Spatial heterogeneity and fragmentation of the consumer market would only be increased by regional initiatives of this sort. The Union government refrained from such regulation. It did not support the idea of a two-level assured supply for the population, involving the introduction of minimum standards over the entire territory of the USSR with the cost defrayed from Union resources and the power to introduce supplementary regional standards according to the resources available in the regions.

Rationed trade had four main forms:

1. sales only to local residents (of the town or region) on production of the appropriate identity card (passport, visitor's permit);
2. sales of goods to labour collectives;
3. sale of a certain list of goods in defined quantities on production of impersonal certificates (cards, coupons and so on). Sugar, vegetable oil, cigarettes, vodka and wine were frequently included in such lists of rationed goods. In practice cards and coupons did not guarantee availability. Supplies were often insufficient to honour even minimum rations, and forged cards (coupons) were common. Resale of cards was a common practice;
4. issue of substitute money as a priority means of payment. The biggest mass experiment was made in the Ukraine. After the autumn of 1990, along with roubles 'coupons' were distributed worth 70 per cent of the amount of the wage, constituting additional means of payment of varying values (three roubles, five roubles and so on) and assuring supply of the goods. People nicknamed these coupons 'perestroika money'.

Attitudes towards this measure varied. The introduction of coupons increased the guaranteed supply. It stifled rising demand within the republic, but at the same time it depreciated those holdings of money (including all savings of the 'pre-coupon' period) which lacked associated coupons, because goods within the republic could be bought for this money only at high commercial (market) prices. 'Couponisation' of the Ukraine came as a considerable shock both to the Union's market in goods and to its monetary system. Firstly, the government of the Ukraine assumed the 'legal' power to prohibit exports of the consumer goods needed in order to honour the coupons. Secondly, 'hot money' lacking associated coupons began to flow towards other republics with relatively free trading conditions, where they had higher purchasing power and there were more chances of finding the desired goods. The coupons became parallel money, in fact, and they laid the groundwork of a separate republic monetary system.

Lithuania had gone over to the system of parallel money ('common coupons') from the summer of 1991. Latvia and Estonia did the same later. The circulation of parallel money was considered by these republics to be a step towards the introduction of their own respective monetary units, Lithuanian and Latvian crowns, in place of the rouble.

Attempts to Stabilise Inter-republic Relations

The 'sovereignisation' of Union republics and their politicoinstitutional alienation from the Union centre significantly accelerated the disintegration of the USSR as an economic spatial entity. The most striking forms of opposition to the centre were typical of the Baltic republics after 1988 and of the Russian Federation after mid-1990. This happened after Boris Yeltsin's accession to power and the Russian Federation's adoption of the declaration of State Sovereignty. The initiation of a constructive dialogue between Soviet President Gorbachev and the leaders of Union republics raised hopes of some move towards reintegration.

In April 1991 the leaders of nine Union republics and the President of the USSR issued a Declaration on joint action and announced their intention of signing an Agreement on the union of sovereign states.[7] This document, entitled 'Agreement 9+1', inaugurated a series of regular meetings which were held at the Novo-Ogarevo residence and known as the 'Novo-Ogarevo process'. The main content of the Declaration comprises principles for the restoration of the integrated economic spatial entity and distribution of powers between the Union and republics, along with a statement on relations with those Union republics which were not signatories to the Declaration. It was envisaged that a very favourable climate for inter-republic economic intercourse would be created within the economic framework of the 'nine'. It was affirmed for the first time that the 'nine' and the centre should maintain normal economic relations with the other republics on the basis of mutual advantage, including price policy.

In the meantime, organisational and legal efforts were being made to counter the centrifugal tendencies of the Union economy and secure its reintegration on a market basis. For example, the USSR's Act 'On the restriction of monopolistic activity in the USSR', adopted in July 1991, introduced the concept of 'all-Union goods turnover'. This meant that the circulation of goods between economic actors within the specified territories and all other economic actors is excluded from the market, whether they act as sellers or buyers, or else their access to it is limited. It also meant the adoption by power bodies and managerial agencies of decisions with regard to centralised distribution of goods and impediments to the movement of goods between one republic and another. But some particularly important articles of the statute were not to come into force until after 1993.

Completely new Union and republic legislation was introduced concerning external economic activity. Enterprises under various forms of ownership were empowered to avail themselves of direct external economic linkages. Foreign investors in the USSR were guaranteed, in principle, the same conditions as those applicable to Russian investors. Decisions were adopted on the domestic convertibility of the rouble and the creation of a legal foreign exchange market. The USSR Act 'On exchange regulation' was based on the idea of a common market. It reads: 'The territory of the USSR is the common exchange territory in which the USSR and component units of the Federation conduct coordinated monetary, credit and international monetary policy with a view to strengthening the purchasing power of the rouble as the only legal means of payment.'

Changes in the practical nature of the political and economic relations between Union republics and centre made it necessary to revise the Agreement on the principles of unification of the republics in the Union state, signed in 1922 (the 'Union Agreement'). The early official variants of the Union Agreement have been under discussion since the middle of 1990. Referendums held in February–March 1991 showed that the populations of the nine republics cited above supported the idea of the Union. The Novo-Ogarevo process intensified the search for a compromise version of the Agreement. Many of the provisions of the draft Agreement gave formal shape to the process of economic integration and the creation of an all-Union market.

The last version of the draft Agreement (summer of 1991) determined the respective spheres of competence of the Union and Union republics. The spheres of Union competence included approval and implementation of the Union budget, the currency issue, Union gold reserves, custody of diamond and hard currency reserves and nuclear power management. The sphere of joint competence of Union and republics included the creation of conditions suitable for the establishment of an all-Union market and the implementation of common fiscal, credit, monetary and tax policies. There were also provisions for insurance and pricing policies based on a common currency; the establishment and use of gold reserves, diamonds and hard currency reserves of the Union; drafting and implementation of all-Union programmes; establishment of all-Union funds for regional development, and so on. On the Agreement's coming into force the signatory states were to enjoy most-favoured treatment in economic and other relations. Relations between the new Union and non-signatory republics were to be regulated on the basis of the USSR legislation in force, bilateral mutual commitments and agreements.

The Agreement was ready for signature at the Kremlin on 20 August 1991. The signing of this Agreement was to mark the legitimate transition from the former almost unitary state to a new federal–confederate state system. Therefore it was no mere chance that the coup staged by supporters of a state with strong central powers was fixed for 19 August. Its primary purpose was to prevent the Agreement from being signed.

Disintegration of the Soviet Union

The failure of the August coup had destructive consequences for the Soviet system as a whole. Two aspects of it are important from the standpoint of our theme: loss of authority and real power by the Union centre (including the President of the USSR) and the decision made by Russia, and by other republics later on, in favour of an accelerated and irreversible transition to a market economy.

After August the principal institutions of the Union state were disbanded: the USSR Cabinet, the Congress of People's Deputies and Supreme Soviet of the USSR, and the Communist Party of the USSR. The interim Inter-republic Economic Committee (IEC) commenced functioning in place of the Union government, the leading roles being played by the representatives of Russia. (I. Silayev, who was at the same time the Prime Minister of Russia, was appointed IEC Chairman.)

The events of August strengthened the political position of 'market adherents'. In late October the Russian President, Boris Yeltsin, declared adoption of the 'new economic policy' and headed the 'government of reforms'. Instant liberalisation of prices, accelerated privatisation and transition to a new tax system formed the most important elements of the new government's programme. This move by Russia caused other republics to speed up the transition to market economics.

As the talks for securing agreement between the centre and Union republics proceeded, ideas concerning the new Union veered sharply in favour of confederation. The Agreement on Economic Community was prepared and signed, but talks on political Union, organised by Mikhail Gorbachev, reached a deadlock. The majority of republics declared themselves independent states, thus narrowing the legal basis of the Union Agreement. The crisis was finally settled in early December, when Russia, Ukraine and Belarus signed the Agreement on the Commonwealth of Independent States (CIS) and abrogated the 1922 Union Agreement. Another eight republics joined this Agreement on terms of equality. The Soviet Union ceased to exist at the end of 1991.

NOTES

1. The term 'territorial (or regional) self-financing' was not a good one in our opinion. It created the illusion of a simple transfer of the existing self-financing of enterprises to the regions.

2. Balances of payments of republics are more general instruments for analysing the equivalence of inter-republic linkages. However, as has already been remarked, many elements of financial (including payments) relations between republics did not exist in the USSR. There was also none of the information necessary for such analysis.

3. In 1988 the USSR's exports at actual external trade prices amounted to 67.01 billion exchange roubles; that is, they exceeded the value of exports at domestic prices by 20.8 billion roubles. Imports at external trade prices were priced at 65.03 billion exchange roubles, thus amounting to 32.6 billion roubles less than at domestic prices.

4. For example, calculations show that, if all the Ukraine's linkages are reduced by 25 per cent, the final product of the Ukraine will decrease by 21.3 per cent. If the linkages with other republics (excluding Russia) are reduced by 50 per cent, the Ukraine's final product could increase by 0.1 per cent; but if linkages with Russia alone are reduced by 50 per cent (and the level of other linkages remains at 75 per cent), the Ukraine's final product will fall by a further 22.8 per cent.

5. The differences between indices describing correlations between indices of Russia and other Union republics combined (α) and correlation of indices of Russia and the USSR (β) are dependent on the size of Russia's share of the all-Union volume (χ). Formulae expressing the correlation between α and β in dependence on χ have the form:

$$\alpha = \frac{(1-\chi)\beta}{1-\chi\beta} \; ; \; \beta = \frac{\alpha}{(1-\chi)+\chi\alpha}$$

For example, labour productivity in a certain branch of production is higher in Russia than in the USSR by an average of 5 per cent ($\beta = 1.05$). Russia produces 75 per cent of this branch output ($\chi = 0.75$). Consequently, $\alpha = 1.235$, that is, labour productivity in Russia is 23.5 per cent higher than in the rest of the USSR. Thus, in this fairly typical case, the difference between Russia and the other republics is 4.7 times greater than the difference between Russia and the USSR.

6. In Figure 3.1 the equilibrium point selected is the starting point of the coordinates. This explains the extension of the peak along the 'Russia' axis and the shortness of the core limits from the starting point of the coordinates for other republics.

7. Russian Federation, Ukraine, Belarus, Kazakhstan, Uzbekistan, Tadzhikistan, Kyrgizia, Turkmenia and Azerbaijan became participants to this agreement. The leader of Armenia attended one of the meetings.

4. Regional development and regional policy in the new Russia

Alexander Granberg

REGIONAL ASPECTS OF THE TRANSITION PERIOD

The gravity of the present socioeconomic situation in the regions of Russia is influenced by the fact that a number of complex transitional processes are going on in the country simultaneously:

- the establishment of a new geopolitical and economic spatial entity following the disintegration of the Soviet Union;
- the collapse of the command economy and transition to an economy of market type;
- the opening of the economy to the external market;
- economic crisis;
- changeover to a state system based on federalism.

The disintegration of the Soviet Union has radically changed the geopolitical and geoeconomic position of Russia in Eurasia. The regions of the Russian Federation are shown in Figure 4.1. New states (republics of the former USSR) separate Russia from Central and Western Europe and the Middle East. The economic linkages between the Russian regions and the republics of the former Soviet Union were severed (exchanges of goods fell by a factor of 3–4), bringing a need to offset the loss by means of domestic production. New frontier regions came into existence: the Russian Federation consists of 26 component territories, each with its own particular infrastructural, production and human problems. A flood of migrants, mainly Russian-speakers, poured into Russia, needing to be settled at the minimum possible social and economic cost. (All in all, 3.8 million people from the 'new' foreign states removed themselves to Russia between 1992 and 1995.) Russia was confronted with the necessity of realigning its defence system and allocating its troops to new regions for the protection of new frontiers.

Any rapid *transition from a command economy to a market economy* in any country which chose to take such a path would be bound to bring social and economic shocks. In Russia this process of transition is complicated and prolonged by its internal heterogeneity as an economic entity and the great

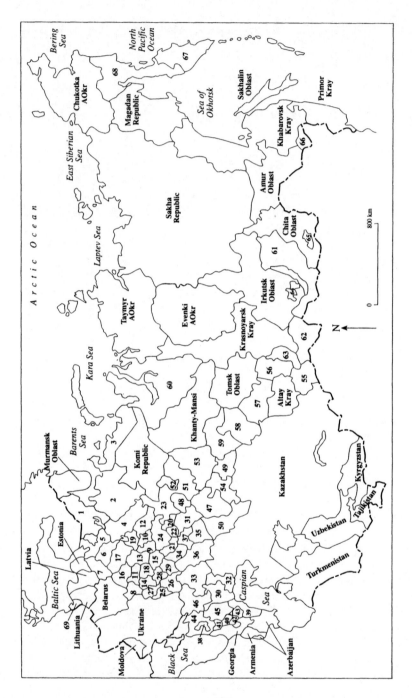

1 Northern economic region
  1 Kareliya Republic
    Komi Republic
  2 Arkhangel'sk Oblast'
  3 Nenets AOkr
    Other Arkhangel'sk Oblast'
  4 Vologda Oblast'
    Murmansk Oblast'
2 Northwest economic region
  5 Leningrad
    St. Petersburg city
    Leningrad Oblast'
  6 Novgorod Oblast'
  7 Pskov Oblast'
3 Central economic region
  8 Bryansk Oblast'
  9 Vladimir Oblast'
  10 Ivanovo Oblast'
  11 Kaluga Oblast'
  12 Kostroma Oblast'
  13 Moscow
    Moscow City
    Moscow Oblast'
  14 Orel Oblast'
  15 Ryazan' Oblast'
  16 Smolensk Oblast'
  17 Tver' Oblast'
  18 Tula Oblast'
  19 Yaroslavl' Oblast'

4 Volgo-Vyatskiy economic region
  20 Mariy El Republic
  21 Mordoviya Republic
  22 Chuvashskaya Republic
  23 Kirov Oblast'
  24 Nizhegorod Oblast'
5 Central Chernozem economic region
  25 Belgorod Oblast'
  26 Voronezh Oblast'
  27 Kursk Oblast'
  28 Lipetsk Oblast'
  29 Tambov Oblast'
6 Povolzhskiy economic region
  30 Kalmykiya Republic
  31 Tatarstan Republic
  32 Astrakhan' Oblast'
  33 Volgograd Oblast'
  34 Penza Oblast'
  35 Samara Oblast'
  36 Saratov Oblast'
  37 Ul'yanovsk Oblast'
7 North-Caucasus economic region
  38 Adygeya Republic
  39 Dagestan Republic
  40 Kabardino-Balkarskaya Republic
  41 Karachay-Cherkesskaya Republic
  42 North Ossetiya Republic
  43 Chechnya & Ingushetiya Republics
  44 Krasnodar Kray
  45 Stavropol' Kray
  46 Rostov Oblast'

8 Urals economic region
  47 Bashkortostan Republic
  48 Urmurtskaya Republic
  49 Kurgan Oblast'
  50 Orenburg Oblast'
  51 Perm' Oblast'
  52 Komi-Permyat AOkr
    Other Perm' Oblast'
  53 Sverdlovsk Oblast'
  54 Chelyabinsk Oblast'
9 West Siberian economic region
  55 Altay Republic
    Altay Kray
  56 Kemerowo Oblast'
  57 Novosibirsk Oblast'
  58 Omsk Oblast'
    Tomsk Oblast'
  59 Tyumen' Oblast'
    Khanty-Mansi AOkr
  60 Yamalo-Nenets AOkr
    Other Tyumen' Oblast'
10 East Siberian economic region
  61 Buryatiya Republic
  62 Tuva Republic
  63 Khakasiya Republic
    Krasnoyarsk Kray
    Taymyr AOkr
    Evenki AOkr
    Other Krasnoyarsk Kray
    Irkutsk Oblast'
  64 Ust'-Ordo Buryat AOkr
    Other Irkutsk Oblast'
    Chita Oblast'
  65 Aga AOkr
    Other Chita Oblast'

11 Far Eastern economic region
    Sakha Republic
    Primor Kray
    Khabarovsk Kray
  66 Yevrey AO
    Other Khabarovsk Kray
    Amur Oblast'
  67 Kamchatka Oblast'
  68 Koryak AOkr
    Other Kamchatka Oblast'
    Magadan Oblast'
    Chukotka AOkr
    Other Magadan Oblast'
    Sakhalin Oblast'
12 Kaliningrad Oblast'

AO – Autonomous Oblast'
AOKr – Autonomous Okrug

Source: Center for International Research, U.S. Bureau of the Census.

Figure 4.1   Regions of the Russian Federation

regional disparities of ability to adapt to market conditions. Three groups of regions are especially vulnerable:

- regions with high concentrations of manufactures which have become unprofitable as a result of the changeover from planned to market prices, or which have suffered a sudden loss of consumer demand for their products;
- peripheral regions whose position has deteriorated because of swingeing rises in transport tariffs relative to the prices of the goods produced;
- regions which formerly received considerable funds from the federal budget by way of capital investment and subsidies but have now lost these sources of finance.

A number of regions fall into two or three of these groups. At the same time the establishment of market infrastructure (and especially of commercial and banking capital) brought new advantages to the metropolitan centres (Moscow, St Petersburg). The acuteness of many regional problems is often influenced by imbalance in the dynamics of market changes. For example, the absence of a real housing market and slow development of small and medium businesses impede automatic regulation of employment and unemployment by the market.

Of course, the *liberalisation of external economic activity* accelerated market changes in the Russian economy and made it possible to exploit the advantages of the international division of labour more actively. But this liberalisation has notably different consequences for different regions. The regions which chiefly gain from it are exporters of products for which there is a stable external demand (oil, gas, non-ferrous metals, diamonds) and large nodal centres of trade (Moscow again, port cities). But the regions with concentrations of manufactures which cannot compete with the imported products, or which depend heavily on expensive imported raw materials (such as the textile regions of the European centre) are caught in a difficult position.

The economic crisis in Russia affected all the regions. Its main symptoms are declining production and investment, contraction of the domestic market, inflation, unemployment and falling personal real incomes. But crisis phenomena display considerable regional idiosyncrasies. The biggest falls in production, and therefore the highest levels of unemployment, are observed in regions with concentrations of defence industries (loss of government orders), investment in engineering and capital construction (investment crisis), light industry (external competition and decline of consumer demand). The explosive inflation of early 1992 inflicted its worst economic damage firstly on the regions forced to hold large sums of circulating capital (to meet the needs of manufactures characterised by long cycles and seasonal goods deliveries) and secondly on the inhabitants of regions with higher levels of money savings. For these reasons the harshest effects of inflation appeared in the north and Far East.

In Russia disparities between the regional markets for goods, capital and labour are evened out relatively slowly because of the large distances and increased cost of transport. Therefore the process of surmounting the crisis will be uneven too. Beginning in 1994, regions with positive growth of gross product and personal incomes emerge against the background of a persistent overall decline of Russian production. Moscow revealed itself to be the biggest market 'growth point'.

The establishment of new economic relationships in Russia goes hand in hand with the transition from the former unitary (in fact) state to *a system of true federalism*. This process has brought numerous clashes in relations, including economic ones, between the centre and regions, for example in the distribution of state property, taxes, financial transfers and so on. The process of dividing up the powers and functions of government between federal authorities, territorial units of the Federation and local authorities has also been accompanied by outbreaks of separatism and inter-ethnic tension. This is most characteristic of the republics, the constituent parts of the Federation and the peripheral regions. Extreme regional diversity makes it impossible for Russia simply to apply some pre-existing approved model of transitional economy 'off the shelf'. Russia has to seek a new synthesis of the world experience.

ESTABLISHMENT OF NEW REGIONAL ECONOMIC MECHANISMS AND REGIONAL FEATURES OF THE ECONOMIC REFORM

In the planned economy, *an individual region* (administrative–territorial unit) was first and foremost a constituent part of the national economy ('single economic complex') and to a lesser extent an economic sub-system (regional economic complex). The internal material and financial linkages of the region were much less robust than the external linkages (within the federal regulatory systems and territorial division of labour). Production, consumption and investment were primarily determined not by regional needs (demand) but by the state plan and the policy of federal departments. In the majority of regions full employment was maintained because there was no economic incentive for enterprises to release superfluous workers, and migration from regions of labour surplus was mainly of a seasonal character. By redistributing financial resources and fixing wage rates, the centre exercised strict control over the money incomes of both enterprises and population, while at the same time ensuring that these incomes had little influence on levels of production, consumption and investment. Thus the economy of the region was a weakly linked sub-system.

Simultaneously with the transition to market economics and true federalism, each region, as a unit of the Federation, has become an economic sub-system with strong interdependence of its main elements. The impact of incomes and an effective demand for regional production, consumption and investment has become appreciably stronger, as also has the impact of production (including services) on employment and incomes. Interregional exchanges now take place on a market basis, so that *a region as a market* is subject to the influence of (external) competing and supplementary markets for goods, labour and capital.

The elements and linkages of regional economic mechanisms in the aggregate formally coincide in the planned and market economies (see Figure 4.2). But during the transition from a planned to a market economy there are changes in the nature and strength of the linkages between the elements of the regional complex and the external environment. Increased strength is typical of the internal linkages, while external linkages will typically be subject to qualitative changes or weakening (see Table 4.1).

Undifferentiated approaches to economic reform are doomed to failure in Russia because of the country's extreme diversity of natural geography, social demography and economic and political conditions, along with its federal system of government. Economic reform in Russia requires a variety of individual approaches to the problems of individual regions combined with consistent general principles for the functioning of the market and common rules governing the interaction between all economic players over the entire territory of the country. Regional diversity of reform requires social and economic stability to be maintained in each region. It imposes limitations on the sequence and terms of the main measures of reform. The pace of reform will differ from region to region. This is why the traditional stages of both the reform and the economic cycle from crisis to resurgence are difficult to distinguish clearly when Russia is viewed as a whole.

Four main models of regional authority economic policy manifested themselves during the initial stage of reform (after 1993):

1. accelerated transformation of markets (Moscow, St Petersburg, Nizhny Novgorod oblast);
2. efforts to increase exports, exploiting the differentials between world and

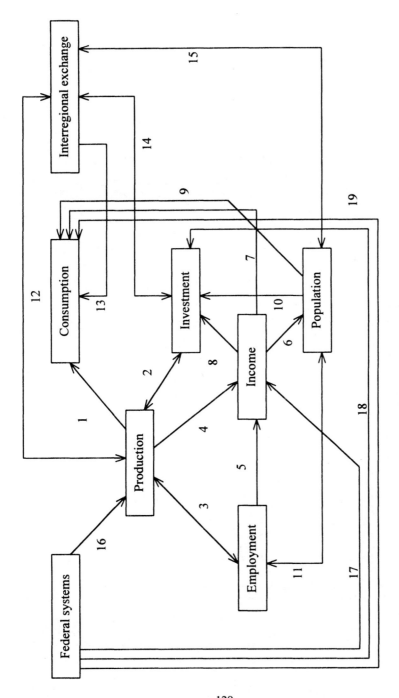

Figure 4.2   Aggregate scheme of regional economic mechanisms

home prices;
3. acquisition of privileges for the region in the form of tax breaks,
    subsidies and investment from the federal budget;
4. retention of considerable elements of the planned economy at the
    regional level (subsidies to agricultural production, price controls,
    rationed distribution of consumer goods and bans on their export and so
    on).

Table 4.1   Strength of the linkages of regional economic mechanisms

Numbers of linkages	Planned system	Transitional economy
A. Internal		
1	M	M
2	W/S	W/S
3	M/S	S/S
4	M	S
5	S	S
6	S	S
7	M	S
8	M	S
9	M	S
10	W	M
11	S/M	S/S
B. External		
12	S/S	S/S
13	S	M
14	S	M
15	W	M
16	S	M
17	S/S	M/M
18	S	M
19	S	M

Note: If the linkage is bilateral (number 2 for example), the numerator is the strength of the
linkage reading from the top (or from the left), and the denominator is the strength of the linkage
reading from the bottom (or from the right). W = weak, M = medium, S = strong.

As the process of liberalising prices and bringing them into line with world
prices went on and regional privileges were abolished (especially after the
spring of 1995), the opportunities for continued reform along the lines of

models 2 and 3 were gradually exhausted. Survival of the 'islands' of planned economy (Ulyanovsk oblast is the most typical case) became more problematical because of growing competition from the surrounding spatial market (at the beginning of 1997, food prices in Ulyanovsk rose by 40–60 per cent). As the authors of government programmes had expected, the first of the reform models cited above – the market proper – became the most widespread, though some regional differences were retained. Regions became more similar in the basic structure of their economic mechanisms.

REGIONAL SOCIOECONOMIC DIFFERENTIATION

Demographic Situation and Migration

Russia's population has been decreasing slowly since 1992 as a result of falling birth rates and rising mortality. The economic crisis has doubtless influenced this development, but it would be naive to assert that market reforms triggered population decline.

In some central and western regions of European Russia the depopulation process had already started in the 1980s, extending gradually to most of the country. In 1996 a natural decrease in population was observed in 69 out of 89 territorial units of the Federation. Positive growth was recorded only in certain republics and autonomous districts (that is, in regions where ethnic minorities are concentrated). Regional differentiation of natural population growth is influenced by differences of sex–age population structure, ethnocultural traditions and socioeconomic conditions. In recent years natural population growth has been negative in all economic regions (see Table 4.2). The most rapid rates of decrease are to be found in the Northwestern, Central and Central Chernozem regions, the lowest rate being in the North Caucasus region, where the proportion of surplus labour is highest and the political situation is unstable.

External and internal migration has a considerable influence on the demographic situation in the regions. In 1993–96 a positive balance of Russia's external migration (accounted for mainly by the republics of the former USSR) exceeded the intensity of interregional migration by three to four times (see Table 4.3). For this reason nine or ten regions out of twelve (including Kaliningrad oblast) have a positive migration balance.

In 1990–96 there was a stable negative migration balance only in the Northern, East Siberian and Far Eastern regions. The most disturbing tendency is the spontaneous outflow of population from the Far East (mainly from the northern districts). The highest increase attributable to migration in

Table 4.2   *Natural growth, migration balance and total growth of population, by economic region of the Russian Federation (per 1000 inhabitants)*

	Natural growth				Migration balance				Population number			
	1993	1994	1995	1996	1993	1994	1995	1996	1993	1994	1995	1996
Russian Federation	-5.1	-6.1	-5.7	-5.5	2.9	5.5	3.4	2.4	-2.2	-0.6	-2.3	-3.1
Northern	-4.5	-5.8	-5.5	-5.0	-6.2	-6.8	-4.3	-3.8	-10.7	-12.6	-9.8	-8.8
Northwestern	-10.9	-11.2	-10.1	-9.2	0.9	5.9	5.0	5.1	-10.0	-5.2	-5.1	-4.1
Central	-9.0	-10.4	-9.6	-9.0	3.8	7.2	5.6	4.7	-5.3	-3.2	-4.0	-4.3
Volgo-Vyatka	-5.7	-7.2	-7.2	-7.0	3.1	6.0	3.7	2.6	-2.6	-1.2	-3.5	-4.4
Central Chernozem	-7.4	-8.1	-7.8	-8.5	11.7	13.0	7.9	6.7	4.3	4.9	0.1	-1.8
Povolzje	-3.6	-4.7	-4.8	-5.2	7.8	9.9	6.2	3.7	4.2	5.2	1.4	-1.5
North Caucasian	-1.7	-1.7	-1.6	-1.7	8.2	9.5	4.9	2.0	6.5	7.8	3.3	0.3
Urals	-4.0	-5.2	-5.0	-4.6	2.0	6.0	3.6	2.4	-2.0	0.8	-1.4	-2.2
West Siberian	-3.4	-4.4	-4.1	-4.3	1.7	7.4	3.3	2.0	-1.7	3.0	-0.8	-2.3
East Siberian	-2.0	-3.2	-2.7	-2.6	-2.5	-0.8	0.4	-0.9	-4.5	-4.0	-2.3	-3.5
Far Eastern	-1.3	-2.0	-2.4	-2.6	-12.9	-19.2	-13.6	-8.8	-14.2	-21.2	-16.0	-11.4
Kaliningrad oblast	-4.6	-5.6	-5.0	-5.3	12.2	20.0	11.3	8.5	7.6	14.4	6.3	2.3

the 1990s (excluding 1995 and 1996) was recorded in the North Caucasus, and this was a factor which aggravated that region's socioeconomic problems.

Until 1996 positive migration balance exceeded negative natural growth in the Central Chernozem, Povolzje and North Caucasian regions and Kaliningrad oblast, but of this group only North Caucasus and Kaliningrad oblast remained by 1996. A different situation is observable in the Northern and Far Eastern regions. Negative natural growth superimposed on negative migration balance caused the annual decline of population numbers here to accelerate from 9 to 21 persons per thousand.

Table 4.3   *Balance of population migration in the Russian Federation, by economic region (thousands)*

Economic region	1990	1991	1992	1993	1994	1995	1996
Northern	−13	−39	46	−37	−41	−25	−22
Northwestern	19	−7	−4	7	48	40	41
Central	71	9	62	113	216	166	139
Volgo-Vyatka	−2	5	22	26	51	32	22
Central Chernozem	23	26	80	92	102	63	53
Povolzje	40	33	104	131	167	105	63
North Caucasian	79	150	103	143	167	86	35
Urals	−23	−4	37	41	124	74	49
West Siberian	−2	−32	37	26	112	50	30
East Siberian	−25	−29	−36	−23	−7	4	−8
Far Eastern	−10	−66	−150	−101	−148	−103	−65
Kaliningrad oblast	6	6	13	11	18	11	8
Russian Federation (external migration)	164	52	176	430	810	502	346
Net interregional migration*	75	177	−	161	196	128	95

Note: * Balance sum with the negative sign.

On the whole the demographic tendencies of the 1990s reinforce the unevenness of population distribution. A shift of population from North and East to the most populated European core is observable for the first time in the history of Russia. The main tendencies of the 1990s will probably persist until 2010 (see Table 4.4). Assuming a total decline of population numbers in

Russia of 4.2 per cent, positive growth is to be expected only in the North Caucasian (+3.3 per cent); with the biggest falls occurring in the Northern (9.3 per cent), Northwestern (9.1 per cent) and Far Eastern (10.9 per cent) regions.

Table 4.4   *Forecast of population numbers in the Russian Federation, by economic region (growth compared to 1996)**

	2000	2005	2010
Russian Federation	−1.0	−2.5	−4.2
Northern	−3.1	−6.4	−9.3
Northwestern	−2.5	−5.8	−9.1
Central	−2.2	−5.0	−7.9
Volgo-Vyatka	−1.1	−2.3	−3.7
Central Chernozem	−0.8	−2.3	−4.0
Povolzje	0.1	−0.0	−1.0
North Caucasian	1.5	2.6	3.3
Urals	−0.6	−1.5	−2.8
West Siberian	−0.6	−1.8	−3.7
East Siberian	−1.0	−2.2	−3.3
Far Eastern	−4.2	−7.9	−10.9
Kaliningrad oblast	0.3	−0.7	−2.9

Note: * Data of the RF State Committee for Statistics.

Production and Employment

In Soviet statistics the sphere of production included industry, agriculture and forestry, and capital construction works, along with 'production' services (transport and communications, service industries and trade). The regions did not officially calculate their own macroeconomic indices (gross social product, produced national income). In the regional analysis, priority was given to comparisons of the dynamics and structure of industrial production, this being justified on the ground that industry's share constituted 60–70 per cent of the volume of gross social product. In recent years Russian statistics have gone over to the international system of national accounting, so that the volume of gross domestic product (GDP) is now regarded as the main indicator of economic development at national and regional levels.

The changes in the methodology of statistical calculations are in line with the structural changes in the Russian economy determined by the evolution of market relationships. Thus, by 1993, industry's share of GDP had already decreased to 38.6 per cent, while the services share had increased to 45 per cent. By 1994 the services share of GDP was almost double the industry share (53.1 per cent compared with 29.3 per cent).

Territorial structure and dynamics of GDP

The analysis made of regional volumes of GDP in 1993–95 is based on figures compiled by SOPS and data furnished by the Ministry of Economy and State Committee for Statistics. The first three places in the territorial structure of GDP are occupied by the Centre, Urals and West Siberia (see Table 4.5). These account for about a half of Russia's GDP (fluctuating between 47.8 per cent and 50.9 per cent in 1993–95). From the aspect of the 89 territorial units of the Federation the analysis shows the growing role of Moscow and a small number of areas in different economic regions (from Northwestern to Far Eastern). The share of the first five units of the Federation was 30.7 per cent in 1995, of the first ten units 44.1 per cent, and of the first 17 units 57.5 per cent (see Table 4.6).

Table 4.5   Territorial composition of GDP (percentage of the Russian Federation total)*

Economic regions	1993	1994	1995
Northern	5.4	5.9	5.8
Northwestern	4.6	4.8	4.5
Central	17.4	20.0	15.6
Volgo-Vyatka	5.3	5.1	5.7
Central Chernozem	4.7	4.6	4.5
Povolzje	11.0	10.6	10.8
North Caucasian	6.5	5.9	4.7
Urals	15.7	15.5	17.4
West Siberian	14.7	13.8	17.9
East Siberian	7.3	6.6	7.2
Far Eastern	7.0	6.8	5.6
Kaliningrad oblast	0.4	0.4	0.3

Note: * According to SOPS figures.

As the general economic crisis continues, growth of the physical volume of GDP is observable in two types of region – centres of banking and commercial capital (primarily Moscow) and regions with producers and exporters of raw materials (chiefly Khanty–Mansi and Yamal–Nenets autonomous districts). At the same time the decline of GDP continues in the depressed and less developed regions. The result of this is an increasing differentiation of regions in terms of GDP volumes per head.

Table 4.6   Shares of the 'richest' units of the Federation in Russia's GDP, 1995 (%)

1. Moscow	13.1
2. Khanty-Mansi AD	5.2
3. Samara oblast	4.5
4. Moscow oblast	4.2
5. Primorsky krai	3.7
6. Perm oblast	3.0
7. Sverdlovsk oblast	2.8
8. St Petersburg	2.7
9. Krasnoyarsk krai	2.5
10. Republic of Bashkortostan	2.4
11. Kemerovo oblast	2.3
12. Republic of Tatarstan	2.2
13. Irkutsk oblast	2.0
14. Yamal-Nenets AD	2.0
15. Nizhny Novgorod oblast	1.7
16. Chelyabinsk oblast	1.6
17. Republic of Sakha (Yakutia)	1.6
Total	57.5

Source: Russian–European Centre of Economic Policy, Review of the Economy of Russia, II, 1997.

The spread between the marginal values of GDP per head in 89 regions in 1995 was amazing, the highest being 1373 times bigger than the lowest! But this is a misleading indicator because the last position is occupied by war-ravaged Chechenya. Nevertheless, the spread between the GDP volumes per head of the regions is very large, even if Chechenya is excluded and even if we compare groups of regions. In 1993 the average value for the first ten regions was six times higher than for the last ten, and in 1995 it was eleven times higher.

Data on GDP volumes per head in the first 16 regions are given in Table 4.7. Along with the first three obvious leaders, territorial units from six economic regions of the Federation are to be found in the list, enjoying sundry advantages (sectoral structure, tax base, high incomes of inhabitants, geographical position and so on) compared with the other 72 units.

Table 4.7   GDP per head of certain territorial units of the Federation, by purchasing power parity (as percentage of the average value for Russia, February 1997)

Khanty–Mansi AD	469.5
Yamal–Nenets AD	420.2
Moscow	258.1
Samara oblast	241.8
Perm oblast	191.3
Arkhangelsk oblast	167.3
Republic of Komi	155.3
Tula oblast	154.2
Lipetsk oblast	149.1
Republic of Tatarstan	144.4
Republic of Sakha (Yakutia)	143.5
Kamchatka oblast	141.5
Khabarovsk krai	132.7
Vologda oblast	131.6
Kemerovo oblast	129.6
Kostroma oblast	127.5

Note: Estimates of the purchasing power parities were compiled on the basis of the cost of a basket of 25 of the most important consumer goods.

Source: Russian–European Centre of Economic Policy, *Review of the Economy of Russia*, II, 1997.

Increasing differentiation of the levels of economic development of regions is a serious problem for Russia, of course, imperilling its economic and political unity. But this is not a problem of direct state action. Its solution does not lie in 'equalising' or restraining the development of 'rich' regions, but in using instruments of economic and social policy to help the 'poor' regions to catch up.

Dynamics and structure of industrial production
The volume of industrial production in Russia halved between 1991 and 1995, according to the official data (see Table 4.8). Differentiation of production indices by economic regions is not very high, varying from 41 per

cent for North Caucasian to 61 per cent for Northern region, but this is explained by the averaging of large differences within each economic region. Differentiation of indices relating to the territorial units of the Federation is significantly higher, ranging from 20 per cent (Republic of Ingushetia) to 77 per cent (Republic of Khakassia and Nenets Autonomous District). In nine units of the Federation (excluding Chechenya) volumes of production decreased to between one-third and one-fifth and in four units to less than a quarter. The average Russian indices conceal not only a catastrophic situation in the industries of a number of regions but surprising growth as well. Thus in 1995 the volume of industrial production grew in 17 units of the Federation, including Lipetsk oblast (14 per cent), Sakhalin oblast (9 per cent) and Kamchatka oblast (8 per cent). Data for 1996 showed the volume of industrial output of large and medium enterprises to have increased in four units of the Federation, but only in two of them (Tatarstan and Kamchatka oblast) had growth begun in 1995.

Table 4.8   Indices of physical volume of industrial output, by economic region (in percentage of 1990)

	1991	1992	1993	1994	1995
Russian Federation	92	75	65	51	50
Northern	95	85	76	63	61
Northwestern	100	84	75	50	43
Central	97	75	66	48	42
Volgo-Vyatka	99	87	82	55	48
Central Chernozem	97	85	77	58	57
Povolzje	97	85	78	59	54
North Caucasian	97	78	66	46	41
Urals	98	81	70	54	50
West Siberian	96	81	72	60	56
East Siberian	96	83	73	61	57
Far Eastern	97	83	72	55	46
Kaliningrad oblast	96	80	66	41	37

The sectoral structure of industry is the main factor determining regional differentiation of the indices of industrial production. The combination of a number of tendencies of the transitional period (termination of artificial supply conditions, declining domestic demand, liberalisation of external trade and so on) led to a situation in which the biggest fall in production occurred in the mechanical engineering, chemical and forest industries (by a factor of

2.2–2.3 on average). This was especially evident in the light industry (a factor of four). Production declined to a lesser extent in the power industry (consumption of electricity is not very elastic in its response to falls in production and personal real incomes – a phenomenon which merits special analysis), sectors with an export orientation (fuel, ferrous and non-ferrous metallurgy) and the food industry (which is better protected from external competition).

In 1991–95, as a result of sectoral differences in the dynamics of production and prices, the sectoral structure of industry changed considerably both in Russia as a whole and in each economic region individually (see Tables 4.9, 4.10 and 4.11). In particular, the proportion of mechanical engineering and light industry decreased from 43.3 to 20.4 per cent, and the proportion of power production, fuel industry, and ferrous and non-ferrous metallurgy increased from 22.9 to 45.5 per cent. It is evident that the concentration of the first group of branches in the region had a negative impact on the regional index of industrial production, whereas the concentration of the second group had a positive effect.

Table 4.9　Indices of the physical volume of output, by industry sector (%)

	1995–90	1994–93
Mining	70	90
Manufacturing	48	76
Power production	83	91
Fuel	69	90
Ferrous metallurgy	54	83
Non-ferrous metallurgy	54	91
Mechanical engineering and metal working	45	69
Chemical and petrochemical	44	76
Forestry, woodworking, pulp and paper	44	70
Building materials industry	47	73
Light	26	54
Food	57	83
All industry	51	79

Table 4.10 Structure of industrial production in 1990 (%)

Economic region	Power production	Fuel industry	Ferrous metallurgy	Non-ferrous metallurgy	Chemical industry	Mechanical engineering	Forestry woodworking and pulp and paper	Building materials industry	Light industry	Food industry	Others
Russian Federation	4.3	7.6	5.3	5.7	7.3	31.2	5.4	3.5	12.1	12.7	4.9
Northern	4.1	6.1	13.8	6.5	4.2	15.6	21.5	4.5	5.0	16.1	2.6
Northwestern	3.4	3.2	0.8	1.8	5.7	44.1	6.2	3.1	12.3	11.5	7.9
Central	3.4	1.9	1.8	5.9	6.2	34.8	3.3	2.9	23.6	10.5	5.7
Volgo-Vyatka	2.4	3.3	3.5	0.5	9.3	44.9	6.3	2.9	12.2	9.6	5.1
Central Chernozem	3.3	0.0	13.6	0.0	9.1	33.4	1.9	4.1	8.1	20.8	5.7
Povolzje	5.2	6.1	2.1	1.7	13.2	39.8	2.3	3.6	9.6	11.1	5.3
North Caucasian	2.7	4.8	1.4	2.5	7.1	27.5	4.5	4.3	13.2	24.2	7.8
Urals	4.7	7.3	15.8	8.2	7.6	31.7	4.1	2.8	5.7	7.9	4.2
West Siberian	5.1	32.2	5.0	1.5	8.0	22.0	3.6	3.6	6.5	8.7	3.8
East Siberian	9.0	9.7	1.0	21.7	4.1	12.0	13.6	4.0	10.9	8.1	5.9
Far Eastern	4.5	5.4	0.9	14.1	2.0	18.7	8.4	6.5	4.1	30.5	4.9
Kaliningrad oblast	0.7	1.1	0.8	0.0	0.1	27.1	10.7	2.7	4.7	43.6	8.5

Table 4.11 Structure of industrial production in 1995 (%)

Economic region	Power production	Fuel industry	Ferrous metallurgy	Non-ferrous metallurgy	Chemical and petrochemical industry	Mechanical engineering and metalworking	Forestry woodworking	Building materials industry [a]	Light industry	Food industry [b]
Russian Federation	13.5	16.4	9.1	6.5	7.5	17.9	5.1	5.1	2.5	14.2
Northern	13.3	10.3	20.1	8.1	4.6	5.9	21.6	3.7	0.8	10.6
Northwestern	11.7	7.5	1.7	3.5	6.9	26.2	8.6	4.8	3.9	21.8
Central	15.6	5.2	2.7	1.5	7.0	25.2	3.9	8.1	6.6	18.9
Volgo-Vyatka	11.8	7.5	3.7	0.5	10.1	35.2	7.1	4.4	3.3	13.4
Central Chernozem	13.7	0.0	34.6	0.0	6.7	15.8	1.3	5.8	1.7	18.9
Povolzje	13.4	13.6	1.6	1.8	15.7	31.0	1.5	4.9	2.2	12.6
North Caucasian	16.1	9.3	3.2	2.7	6.5	16.9	3.2	8.8	2.9	28.6
Urals	12.4	13.6	21.6	8.1	9.1	15.8	3.1	4.6	1.3	9.1
West Siberian	11.5	51.5	9.2	1.4	5.4	8.3	1.5	3.2	0.9	7.8
East Siberian	11.9	15.3	1.6	32.2	3.9	7.6	12.2	3.9	1.0	8.8
Far Eastern	19.3	10.5	0.5	20.7	0.7	8.5	5.4	4.2	0.6	27.3
Kaliningrad oblast	13.9	6.8	1.8	0.3	0.5	10.6	21.3	2.7	2.3	36.2

Notes:
a Including glass and porcelain and pottery industries.
b Including flour-cereals and fodder industries.

Table 4.12 compares the rankings of economic regions on the basis of three characteristics: index of industrial production, weighting of the group of sectors with the most rapidly declining production and weighting of the group of sectors with the least rapidly declining production. For such regions as Northern, Northwestern, Central, West Siberian and East Siberian, the ranking according to the production index is satisfactorily explained by the combination of rankings based on the second and third characteristics. For other regions this approach is unsatisfactory; it is necessary to take account of the differing competitiveness of the goods produced (including the effect of intrasectoral structure) and other factors, including non-economic ones. For example, in the Far East a considerable part of the decline in production is explained by increased transport costs. In North Caucasus the decline is explained by political instability resulting in armed conflicts.

Table 4.12 Ranking of economic regions on the basis of industrial production indices and shares of the groups of sectors with the most and least rapidly declining production levels in the total volume of industrial output of the economic region

Economic regions	By index of industrial production [a]		By share of sectors of group 1 [b]		By share of sectors of group 2 [c]	
Northern	1	(61)	1	(20.6)	4	(30.5)
Central Chernozem	2–3	(57)	7	(41.5)	6	(16.9)
East Siberian	2–3	(57)	3	(22.9)	2	(41.4)
West Siberian	4	(56)	4	(28.5)	1	(43.8)
Povolzje	5	(54)	8	(49.4)	7	(15.1)
Urals	6	(50)	5	(37.4)	3	(36)
Volgo-Vyatka	7	(48)	10	(57.1)	10	(9.7)
Far Eastern	8	(46)	2	(22.8)	5	(24.9)
Northwestern	9	(43)	9	(56.4)	11	(9.2)
Central	10	(42)	11	(58.4)	8	(13.0)
North Caucasian	11	(41)	6	(40.7)	9	(11.4)

Notes:
a In brackets – indices of industrial production (1995 in % of 1990).
b In brackets – shares of products of mechanical engineering and food industry in the total volume of industrial output in 1990 (per cent).
c In brackets – shares of products of power production, fuel industry, ferrous and non-ferrous metallurgy in the total volume of industrial output in 1990 (per cent).

Employment and unemployment

Ever since the start of the economic reforms, employment in Russia has been shrinking gradually while both total and registered unemployment has been growing (see Table 4.13). In spite of the mitigating factor of artificial job creation (partly a relic of the socialist past and partly the result of state assistance to town development projects), unemployment is becoming an increasingly serious social problem.

Table 4.13   Total and registered unemployment in the Russian Federation

	1992	1993	1994	1995
Total number of unemployed (thousands)	3594	4160	5478	6431
% of occupationally active population	4.8	5.5	7.4	8.7
Number of registered unemployed (thousands)	578	836	1637	–
% of occupationally active population	0.8	1.1	2.2	–

The levels of total and registered unemployment vary considerably from region to region. The lowest levels of total unemployment in 1995 are shown in Table 4.14. Six regions in this group are among the leaders by volume of GDP per head (see Table 4.7). The others belong to the category of regions which are favourably placed economically. It should be noted that in Chukotka Autonomous District the proportion of registered unemployed is higher than the average Russian value. This category of the occupationally active population is the source of labour emigration.

The regions of highest unemployment (see Table 4.15) are either poorly developed regions with a constant pool of surplus of labour or else depressed regions. The highest level of registered unemployment is in Ivanovo oblast. In the republics of the North Caucasus, where there are traditions of labour mobility, it is not high. In addition to the districts of the Federation territorial units cited, the employment problem manifests itself in acute form at local level in the majority of the Federation's units. This also applies to small and medium-sized towns with concentrations of defence and light industries, at the unfinished construction sites of large-scale undertakings, in mining settlements of the extreme north, and in the 'closed' zones.

Table 4.14   Regions with lowest unemployment, 1995

	%	%
Moscow	5.2	(0.3)
Omsk oblast	5.2	(1.4)
Chukotka AD	5.2	(3.4)
Belgorod oblast	5.5	(0.7)
Tula oblast	5.9	(1.0)
Kursk oblast	6.0	(1.6)
Tyumen oblast	6.1	(1.7)
Lipetsk oblast	6.3	(1.2)
Republic of Sakha	6.4	(0.8)
Republic of Tatarstan	6.4	(0.8)

Note: Level of registered unemployment in brackets.

Table 4.15   Regions with highest unemployment, 1995

	%	%
Republic of North Ossetiya	24.0	(2.6)
Republic of Karachaevo–Cherkessia	24.0	(2.6)
Republic of Dagestan	22.3	(5.7)
Republic of Kalmykia	19.8	(5.8)
Jewish autonomous oblast	15.9	(1.6)
Ivanovo oblast	14.9	(8.9)
Republic of Kabardino–Balkar	14,7	(2.7)
Republic of Tyva	14.2	(1.6)

Note: Level of registered unemployment in brackets.

Personal Incomes

Changes in the mechanisms for establishing and distributing personal incomes reinforce social differentiation, including the regional aspect. Given the fall in average real income per head (after inflation), the gap between the regions with the highest and lowest levels of incomes has been growing: 6.06 times by December 1994, 14.5 times by 1995, 16.7 times by April 1997 and 14.1 times without distinguishing autonomous districts (see Table 4.16). The breakdown into 'richest' and 'poorest' regions is fairly stable. The former group includes Moscow, oil-gas producing regions and Far Eastern regions with the highest cost of living. The latter group includes the republics of North Caucasus, Kalmykia and Tyva and a number of autonomous districts and some agricultural regions in close proximity to them. The social situation in Russia is exacerbated by the fact that, in the 'poor' regions, real incomes per head are continuing to fall, in contrast to the notable growth of real incomes both in Moscow and in certain regions benefiting from their exceptional position during the transitional period.

Table 4.16   Incomes per head in April 1994 and average monthly incomes, 1995 (thousand roubles)

	1994	1995
Average for the Russian Federation	925.7	532.9
Regions with highest incomes		
Yamal–Nenets AD	3911.3	–
Moscow	3663.0	1707.8
Khanty–Mansi AD	2998.7	–
Tyumen oblast	2314.3	1140.5
Chukotka AD	1668.0	1185.6
Magadan oblast	1614.2	1151.8
Kamchatka oblast	1410.6	1108.1
Regions with lowest incomes		
Ust-Ordynsk Buryatsky AD	233.7	–
Aginsky Buryatsky AD	254.4	–
Republic of Ingushetia	260.3	117.6
Republic of Dagestan	279.1	185.5
Republic of Tyva	365.5	302.2
Komi–Permyak AD	379.3	–
Republic of Adygea	445.8	295.2
Republic of Kabardino–Balkar	452.2	280.2
Altai krai	478.1	349.9

It is evident that regions differ considerably not only in average income per head but also in the distribution of population according to average income per head (see Table 4.17). It is hard to believe that such wide variations can exist within a single country, or to conceive of the consequences to which this could lead. Whereas in the first group of regions over 40 per cent of the population had an average monthly income per head exceeding one million roubles in 1995, in the second group a similar proportion had incomes below 200 000 roubles. The data in Table 4.18 illustrate the unique degree of social differentiation not only between the regions but also within the majority of them.

Table 4.17   Distribution of population according to average income per head, 1995 (%)

	Average income per head (thousand roubles per month)					
	Below 200	200.1– 400	400.1– 600	600.1– 800	800.1– 1000	Over 1000
Russian Federation		32.9	22.4	12.7	7.0	10.5
Regions with highest average income per head [a]						
Moscow	14.5	21.1	17.0	10.1	6.1	40.1
Magadan oblast	1.4	10.1	15.6	15.4	12.9	44.6
Tyumen oblast	4.6	15.1	16.1	13.6	10.7	39.9
Kamchatka oblast	1.6	11.0	16.4	15.7	12.9	42.4
Republic of Sakha	1.1	11.1	18.3	17.7	14.2	37.6
Regions with lowest average income per head [b]						
Republic of Kalmykia	49.5	41.8	7.1	1.2	0.3	0.1
Karachaevo–Cherkessia	42.2	43.9	10.6	2.4	0.6	0.3
Republic of Mari-El	34.9	52.5	10.5	1.8	0.3	0.1
Republic of Kabardino–Balkar	36.3	46.1	13.0	3.3	0.9	0.4
Kurgan oblast	33.9	48.6	13.3	3.1	0.8	0.3

Notes:
a   No data available for the autonomous districts, including the richest (Khanty–Mansi, Yamal–Nenets and Chukotka).
b   No data available for the poorest republics, including Chechenya, Ingushetia and Dagestan.

Over the country as a whole, the 20 per cent of inhabitants with the highest average incomes per head had a volume of income 8.5 times larger than the same proportion of inhabitants with the lowest incomes. Regions with higher average incomes per head exhibit greater social differentiation as a rule. Moscow is the 'leader', its ratio between the total incomes of the fifth and first groups respectively being 19.7:1 in 1995. The capital city also has the lowest share of income earners in the first group and the biggest share in the fifth 20 per cent group (59.2 per cent). The most even distribution of incomes occurs in Sakhalin oblast, with a ratio of 3.3:1 between groups five and one. This region has the highest share of income earners of all regions in the first group (10.1 per cent) and the lowest share of all in group five (33.8 per cent). Thus, to a considerable extent, the phenomenon of 'rich on average' and 'poor on average' regions (by incomes per head) is the outcome of intraregional differences in social stratification.

Table 4.18 Distribution of the total volume of money incomes, by population groups with different incomes, 1995 (%)

	By 20 per cent groups of population				
	First	Second	Third	Fourth	Fifth
Russian Federation	5.5	10.2	15.0	22.4	46.9
Regions with highest average income per head [a]					
Moscow	3.0	5.5	9.2	23.1	59.2
Magadan oblast	6.2	11.1	15.9	22.9	43.9
Tyumen oblast	4.7	9.2	14.3	22.3	49.6
Kamchatka oblast	6.2	11.1	15.9	22.9	43.9
Republic of Sakha	7.1	11.9	16.6	23.1	41.3
Regions with lowest average income per head [b]					
Republic of Kalmykia	8.7	13.5	17.7	23.1	37.0
Karachaevo–Cherkessia	8.1	13.0	17.3	23.2	38.4
Republic of Mari-El	9.5	14.2	18.1	23.0	35.2
Republic of Kabardino–Balkar	8.1	13.0	17.4	23.1	38.4
Kurgan oblast	8.5	13.4	17.6	23.1	37.4

Notes:
a   No data available for the autonomous districts.
b   No data available for the poorest republics.

Revolutionary changes occurred in the pattern of money incomes of the population of Russia during the second half of the 1980s. These reflected the transition from socialist planning to the market economy. Between 1980 and 1994 the reward to labour declined from 77.4 to 46.4 per cent of total money incomes and the reward to property ownership and entrepreneurship increased from 6.9 to 36.2 per cent. The disparities between average wages by regions are smaller than those between money incomes per head. The maximum disparity in 1995 was 10.2 times (excluding Chechenya), while the difference in incomes per head was 14.5 times (see Table 4.19). Wage disparities are growing. Data for May 1997 show them to have reached 11.9 times (excluding Chechenya).

Table 4.19   Average monthly wages of workers in enterprises and organisations, 1995 (thousand roubles)

Regions of highest wages	
Yamal–Nenets AD	1758.8
Chukotka AD	1681.4
Koryak AD	1454.4
Khanty–Mansi AD	1392.0
Taimyr AD	1369.6
Kamchatka oblast	1213.8
Tyumen oblast	1160.6
Republic of Sakha	1154.0
Magadan oblast	1107.4
Regions of lowest wages	
Ingush Republic	172.1
Republic of Karachaevo–Cherkessia	237.0
Republic of Kalmykia	243.8
Republic of North Ossetiya	244.8
Republic of Chuvashia	253.0
Republic of Mari-El	254.4
Orel oblast	299.9

Sectoral structure of the economy is the main factor determining regional differentiation of average wages. In 1994 average sectoral wages compared with average wages in the national economy were 237 per cent in the fuel industry, 208 per cent in finance and insurance, 205 per cent in electric power production, 150 per cent in transport, 80 per cent in mechanical engineering, 69 per cent in education and 50 per cent in light industries. In addition there are significant effects from payments to the workers of eastern and northern regions for purposes of regional regulation of wages, as well as differences in the cost of the labour force. This explains why only northern and eastern mining regions are to be found among the leaders as regards wage levels while southern republics of labour surplus, with their relatively low cost of living and adjacent individual areas with a large proportion of agricultural production, occupy the bottom places. In 1995 Moscow came twenty third for wage levels, and in St Petersburg wages were lower than the average value for Russia. In these two largest cities, having the status of territorial units of the Federation, the growth of personal incomes is associated chiefly with income from property ownership, entrepreneurship and finance and credit operations. A favourable economic climate stimulates the labour market and conduces to rising wages. In May 1996 average wages in Moscow exceeded the average Russian value by 38 per cent (in 1995 by 24 per cent) and in May 1997 by 42 per cent (sevententh place in Russia). The corresponding figures for St Petersburg are 8–9 per cent higher than the average Russian value.

Regional differentiation of prices for consumer goods and services has a considerable influence on the living standard of regional populations. Because of the climatic conditions and peripheral location, the highest cost of living is to be found in the northern and eastern regions; the lowest is in the central zone of Russia (see Figure 4.1). The cost of the basket of 25 main food products varies by a factor of 3.9 in the regions, and the average subsistence wage per head by 3.8 (see Table 4.20). The actual differentiation according to the second index is underestimated because of lack of data concerning autonomous districts, where the cost of living is especially high. It should be noted that the liberalisation of imports has offered northern and Far Eastern port cities and frontier territories favourable opportunities for making imported consumer goods cheaper, especially food. The fact that advantage is not taken of them is evidence of imperfection in the forming of regional consumer markets.

The ratio between money incomes and subsistence wage is used as the main statistical index for comparing regional living standards. In 1995 the value of this index amounted on average to 202 per cent in Russia, and the difference between maximum and minimum in the regions was 8.5 times (see Table 4.21). The group with the highest ratio includes a number of regions with the highest average incomes per head (Moscow, Tyumen and Kamchatka oblasts) and other regions showing favourable figures for both indices (St Petersburg, Orel oblast). The group with the lowest ratio includes the republics of North Caucasus, Kalmykia and Mari-El, regions with high living costs (Chita oblast) and backward agricultural regions. In four regions the average incomes per head are lower than the subsistence wage.

The proportion of population with money incomes lower than the subsistence wage is a more direct (socially concrete) characteristic of poverty in the region. In 1995 in Russia, this proportion amounted on average to 24.7 per cent, in 1992 to 33.5 per cent, in 1993 to 31.8 per cent and in 1994 to

Table 4.20   Cost of living indices for the regions of the Russian Federation

	Cost of the basket of 25 main food products, May 1997 (% of the average Russian value)[a]	Average monthly subsistence wage per head in 1995 (thousand roubles)[b]
Russian Federation	100	264.1
Regions with the highest cost of living [c]		
Evenk AD	302	–
Koryak AD	300	–
Chukotka AD	298	–
Kamchatka oblast	240	524.4
Taimyr AD	229	–
Republic of Sakha	214	585.5
Magadan oblast	192	570.1
Yamal–Nenets AD	185	–
Sakhalin oblast	185	490.2
Chita oblast	162	426.0
Nenets AD	161	–
Khanty–Mansi AD	143	–
Murmansk oblast	125	416.6
Tyumen oblast	124	393.9
Regions with the lowest cost of living [c]		
Republic of Tatarstan	77	192.2
Ulyanovsk oblast	80	153.6
Republic of Chuvashia	80	196.5
Republic of Mari-El	80	220.8
Kaliningrad oblast	83	261.6
Kirov oblast	83	280.2
Tambov oblast	84	166.5

Notes:
a   The cost of the basket was calculated using standards customary in average Russian consumption.
b   Autonomous districts were not specified separately.
c   Ranked according to cost of the basket.

24.4 per cent. The lowest proportion of population living below the poverty line is in Kemerovo (16.1 per cent), Tula (16.2 per cent) and Ulyanovsk oblasts. It is noticeable that in Moscow, the 'richest on average' of the Federation's territorial units, this proportion is higher (19.1 per cent). The largest proportion of population with incomes below the subsistence wage is in Tyva (73.2 per cent), Chita oblast (66.5 per cent), Kalmykia (60.3 per cent) and Buryatia (55.2 per cent). It is interesting that this list does not include any republic of North Caucasus, a characteristic feature of which is the more even, 'fair' distribution of small average incomes per head.

It is evident that there is a considerable and growing differentiation of the regions of Russia by various statistical indices of living standards. This differentiation could probably be evened out if we were to take account of incomes in kind (especially in the form of food products produced in households) and incomes derived from the black economy. But there is no reason to expect much equalisation of incomes to result from more comprehensive accounting.

Table 4.21   Ratio of money incomes to subsistence wage in the regions of the Russian Federation, 1995*

Russian Federation	202
Regions with the highest ratio	
Moscow	520
Tyumen oblast	290
Kemerovo oblast	254
Krasnoyarsk krai	246
St Petersburg	229
Orel oblast	214
Kamchatka oblast	211
Regions with the lowest ratio	
Ingush Republic	61
Republic of Tyva	84
Republic of Dagestan	86
Chita oblast	99
Republic of Kalmykia	100
Kurgan oblast	113
Orenburg oblast	115
Republic of Mari-El	120

Note: * Autonomous districts were not specified separately.

Against a background of serious differences in the 'material' elements of the standard of living, the negligible differences of life expectancy between regions appear paradoxical (see Table 4.22). If we bear in mind especially that life expectancy in Russia lags 10–20 years behind that in many other countries, it is hard not to agree that Russians live in a country unlike any other!

Table 4.22   Life expectancy at birth in the economic regions of the Russian Federation, 1995

	Life expectancy			Deviation from average		
	Total population	Males	Females	Total population	Males	Females
Russian Federation	64.64	58.27	71.70	–	–	–
Northern	63.07	56.76	70.61	–1.57	–1.51	–1.09
Northwestern	64.48	58.03	71.37	–0.16	–0.24	–0.33
Central	64.54	57.77	71.99	–0.10	–0.50	0.29
Volgo–Vyatka	65.28	58.67	72.50	0.64	0.40	0.80
Central Chernozem	66.92	60.46	73.88	2.26	2.19	2.18
Povolzje	66.43	60.17	73.13	1.79	1.90	1.43
North Caucasian	66.59	60.54	73.03	1.95	2.27	1.33
Urals	64.61	58.23	71.68	–0.03	–0.04	–0.02
West Siberian	64.13	57.96	71.08	–0.51	–0.31	–0.62
East Siberian	61.86	55.48	69.46	–2.78	–2.79	–2.24
Far Eastern	62.29	56.74	68.94	–2.35	–1.53	–1.76
Kaliningrad oblast	64.81	58.88	71.42	0.17	0.61	–0.38

TYPOLOGY OF RUSSIAN REGIONS

The main socioeconomic indices in combination reveal a highly variegated pattern of differentiation between the regions. Therefore it is necessary to create a system of classification or typology, applicable especially to the 89 territories of the Federation, to enable the problems of the regions to be described and analysed and the objectives of state regional policy to be achieved. Clearly the time has passed when the centre attempted to pursue individual policy in relation to individual territorial units of the Federation by providing direct financial assistance or economic privileges of some sort. The new regional policy will best be conducted on the basis of all-Russian

Table 4.23 Typology of the territorial units of the Russian Federation based on the main problems of regional development

Types	Regions*
	I. BASIC PROBLEMS: ECONOMIC
1. Traditionally backward a) unfavourable natural climate	Republics *Ingush, Kalmykia-Khalmg Tangch, Tyva; Jewish Autonomous Oblast*; autonomous districts: *Aginsky Buryat, Komi-Permyak, Koryak, Nenets, Taimyr, Ust-Ordynsky Buryat, Evenk*
b) favourable natural climate	Republics *Adygeya, Dagestan, Kabardino-Balkar, Karachaevo–Cherkessia, North Osetia*
2. Depressed a) pre-reform	Republics *Buryatia, Chuvash; Altai krai*; oblasts: *Amur, Kirov, Kurgan, Chita*
b) new	*Republic of Udmurtia, Arkhangelsk oblast, Ivanovo oblast, Khabarovsk krai*
3. Traditionally developed a) not adapted to the new economic conditions (critical: import- and export-oriented, conversion)	*Republic of Mordovia*; oblasts: *Kamchatka, Kostroma, Moscow, Novosibirsk, Rostov*, Magadan; Primorsky krai
b) better adapted to the new economic conditions (not associated with problem regions)	Republics *Bashkortostan, Karelia, Mari El, Tatarstan, Khakassia*; federal metropolitan units of the RF: *Moscow, St Petersburg*; krais: *Krasnodar, Krasnoyarsk, Stavropol*; oblasts: *Astrakhan, Belgorod, Bryansk, Vladimir, Volgograd, Voronezh, Vologda, Irkutsk, Kaluga, Kursk, Leningrad, Lipetsk, Nizhny Novgorod, Novgorod, Omsk, Orenburg, Orel, Penza, Perm, Ryazan, Samara, Saratov, Sverdlovsk, Smolensk, Tambov, Tver, Tomsk, Tula, Tyumen, Chelyabinsk, Ulyanovsk, Yaroslavl*
4. Developing (resources) a) existing	Republics *Komi, Sakha (Yakutia)*; oblasts: *Kemerovo, Magadan*, Murmansk; autonomous districts: *Khanty–Mansi, Yamal–Nenets*
b) perspective	Evenk AD; Sakhalin oblast
	II. BASIC PROBLEMS: GEOPOLITICAL
1. Frontier a) strategic	Oblasts *Kaliningrad, Murmansk, Sakhalin*, Amur, Kamchatka, Chita; *Primorsky krai*
b) new	*Pskov oblast*; Altai krai
	III. BASIC PROBLEMS: ETHNIC
1. Ethnocultural–religious conflicts	Republics *Chechenya*, Ingush, North Osetia, Bashkortostan, Tatarstan, Tyva
	IV. BASIC PROBLEMS: ENVIRONMENTAL
1. Inherent dangers a) disaster	Republics Dagestan, North Osetia; Sakhalin oblast
b) industrial and transport pollution	Autonomous districts Taimyr, Khanty–Mansi, Yamal–Nenets; Altai krai; oblasts: Bryansk, Irkutsk, Kemerovo, Chelyabinsk
c) specially protected territories	Republics *Altai*, Buryatia, Karelia; autonomous districts: *Chukotka*, Komi–Permyak, Koryak, Khanty–Mansi, Evenk, Yamal–Nenets; oblasts: Irkutsk, Kamchatka

Note: * Regions whose types predominate are italicised.

legislation applied to *types of regions* identified in terms of their objective economic, social, natural and geopolitical conditions. Several methodological approaches have been employed in recent years to create a typology of Russian regions. The results of two studies are considered below.

The typology of regions devised at the instance of the Ministry of Nationalities and Federal Relations uses a variety of criteria to identify *problem regions* in need of state assistance. The typology of Federation territorial units takes account of four aspects of regional problems: economic, geopolitical, ethnic and environmental. Several types of region were identified within the category of each aspect ('basic problem' in the table). In Table 4.23 all regions of Russia are distributed according to type of region.

The SOPS typology of regions is based on more than 40 indices. Three types of *problem* region are distinguished for purposes of regional economic policy: weakly developed (about15), depressed (about 20) and crisis (about 15). The crisis regions in the European part of the country form three crisis belts: Central, Southern and Urals. The largest is *Central*, comprising parts of the Northwestern, Central, Volgo-Vyatka, Central Chernozem and Povolzje economic regions. A total of 17 territorial units of the Federation are located here, all of them deemed to be either in or approaching a crisis associated with declining production: 13 of them have environmental problems, 19 are experiencing rapid depopulation, 14 are suffering rising unemployment, 7 exhibit poverty at crisis levels and 19 are in financial difficulties.

The *Southern* crisis belt comprises adjoining regions of the North Caucasus and Povolzje. The rate of production decline marks the republics of North Caucasus and five other Federation territorial units as being at a pre-crisis stage. There are serious inter-ethnic conflicts in these belts, crisis phenomena in the employment sphere (7 Federation territorial units), in living standards (12 regions) and in financial conditions (12 regions). There are also large numbers of refugees and economic migrants concentrated here.

The *Urals* form the third crisis belt. Here there are four territorial units of the Federation with steeply declining production, five regions in crisis or pre-crisis related to technological factors, three experiencing high unemployment, five facing poverty problems and two with unsatisfactory finances. Despite the relative compactness of this crisis belt, it poses a significant threat to Russia's national security because basic industrial sectors, large defence installations and industries and the atomic energy industry are concentrated on its territory.

A fourth, southeastern, crisis belt is currently taking shape, comprising the republics of Altai, Tyva and Buryatia, along with Altai krai and Chita and Amur oblasts. Weak finances and low living standards are typical of most of them.

TERRITORIAL ECONOMIC DISINTEGRATION

Following the collapse of the Soviet Union, tendencies towards political and economic disintegration have manifested themselves in the Russian Federation. Various phenomena symptomatic of disintegration typify the Russian economy:

1. Diminution of interregional trade linkages resulting from the growth of transport tariffs, uncompetitiveness of producers, insolvency of consumers and reorientation of regions (producers and consumers) towards external linkages. Decreasing exchanges of interregional goods are more significant than declining production.
2. Unsatisfactory functioning of monetary and financial systems: regular cash deficits in individual regions, long-term accumulations of indebtedness between regions with cash settlement continually postponed, growth of debt default, disputes between centre and regions over transfers of tax-money and so on.
3. Repeated outbreaks of economic separatism, manifested in attempts to exploit natural resources unilaterally, to retain tax revenues within the subordinate territory or to ban the export of consumer goods beyond its borders.
4. Diminution of human contacts between the regions, primarily as a result of rises in passenger transport fares.

Russia's viability as an economically integrated spatial entity is complicated not only by economic but also by political factors during this transitional period. These latter include the asymmetry of the Russian Federation, that is the coexistence within the Federation of territories enjoying different kinds of status, the as yet unfinished process of determining the distribution of powers between centre and regions, and the practice of conducting relations between the centre and certain regions on an exclusive basis (especially on the eve of presidential and parliamentary elections).

The new constitution has consolidated the legal principles of the all-Russian market and removed most of the economic discrimination between different Federation territorial units. But the crisis of 1998 is not the least of the factors indicating that there is still a danger of economic collapse. It is clear that the *political* dangers of collapse have diminished, but the tendency towards disintegration of the economy has not yet been dispelled. The main positive change is that factors favouring integration, such as the interest of goods producers in overcoming limited demand and enlarging the market, have started to operate actively. This interest is now supported by regional authorities as well, since expanded production and marketing increase both public revenues and personal incomes, while also reducing unemployment.

The considerable degree of heterogeneity characterising the present economic spatial entity called 'Russia' does not constitute an insurmountable obstacle in the way of integration on a market basis. But it does restrict the scope for market self-regulation (especially in problem regions) and diverts substantial state resources to assist weak regions. Normal market regulation implies a strengthening not only of the *integrity* (connectedness) of the economy but of the *homogeneity* of the economic spatial entity as well.

New economic space is created as the system of markets for goods, labour and capital takes shape on the ruins of the socialist market, bringing new efficiency criteria. Therefore the weakening or rupture of many former economic linkages is inevitable and rational. This applies, for example, to cooperative supplies under contract to government departments, long-distance transport of products formerly in short supply and replacement of home suppliers and consumers by foreign suppliers and consumers in the peripheral regions. These consequences follow from the need to alleviate hyperconcentration of production and hyperspecialisation of the regions.

A more rapid diminution of interregional exchanges relative to the decline of GDP and industrial and agricultural production is the indicator of a continuing process of narrowing and fragmenting of the Russian market for goods. As a result, the proportion of interregional trade turnover decreased in proportion to GDP from 22 per cent in 1990 to 16 per cent in 1994 and continued to decrease in 1995–96. At the same time the proportion of raw materials, competition for which is relatively low among buyers, increased appreciably (from 47 per cent to 72 per cent) in interregional exchanges, and a fall therefore ensued in the proportion of interregional trade in goods objectively enjoying greater advantages in market competition. A substantial proportion of barter transactions still persists in interregional intercourse.

The chief reason for the rapid diminution of interregional exchanges is the relative rise in transport costs. This was what made many economic linkages inefficient, especially between the Far East, Siberia and European regions of the country. For a number of years a critical situation persisted with regard to supplies of food and fuel to the regions of the extreme north because of insolvency of consignees, unprofitable terms of shipment and increased risk for producers and transporters of goods.

It is clear that the volumes of cargo shipped decreased more rapidly than the volumes of production, diminishing by a factor of more than three in five years (see Table 4.24). In recent years the dynamics of shipment by Russian transport enterprises has been influenced not only by the fall in domestic demand but by the participation of foreign companies in motor and sea transport.

Under present conditions, interregional exchanges of goods remain of paramount importance as the factor of economic integration. This may seem strange, bearing in mind the rapid development of the *financial market* in Russia. But concentration of financial capital in Moscow and a small number of large centres still remains a dominant tendency, drawing financial resources away from the majority of Russian regions. This is why it is premature to speak about the integrating role of financial markets and institutions.

Table 4.24   Changes in volumes of cargo carried by different means of transport (%)

	1992–91	1993–92	1994–93	1995–94	1996–95	1996–91
Railway	84	83	78	97	89	47
Road	68	60	70	–	–	–
Sea	89	93	83	93	84	54
Inland water	60	70	71	–	–	–
Air	72	77	80	–	–	–
Pipeline	91	92	92	98	100	76
Total	76	75	76	90	82	32

The current interregional *labour market* is also contributing a little to the economic integration of Russia at present. As already noted above, the main flows of labour migration consist of refugees and migrants from the republics of the former USSR, usually settling in regions of labour surplus. There are also movements from the regions of the extreme north, which likewise increase the burden on the labour markets of the regions with more favourable climatic conditions. The underdeveloped housing market for the people of average and low incomes presents a serious obstacle to the intensification of desirable forms of labour migration which otherwise would disperse structural unemployment and create more jobs.

The fragmentation of human occupancy and usage of space in Russia should also be considered at this point. It is manifested most clearly in decreasing passenger journeys, especially between distant regions. The number of passengers using public transport in 1994 was 25 per cent lower than in 1991. The figure for those travelling by air – the only available means of transport for the inhabitants of the greater part of the country – more than halved (from 86 million passengers in 1991 to a mere 34 million in 1994).

Thus factors for territorial economic disintegration are still in being in Russia. The most serious tendency is the gradual isolation of the Russian enclaves (Kaliningrad oblast and the remotest parts of the Far East) from Russia's economic core. The feature shared by these geographical extremities is proximity to more developed or rapidly developing countries. Actual breakaway to form separate states – a favourite theme of Russian journalists – does not necessarily follow from this, however. Such a result is only a reality for Chechenya. In spite of some weakening of the *economic* integrity of Russia there are fairly strong political, legal, social and cultural factors at work in favour of the integrity of the *state*.

REGIONAL POLICY OF THE CENTRE: INTENTIONS AND REALITIES

Only in the late 1980s was the term 'regional policy' introduced into the Soviet political lexicon. In the new Russia, 'regional policy' progressed very rapidly through the stages of official recognition as a special sphere of state and public activity, consolidation of its status and finally its metamorphosis into an arena of political fashion and manoeuvre. As the main political parties and movements jockey for position and seek to enlarge their appeal to the electorate, very few of their manifestos fail to include ringing declarations regarding the importance of regional policy.

All the Russian government's economic programmes since 1992 have included sections on regional policy. The problems of regional policy receive considerable attention in Boris Yeltsin's annual Presidential Address to Russia's Federal Assembly. A number of major provisions on the subject of regional policy are consolidated in the new Constitution of the Russian Federation. Special committees concerned with regional policy are established in both chambers of the Federal Assembly, and there is a group of deputies for 'Regions of Russia' in the state Duma. The programmes of many parties and movements contain sections on regional policy.

In July 1996 President Yeltsin approved the 'Main provisions of regional policy in the Russian Federation'. Regional policy signifies the scheme of objectives and responsibilities of the state and its agencies with respect to the management of the political, economic and social development of the country and to the mechanisms existing for that purpose. The following objectives of regional policy are set forth in this document:

- establishment of economic, social, legal and organisational principles of federalism in the Russian Federation and creation of an integrated

economic spatial entity;
- provision of common minimum standards and equal social security, ensuring the social welfare of citizens as established in the Constitution of the Russian Federation, independently of the economic potentialities of the regions;
- equalisation of the conditions of social and economic development of the regions;
- prevention of environmental pollution and elimination of its consequences; integrated environmental protection of the regions;
- priority development of regions of special strategic importance;
- maximum use of natural climatic features individual to the regions;
- establishment and provision of guarantees for local self-government.

There is not much that is new in this list compared with former programmes, including the declarations of the Soviet period. Perhaps the sole exception is the second objective, which is specified in greater detail: provision of common minimum standards and equal social security, independently of the economic potentialities of the regions. Unlike the others, the achievement of this objective could be checked.

The 'Main provisions' not only specify objectives and responsibilities but also contain sections on federal relations and local self-government, regional economic and social policy, and the legal framework and regional aspects of national–ethnic relations. In these sections the principles for fulfilling the various objectives and responsibilities are set out schematically. They constitute a declaration of intent. But the question is what power the state really has to implement them.

We must first take note of changes in the objective conditions under which state policy operates. At the present time the main process of 'privatisation' of the Russian economy has been completed. More than 70 per cent of total property is now in the private sector, and a significant proportion of state property has been devolved into the ownership of Federation territorial units and local authorities. The institutions of a market economy have been created. The power of the centre to manage the economy of the regions administratively has been substantially reduced. Interaction between *direct (specifically regulated) and general economic regulation of regional development* is now a primary factor in the dialogue between centre and regions. In recent years the federal centre has made use in varying degrees of five main forms of direct (targeted) influence on the regional economy.

Distribution of Financial Resources from the Federal Budget between Federation Territorial units

The major proportion of funds from the federal budget (transfers) reaches the regions from the Federal Territorial Units Support Fund (FTUSF); its assets are established at 15 per cent of total tax revenue excluding customs and import duties. It was intended that financial assistance should be channelled only to regions of especially acute need, but matters did not turn out that way in practice. By 1997 there were 81 recipients out of 89 Federation territorial units. There are only eight donor regions: Moscow, the oblasts of Lipetsk, Samara, Sverdlovsk, Republic of Bashkortostan, Khanty–Mansi and Yamal–Nenets autonomous districts, and Krasnoyarsk krai. It should be emphasised that the share of each Federation territorial unit in FTUSF monies is laid down under the law on the federal budget, and that the actual sums transferred depend on implementation of the budget as related to tax revenues.[1]

Financial assistance to the territorial units is transferred from the federal budget via other channels besides FTUSF. In particular, 1300 billion roubles were allotted to the regions of the Far East in 1997 to subsidise electric power tariffs. A further sum of 3500 billion roubles was allocated to the extreme north to subsidise fuel supplies and another 2735 billion roubles to subsidise the budgets of 'closed' towns and settlements.

Compilation of the Russian Federation budget is in the process of being changed over from individual contracts to the standard-calculation method of determining interbudgetary transfers. The 'rules of the game' have not yet been completely formalised and are therefore not stable. The result is that negotiations and lobbying can occur. Competition for interbudgetary transfers provides the main arena for financial dialogue between the 'centre' and the regions. The centre retains the power to impose sanctions against regions failing to observe federal agreements, bilateral agreements and other commitments.

Financing of Federal Programmes of Regional Development and Other Federal Programmes Implemented in Certain Territories

The major proportion of centralised investment is assigned to the implementation of federal programmes. Naturally, any general reduction of centralised investment will have an adverse effect on the financing of federal programmes in progress, since these are medium-term or long-term programmes as a rule. But the number of federal programmes of regional development and individual government decisions to furnish financial assistance to individual regions has increased constantly. Such programmes and decisions have usually been adopted in the course of the election campaigns of the president and party in power.

In 1991–95 the implementation of the regional programmes and resolutions adopted required 17.9 trillion roubles (including 11.7 trillion roubles from the federal budget). Actual allocations in this period amounted to 498.1 billion roubles.[2] What may be termed 'the sobering-up process' began in the first week following the election of the RF president. It was stated at the RF government meeting on 11 July 1996 (the second round of the presidential election having taken place on 3 July) that the programmes of state assistance to regions adopted in 1991–96 were 'unsystematic, uncoordinated and lack financial provision'. They would require 40 trillion roubles for 1996 alone, while the whole federal investment programme envisaged 29.2 trillion roubles. (Less than one quarter even of this programme was actually financed.) The Ministry of Economy proposed to modify the list of regional programmes every half-year in the light of the financing possibilities available. This means that official approval of a programme by government or president does not guarantee its implementation but is merely evidence of goodwill, which may bear fruit but, equally, may be repudiated or forgotten. This Russian reality needs to be kept in mind when assessing the feasibility of new federal programmes, especially those concerned with development of the Far East and Siberia.

Allocation of Orders for Government Supplies

This form of state participation in the economy could be used in order to achieve the ends of regional policy. Regional social and economic consequences need to be taken into account when allocating state purchases. For example, it is expedient if military orders, purchases of strategic materials and so on are allocated, if possible, to localities where new town projects are under way. There is no convincing evidence yet that the centre deliberately applies any such approach. But many instances are known where the state, by failing to pay for the products purchased, puts not only the supplying enterprise but also the population of the town or entire region depending on the enterprise in a critical position. This is a typical occurrence in defence industry centres, for example. Another example is furnished by the repeated delays in payment for the gold purchased from the goldminers of Magadan oblast, the Republic of Sakha and other territories of the Far East. These cause great damage to the gold-mining industry of the Russian East, where output has already been decreasing for a number of years. At the same time, the state impedes liberalisation of the gold market by failing to abolish the enforced selling of gold by producers.

State Participation in Investment Projects

In order to encourage private investment in the economy the government adopted a resolution in 1994 to invite competitive tenders from private entrepreneurs for investment projects. The successful applicants were promised financial assistance from the state amounting to not less than 20 per cent of the project cost. Clearly, a factor which ought to have been taken into account when selecting the winning proposals was the impact they would have on social and economic conditions in the regions involved (job creation, market expansion, development of social infrastructure and so on). Competitive tendering was organised in 1995–97, but the government fell down very badly on its financial commitments to the successful applicants. It was reported at the cabinet meeting of July 1997 that only 'practically negligible volumes' of investment debts relating to these commercially highly efficient projects had been repaid.

Granting of Privileges and Preferences to the Regions

In the initial stage of economic reform it was common practice in Russia to grant tax and credit privileges, subventions, exemptions from the normal terms of external trade and other such preferences to individual regions. In the first Programme of economic reforms (1992) it was considered important for the state to regulate economic life to take account of varying regional conditions. But since 1994 the ideology of unification and a level economic playing field has prevailed. The main argument for this was the need to increase federal budget revenues. But there was another argument based on the practical political realities: exemptions from general economic rules for individual regions provoked other regions to attempt to secure the same privileges, and subjectivism in the selection of 'deserving regions' created a fertile ground for corruption. Nevertheless, the distribution of privileges and preferences continued. One of the most notorious examples is the Decree of the RF president 'On indexing state pensions in Samara oblast'. This was signed by the president while on vacation, and its terms provided for all pensions in this particular oblast to be increased by 51 per cent commencing on 17 September 1994, the RF government being charged with finding the finance for the purpose. A week later this Decree was in effect disavowed by another Decree wherein it was explained that the financing of the increased pensions was to be effected by the administration of Samara oblast. That is to say, the Samara administration was given permission to spend money from its own budget – a power which it already possessed without the need for presidential decrees.

Most of the privileges and preferences of regions were abolished by the president and government in March 1995. Exceptions were made for free economic zones and regions of natural disasters.[3] What have been the consequences? On the one hand a level playing field for all regions taking part in the economic game prevents abuses in the distribution of privileges. On the other hand (to change the metaphor) the baby is thrown out with the bath water, in that it is no longer possible to pursue an active regional policy by reasonable differentiation of economic regulators. Thus, of the possible means of producing a specific impact on regional development, it is mainly the federal budget that is used. The budget therefore cannot be regarded as merely an expression of 'centre' policy: it is the outcome of a series of compromises, including those between the centre and regions. Specific decisions concerning economic assistance to individual regions have an ad hoc character as a rule and are limited to 'hot' spots (zones of conflict or natural disaster).

It is still not regional, but *general economic policy of the centre,* and empirical changes wrought by macroeconomic events that influence the economy of the regions. Regions alone have no power in principle to change an unfavourable investment climate, the parameters of money circulation, the rouble rate in relation to foreign currencies, the dynamics of prices and tariffs, the solvency of partners in other regions and so on. At the same time, the impact of general economic policy and general economic trends on different regions will produce divergent and often even contradictory results. Physical controls introduced in 1989–92 impeded the development of an export trade in Siberian engineering products. The policy of resisting changes in the dollar rate hampers exports and prevents their diversification.[4] It could be added that runaway rises in railroad tariffs, regulated by the state, robbed exports of coal, oil products, timber and mineral fertilisers of much of their competitiveness. New financial problems associated with the establishment of large private financial–industrial interests emerged in the relations between the centre and the regions. Some of these problems arose in connection with the accumulation of revenues, at the Moscow headquarters of companies and in commercial banks, from sales of raw materials. Others were caused by efforts on the part of Moscow banks (often in association with foreign companies) to secure control of and block shareholdings in the biggest enterprises of the oil and gas industry, electric power production and non-ferrous metallurgy.

The constantly lagging tendency of the legal basis of the new economy is one of the most acute of the problems facing Russia. This applies particularly to certain aspects of the legal regulation of relations between the centre and the regions. The attitude adopted by the regions in the legislative dialogue is somewhat pragmatic: if the centre cannot give money, then let it give the regions their economic freedom. Regional authorities approach their deliberations on legislative proposals involving budgetary and tax systems, exploitation of natural resources, external economic activities and so on on the basis of this stance. In 1997 the main disputes concerned the proposed tax and budgetary codes of the Russian Federation. On the whole, federal legislation is moving in the direction of devolving power from the federal centre to the Federation territorial units and local organs of self-government. Under the current policy the centre displays particular willingness to delegate responsibility for social affairs to regional authorities, examples being the payment of wages and pensions, housing and other local services.

In addition to the RF Constitution and Federal Agreement, the RF government and the administrations of the most 'freedom-loving' RF territorial units have signed agreements on the distribution of powers in the main spheres (ownership, use and disposition of land, mineral wealth, forest resources; international and external economic linkages and so on). Interregional groupings for purposes of economic interaction, called 'associations', have brought federal territorial units together according to shared economic geographical characteristics as part and parcel of the process of distributing powers between the centre and the regions. All in all eight such associations have been established to cover the entire territory of Russia.[5] The political importance of interregional associations[6] and their potential for integration make the federal authorities eager to establish direct partnership with them (though not with the individual federal territorial units) for the purpose of dealing with many economic and other matters of joint concern. The future development of this partnership in the economic sphere will probably be along the lines of joint financing and management of interregional programmes, accompanied by development of coordinated regional policies.

NOTES

1. The plan of the first half of 1997 for tax revenues, excluding import custom duties, was fulfilled for 61.1 per cent.
2. Data of the RF Ministry of Economy.
3. In March 1996 the Decree of the RF president 'On some measures for the promotion of investment activity in the free economic zone "Nakhodka" was signed, which provides tax privileges for Russian and foreign juridical persons.
4. The rate of the dollar, as of 1 January 1992, was 150 roubles and increased by the end of 1995 to 5600 roubles, that is by 37 times. At the same time the GDP

index-deflator increased 1807 times between 1995 and 1991: that is, the conventional purchasing capacity of the dollar (in relation to the total GDP) fell by almost 49 times.

5. Division of the territory of Russia between associations is rather close to the division by economic regions (8 and 11). Some associations unite territories of two economic regions, for example associations of the Northwest, Centre and 'Siberian Agreement'. Some subjects of the Federation are at the same time members of two associations: for example, the Republic of Buryatia, Chita oblast and Aginsky Buryatsky Autonomous District are in the 'Siberian Agreement' and 'Far East and Trans-Baikal Regions' associations.

6. The supreme body of each association – the board – includes heads of administrations and legislative bodies of the Federation subjects; that is, it is a part of the upper chamber of the Russian Parliament, the Council of the Federation.

5. Collapse or a new dynamism?

Hans Westlund

The grave economic crisis which was shaking Russia during the autumn of 1998 still shows no signs of moving towards a solution. It has triggered renewed speculation as to whether Russia is facing not merely an economic but a territorial collapse of the type precipitated by the dissolution of the Soviet Union. A territorial fragmentation of Russia would alter the prospects for peace, stability and economic development in this part of the world more drastically than the disintegration of the Soviet Union did. The latter event was set in motion by the exit of the Baltic republics from the Union, among other factors, but it was soon apparent, even to Moscow, that dissolution of the Union was the only possible course. Constitutional factors played a large role in facilitating dissolution. In the formal sense the Union consisted of independent republics with a partial 'state apparatus' of their own capable of taking over power. Any dissolution of Russia will certainly be resisted by Moscow with all the means at its disposal, as the example of Chechenya has clearly shown. Even though the Russian republic has a type of administrative division represented by krays, oblasts, okrugs and autonomous republics, these units are considerably less well equipped for managing state power than were the former republics of the Union.

During the early 1990s, in the aftermath of the Soviet Union's fall, a fairly broad debate broke out over the question whether the dissolution of the Union would soon be followed by the break-up of Russia. 'Will Russia Disintegrate into Bantustans?' was the provocative title of an article (Szhajkowski, 1993). Russia's possible regional fragmentation has also been discussed, for example, by Blum (1994) and Khrushchev (1994) and by several authors in Segbers (1994).

Aspirations to independence were observable in a number of regions. The predominant conclusions were that the decentralisation of power which was continuing in Russia as well might in the long run bring in its train a threat to the cohesion of the Federation. From this perspective the war which broke out in Chechenya could be regarded as a sign that an early collapse of Russia was near. But the fact that Russia managed to prevent Chechen independence by the application of military force sent a clear signal to other groups working for increased independence from Russia. Russia's unity seemed to have been secured and discussion of Russia's collapse died down.

In the light of the current political and economic crisis and the widening regional rifts inside Russia there are grounds for attempting to analyse which are the factors conducing respectively to unity and disintegration of the country. The concept of interaction costs is assigned a key role in the analysis conducted in this chapter. Interaction cost may be defined as the cost arising from interaction in some type of network (economic, social and so on). In the typical case, interaction cost may be regarded as identical to the marginal utility of the interaction. Therefore no interaction takes place in those instances where interaction cost exceeds marginal utility. The very existence of states may be regarded as an expression for minimising the interaction costs within a particular given territory. A fundamental assumption here is that, if the aggregate interaction costs for the various parts of Russia would become lower as a result of remaining within Russia compared with what would be the case if they tried to break away, then they would remain part of Russia.

Interaction costs consist of a number of different component costs generated by a number of different factors. In Table 5.1 a group of such factors are deployed according to potential for change, from rapid to very slow. The table is discussed in detail in Westlund (1999). Here follows a short summary. In the grouping set out in Table 5.1, the *technical–logistical factors* form the group possessing the potential for the most rapid change. Such a view is entirely in agreement with the mainstream of economic history research. The 'galloping' developments in the field of data and information technology during the past 30 years can be seen as a modern confirmation of this. Nevertheless, it has to be underlined that the relative importance of the changes in the various technical–logistical factors have varied over time. The relative technical–logistical costs have evolved differently for different sectors and thus resulted in relative price changes, market changes and pressure for change on other factors generating interaction costs. Not only should the relative price changes over time be stressed; in a spatial context, the most important impact of these factors is that their effects are not similar in all regions. In a spatial context, the technical–logistical development is never neutral, since the prerequisites for taking advantage of the development differ between regions.

Throughout history, changes in *political–administrative factors* have very clearly had differing effects at different spatial levels. Obstacles have been overcome at one spatial level but have simultaneously been created at another. The rise of the nation state was itself a result of technical–logistical advances within both the military and public administration. These advances also created institutional and market conditions which were instrumental in the gradual move towards industrialisation, a feat which the earlier trade network failed to accomplish to the same degree. From its origins as a weapon against mercantilistic regulation, economic nationalism evolved to become a serious obstacle to economic progress. The European free trade which accompanied the definitive breakthrough of industrialisation in the second half of the 19th century was soon replaced by growing protectionism when individual countries' 'own' agriculture and industries began to be faced with foreign competition. Since the Second World War, the trend has been the reverse and this trend has been strengthened by the collapse of socialism in eastern Europe.

In Table 5.1 the *economic–structural factors* have been placed in the middle of the scale showing the velocity of potential for change. In the short-term perspective, economic structures can be regarded as given, but in the longer term they undergo great changes. The economic–structural factors consist largely of what was called 'social overhead capital' in the 1950s and 1960s. It has long been a fact that exchange between highly developed economies is more extensive than exchange between these economies and less developed ones. This is because the economic–structural differences limit the potential number of interaction areas. The interesting aspect of economic–structural obstacles to interaction is that, while they can be considerable in size, they contain within themselves the solution to the problems they create. Investment in education and infrastructure are not short-term solutions to increasing regional differences – there are no short-term solutions – but they are instruments which cause the increase in differences to slow down, and eventually turn towards decreasing differences.

The *cultural–historical obstacles* to interaction have been built up over a period of hundreds or thousands of years of friction. Some of these obstacles, such as nationalities characterised by specific languages, religion and mentalities, have developed as a result of low contact frequency. From an interaction cost standpoint, these cultural–anthropological phenomena can be seen as time-bound rational solutions to man's economic and social needs.[1] Interaction costs were internalised and minimised through fusion into groups which eventually developed into tribes and nations with common cultures. External interaction costs remained at a high level, however, increasing in step with the strengthening of the internal culture. As long as a society remained at such a level that the group/tribe/nation was self-sufficient, the low internal interaction costs outweighed the high external costs. As the economy progressed and a demand for spatial expansion developed, a more palpable conflict would arise between internal and external interaction costs. The traditional solution to such conflicts was war, conquest and forcible assimilation of new peoples and regions.

Table 5.1   Factors which generate interaction costs in and between networks, grouped by potential for change

Very Rapid				Very slow
Technical–Logistical Factors	Political–Administrative Factors	Economic–Structural Factors	Cultural–Historical Factors	Geographical and Biological Factors
• Costs of production and transport of goods • Costs of transport of people • Costs of capital and capital transfer • Costs of information and information transfer	• National/regional rules and regulations • Customs duties, etc • Tariff zones	• Economic development level / demand patterns for goods and services • Economic structure • Educational level • Compatibility and standard of infrastructure	• Language • Religion • Mentality • Ethnicity • Population density • Power structure and property rights	• Physical distance • Geographical obstacles (e.g. rivers) • Time zones • Human biology

Source: Westlund (1999).

A very significant cultural–historical factor is the spatial distribution of population and the population base as a basis of economic diversification. Spatial distribution of population is a very intractable factor. Viewed as an obstacle to interaction, its importance resides primarily in the differences of economic diversification to be found in different localities. This mechanism leads to there being relatively more contacts between densely populated areas with high levels of diversification than there are between them and sparsely populated regions or between the sparsely populated regions themselves.

Power structures and property rights of various types occupy an important position among the cultural–historical obstacles to interaction. Works of economic history such as North and Thomas (1973), North (1981) and Rosenberg and Birdzell (1986) have debated the question why the industrial revolution and the subsequent increase in prosperity took place in what we today call the Western world. Their answer, in brief, has been that the division of power between Crown, nobility, Church and burghers which arose in the late Middle Ages created property rights favourable to economic change and growth. Mafia power and the absence of sufficiently favourable property rights are regarded today as the fundamental obstacles to economic progress in the former Soviet Union. Despite important differences, similar causes can be seen at work in the stagnation of southern Italy compared with the much more dynamic north. Both of these areas are examples of the way in which organised crime can operate above the legal system, thereby creating increased interaction costs for actors in the economy. These examples also illustrate the fact that property rights are not merely a question of *legislation*. What is fundamental is how strongly these laws are rooted in the legal consciousness of the public or, at a more general level, how firmly civil society is established (cf. Putnam, 1993). Property rights thus become an intractable cultural–historical issue rather than a political–administrative one.

The last of the factor groups in Table 5.1 comprises *geographical and biological factors*, along with the 'administrative' obstacles associated with geography, such as time zones. Changes in geographical obstacles happen at the same speed as other global changes: that is to say, infinitely slowly, with the exception of earthquakes and other sudden natural disasters. The *external* influence of humans on these geographical obstacles (both direct and indirect) has increased in step with technological progress. The increasing ability to overcome technical obstacles to interaction by developing an infrastructure network on, under and above the earth has dramatically reduced the importance of these geographical obstacles to interaction. Other very intractable factors are those associated with human biology. The conception of time-geography developed by Hägerstrand implies that the rhythm of the days and the biological conditions by which man is circumscribed form absolute restrictions whose effects go beyond all cost calculations. Finally, man's own capacities constitute the ultimate obstacle to the obliteration of interaction costs.

The chapters of this book deal with various factors in these five groups. Chapter 1 centres on the economic–structural factors as well as on several of the cultural–historical factors as determinants of the long-term disparities in the spatial production pattern. Chapter 2 deals mainly with the politico-administrative factors in Soviet regional policy, but also with the impact of the power structure on the regions. The description of the economic consequences of the dissolution of the Soviet Union in Chapter 3 is based mainly on the politico-administrative perspective. However, Chapter 3 stresses the economic–structural problems which also arose as consequences of the politico-administrative breakdown. The analysis of Russia's regional situation in Chapter 4 embraces factors from all the five groups, but the politico-administrative and economic–structural factors are of course among the main determinants of the creation of a new, modern regional policy. The issues raised in this final chapter are viewed in the light of all the factor groups.

What, then, is shown by an analysis of Russia in the perspective established in Table 5.1? During the Soviet period, costs in the sense understood by neoclassical economic analysis were an unknown quantity. There was a deliberate endeavour to minimise the subversive, revolutionising function exercised by changes in technical and logistical factors in the market economy. Political control of the economy would create stability and help to keep the Union together in spatial terms.

Capital costs played a very subordinate role in investment. The alignment and location of production were determined by political decisions. In the best case – that is to say in theory – volumes of production too were determined by political decisions. The laying down of infrastructure and the use made of it, and the tariffs of charges for transport and communications, were politically determined in the main, since most of the transport supply was collective in form. The supply of information was strictly controlled by the state.

Thus, in most respects, the Soviet planned economy reduced the technical and logistical factors to a fraction of their importance in countries with market economies, a fact which gave other cost-creating factors a larger role (see below). However, the abandonment of the planned economy in the 1990s has radically changed the levels of the technical and logistical factors, both in absolute respects and as regards their relative spatial levels. Capital, production and transport have become associated with visible, tangible costs inasmuch as supply and demand have been partially allowed to assert themselves. The state's monopoly of large parts of the information sector has been dissolved, Russia has become a part of the world economy and numerous entirely new markets have made their appearance. But the need for social and political stability has prevented market forces from being given totally free rein. Many state enterprises which are bankrupt in terms of market economics continue to function in order to avoid mass unemployment and its social consequences.

In spatial terms the events of the past mean that disparities of productivity between different parts of Russia which were formerly compensated by political measures (cf., for example, Westlund, 1998) are now free to operate with considerably less hindrance. Despite the state's having restrained market forces, the disparities between the centre and the periphery, in both economic and geographical respects, have increased considerably more rapidly than during the Soviet epoch.

The fact that regional disparities of productivity have emerged more starkly does not enhance Russia's cohesiveness, of course, but at the same time it is not in itself a factor driving Russia along the road to actual break-up. It is true that its centre (Moscow) is one of Europe's biggest urban conurbations and is becoming more and more integrated into the world economy, but without the rest of Russia Moscow would not be the centre it is today at all. Possibly the region which in strictly economic respects would have most to gain by cutting itself off from Russia is that of St Petersburg. Many regions on the geographical and economic periphery have scarcely anything to gain in economic respects by breaking free of Russia. On the other hand there are certain regions with raw materials commanding favourable world market prices which have an incentive to liberate themselves from Moscow. Examples of such regions are Tatarstan and Bashkortostan in the Volga region; the Tyumen region and its two autonomous okrugs Khanty–Mansi and Yamalo–Nenets in West Siberia and Sakha (Yakutia) and the Chukot republic in the northeast. However, any increased profit for these regions, and for St Petersburg, has to be weighed against the increased costs which would be involved in establishing their own centres of state power, including the costs of the conflicts with Moscow which this would entail.

The conclusion is that the increased importance of technical logistical factors since the collapse of the Soviet Union have weakened the forces for unity but that these factors do not seem sufficiently strong in themselves to precipitate the dissolution of Russia.

As regards political and administrative interaction costs, dissolution of the Soviet Union has brought in its train the establishment of a number of new political and administrative frontiers between Russia and the new independent states. In varying degrees the new national frontiers have placed obstacles in the way of intercourse between Russia and the new states and thus have affected the costs of raw materials, semi-manufactures and finished products. However, as far as exchanges with the rest of the world are concerned, the collapse of the Soviet Union has brought more open frontiers and reduced political and administrative obstacles to intercourse.

In these ways political and administrative changes have, in principle, modified production and consumption conditions for all regions of Russia. The new frontiers to the new states have created a need for new networks, both inside Russia and *vis-à-vis* other countries. The lowering of barriers to trade with the Western world, *ceteris paribus*, has reduced the need for certain of the trade links inside Russia. But in the long run increased intercourse with the West and the accompanying economic diversification may lead to the emergence of new networks inside Russia as well.

Within Russia, political and administrative interaction costs have been reduced, compared with the Soviet period, generally speaking. State controls over the mobility of people, goods, information and capital have been dropped. In general terms this can manifest itself in both centralising and decentralising trends. *In an administrative perspective*, Russia went through a period of decentralisation due to the weakened power of the state and Yeltsin's ambitions to replace Gorbachev as head of state, during the first half of the 1990s. Since then, regional governments have continued to strengthen their power at the expense of Moscow. However, there is no doubt that deregulation, in combination with the increased importance of technical and logistical interaction costs, at present favours spatial centralisation of new activities, thereby strengthening the centre and weakening the periphery *in an economic sense*. Foreign investments concentrate on Moscow and St Petersburg, and it is in these great metropolises that most of the new economic activities are emerging.

In itself, change currently taking place in the balance between centre and periphery in Russia may lead to new reactions in the form of liberation movements on the periphery. Nevertheless, the periphery responsible for any such possible movements is in general a weakened one. The resource transfers from 'rich' to 'poor' regions have diminished considerably. Only the peripheral regions with raw materials discussed above have, depending on the world market prices, sometimes found their positions improved – but sometimes worsened. The conclusion is that, from the political and administrative standpoint, present events in Russia are not reinforcing a centralised unity by strengthening the centre, but even if this means increased power for regional actors it does not mean any automatic dissolution.

Like the British and French colonial empires, the Tsarist empire contained enormous differences with respect to economic structure and development level. The vast transfers of resources to Siberia and the Asiatic republics during the Soviet epoch meant that these differences diminished radically. However, complete regional equalisation was never achieved in the backward regions despite massive investment in industrialisation, transport infrastructure and education during most of the Soviet epoch. Educational levels and transport infrastructure were among the areas in which the equalisation policy was most successful, but in certain other respects, industrial production per head for example, the disparities were increasing during the final decades of the Union.

Regarded as a single whole, Russia has always been one of the most advanced republics of the former Soviet Union with respect to economic structure. Yet even within Russia the differences of economic diversification, particularly between the Moscow and St Petersburg regions, for example, on the one hand, and Siberia and the Far East on the other, were and remained large, while the disparities of educational level and transport infrastructure diminished considerably.

Accordingly, it is in the level of economic development and in the form of differences in degree of diversification and demand patterns that the big disparities are to be found in Russia. Just as in the case of the more rapidly changeable factors, however, it is very doubtful whether the less advanced and less diversified regions have anything to gain by attempting to cut themselves off from Russia, especially bearing in mind the price that would be entailed.

The geographical boundaries of states have been determined mainly by cultural–historical factors. Until the middle of the 19th century it was power structures, dynasties and property rights that determined the shaping and reshaping of the frontiers of European states. Since then, factors associated with population have come to play a larger role. Language, religion and ethnic affiliation have helped to shape different mentalities over the centuries. These factors assumed crucial importance in the new wave of creation of nation states which started during the 19th century and took a leap forward after the First World War.

The break-up of the Soviet Union, Yugoslavia and Czechoslovakia into separate states marked the end of the formation of nation states in Europe. At the same time, supranational cooperation in the European Union grew more strongly, thereby possibly marking a new phase of Europe's history. From this perspective the Soviet state, with its numerous distinct ethnic groups, with dissimilar languages, mentalities and religions, can be viewed in two ways: either as an attempt, hopeless in the long term, to hold together a multi-ethnic former empire or as an unsuccessful endeavour to 'jump over' the nation state phase by using commando methods and bring dissimilar peoples together in a Union. The result was the same irrespective of which interpretation is chosen. In the end the divisive cultural and historical forces became too strong for it to be possible to hold a state together when the unifying factor of power structure was weakened.

Present-day Russia differs from the Soviet Union at several important points with respect to the cultural–historical factors. Above all Russia, with half of the former Soviet Union's population, is considerably more homogeneous as regards ethnic composition, language, religion and probably mentality as well. More than 80 per cent of the population are Russians and speak Russian as their mother tongue. The Russian Orthodox religion is entirely predominant. Compared with many of the factors discussed above, present-day Russia is therefore considerably more cohesive than the former Soviet Union in terms of its culture and history.

At the same time, there are a number of Union republics and other units (krays, oblasts and okrugs) within the Russian Federation which exhibited aspirations to independence in various ways following the collapse of the Soviet Union. The best-known example is Chechenya, whose struggle for independence developed into open military conflict with Russia. However, Moscow realised that what happened in this tiny republic in the Northern Caucasus would set a precedent. If Chechenya became independent, other regions would join the queue. For Moscow the war to keep Chechenya inside the Russian Federation was a war to preserve the cohesion of the Federation. The Chechenya war was a palpable ethnic conflict in which a people was striving for independence, with Russians in a clear minority. Table 5.2 shows the sizes of the Russian and largest non-Russian population, respectively, in most of the regions which in one way or another have been agitating for increased independence. As the table shows, Russians form the largest population group in almost all other regions, with the exception of some of Chechenya's neighbours in the Russian Federation in the Northern Caucasus (Ingushetia, Kabardino–Balkariya, Dagestan, Kalmykia and North Ossetiya–Alaniya). Of a total of 72 other Russian regions (including those not shown in the table) it is only in five that a non-Russian population forms the largest ethnic group. These are the sparsely-populated Tuvinian and Agin–Buryat on the border with Mongolia, and Tatarstan, Chuvashiya and Komi–Permyak around the central Volga and Vyatka rivers.

Power structures and property rights are in a state of change in Russia. Although many of the decision-making and administrative organs of the Soviet epoch remain in being more or less unaltered, the transition to democracy and Russia's economic decline have palpably weakened central power. That the war in Chechenya ended somewhat inconclusively is only

Table 5.2   *Share of Russians and biggest non-Russian ethnic group, 1989,*
in territorial units with a big share of non-Russians and units
which have demanded greater autonomy

Territory	Inhabitants	Percentage Russians	Biggest non-Russian group Name	Share	Ethnic groups
Northern Caucasus					
Chechenya–Ingushetia*	1 270 429	23.12	Chechenian	57.82	8
Dagestan*	1 802 188	9.21	Avarian	27.53	15
Kalmykia*	322 579	37.67	Kalmykian	45.36	11
North Ossetiya–Alaniya*	632 428	29.91	Osetian	52.95	7
Kabardino–Balkariya*	753 531	31.95	Kabardinian	48.24	5
Karachaevo–Cherkessia	414 970	42.40	Karachayev	31.19	5
Volga–Vyatka					
Bashkortostan	3 943 113	39.27	Tatarian	28.42	6
Chuvashiya*	1 338 023	26.78	Chuvashian	67.78	4
Komi–Permyak	158 526	36.13	Komi–Permyak	60.19	2
Mordova	963 504	60.83	Mordvinian	32.53	3
Tatarstan*	3 641 742	43.26	Tatarian	48.48	8
Mari-El	749 332	47.51	Marian	43.29	3
Tyumen	3 097 657	72.58	Ukrainian	8.40	12
Khanty–Mansi	1 282 396	66.31	Ukrainian	11.57	6
Yamal–Nenets	494 844	59.17	Ukrainian	17.18	7
Baykal area					
Agin–Buryat*	77 188	40.77	Buryatian	54.88	2
Tuva*	308 557	32.03	Tuvinian	64.31	4
North-East					
Chukot republic	163 934	66.06	Ukrainian	16.84	8
Sakha (Yakutia)	1 094 065	50.30	Yakutian	33.38	8
Russian Federation	147 021 869	81.53	Tatarian	3.76	93

Note: Units where non-Russians constitute the biggest ethnic group are marked with a *.

Source: USSR Census, 1989.

one sign of this. In the long run Moscow's weakened grip on the regions therefore probably means a continuance of ethnic conflicts and aspirations to independence in some of the regions where non-Russians form large population groups, chiefly and most likely in Northern Caucasus.

However, although the decentralisation and regionalisation which took place during the 1990s continues, there is no automatic presumption that the great majority of Russian-dominated regions would like to try to declare themselves independent states. Increased nationalism on the part of minority ethnic groups can be opposed by strong counterforces if the Russian inhabitants feel threatened and reply by strengthening their links with the Federation. Nationalism has played a very important role in Russia's history and is absolutely not to be underestimated. The strength of the reaction provoked by the Nato bombing of Yugoslavia in March/April 1999 highlights the resemblance between Russian nationalism and a sleeping bear. The right (or wrong) leader after Yeltsin may very well wake the bear up and put the current regionalisation process swiftly into reverse.

Density of population is the cultural and historical factor not dealt with in this chapter. It expresses itself chiefly in spatial dissimilarities of degree of economic diversification, which have been discussed earlier with regard to factors changeable in the medium and short term. Density of population as a separate factor ought not to have any real influence on the question of Russia's unity or break-up.

Thus, to sum up: the costs of interaction in cultural and historical respects in present-day Russia are lower, generally speaking, than in the former Soviet Union, since Russia is more homogeneous. However, Northern Caucasus is the region which diverges most from this culturally and historically based solidarity. The example of Chechenya suggests that the rest of Russia, headed by Moscow and regardless of president or government, is prepared if necessary to pay a high price to keep these territories under the Russian flag. Should these regions nevertheless succeed in breaking away this would obviously represent a severe loss of political prestige for Russia, but hardly a threat to the cultural and historical solidarity which unites the Russia in which Russians are in the majority.

The natural geographical and biological factors have not changed following the Soviet Union's collapse, but the fact that Russia's surface is a quarter smaller in area than that of the Soviet Union does of itself mean that the country is easier to hold together. Russia became a geographical giant even before the emergence of modern means of transport and communication. From this perspective, therefore, the prospects of preserving the country's unity are probably better now than they were before.

Even though an overriding aim of Soviet policy was to increase production, it is important to underline that important elements of Soviet policy with respect to the regions were focused on the most intractable factors: the cultural–historical and even geographical and biological factors. One major objective was to create a new 'Soviet man', with a new mentality and standing above the multi-ethnic mosaic of which the Union was composed. Lysenko's infamous biological experiments may be viewed as a special case during a very special period. But belief in mastery over nature was deeply rooted in the Soviet ideology, manifesting itself, for example, in proposals to divert the flow of Siberian rivers. Environmental disasters were the results of this belief. Neglect of the rapidly changing costs factors was the other side of Soviet policy. *Viewed in this perspective, the concentration on long-term factors without any understanding of the mutual dependence between various groups of factors – not least the importance of costs – was the ultimate reason for the collapse of the socialist Soviet Union.* Present Russia still suffers from this heritage.

Thus, from the perspective of interaction costs which has been established, there is little to suggest a regional collapse of Russia. Even if the Federation does not collapse, however, Russia has a sufficiency of problems in other fields, mainly economic. Capitalism has not by any means been the motor of success for Russia that was expected. Why does the market economy not function in Russia? What are the chances of reversing the decline which has been going on practically all through the 1990s? Where is the new economic dynamism? What are the obstacles to economic development? What are the possibilities? An analysis of these questions may also benefit from being linked to the interaction cost perspective utilised above. Economic dynamism and development are indissolubly associated with (new) interaction between (new) economic actors. The conditions for economic growth are a matter of conditions for new and enlarged economic interaction.

The analysis above showed several factors which have an influence not only on Russia's unity but also on economic development. The direct effects of the technologistical changes, most notably the increased transport costs – which came about with the Soviet economy's collapse have probably died out after nearly a decade. It is self-evident that the technologistical changes formed a very important factor in demolishing the Soviet production and consumption system, this being itself a basic prerequisite of market economy dynamism. At the same time, it is obvious that realigning these costs to suit a market economy was far from being a sufficient factor to generate any new dynamism. Production and sale on the Russian market seem to require very high risk premiums, a circumstance which seriously disturbs the market economy in Russia.

Then why does the market economy not function in Russia? There is an obvious temptation to cite political and administrative factors such as legislation, controls and lack of clarity as regards the distribution of powers between central and regional levels. Many commentators have singled out the need for a new constitution and a code of commercial law (which has never existed in Russia), but it is very doubtful whether it is simply the legal system *as such*, along with the formal division of power between state and regions, that constitutes the crucial problem. These uncertainties have not placed any decisive obstacles in the way of Russia's incorporation into the world economy. Neither did they form any impediment to the rise of the system of booths and market-places in the early 1990s. Perhaps it could be asserted that the lack of clarity in the legal system contributed to the rapid growth of the black economy and the mafia system. Here too, however, it is not primarily the absence of laws and rules which has been the problem but their survival and rootedness in the popular consciousness, which are factors of quite a different character.

Is it then structural economic factors that form the reason for the market economy's failure to expand? To a certain extent the answer is yes. The economic structure built up under the command economy of the 1980s was not adapted for a smooth and swift changeover to market economics of course. Certain sectors of the economy, notably the defence industry, have felt the effects of catastrophically reduced demand. Other economic sectors have not managed to respond to the new demand either qualitatively or quantitatively, and this has resulted in quantities of consumer goods being imported instead. In spite of this 'spectre at the feast', it could still be argued that it ought to have been possible to modernise the economic structure of Russia to a considerably greater extent during the 1990s if this had really been the only obstacle in the way of expansion of the market economy. The three former Soviet Baltic republics, like practically all the countries of the former Eastern bloc, have enjoyed far better economic progress than Russia during the 1990s, despite the fact that their economic structures have not been essentially different from Russia's.

Neither was the infrastructure for transmission of information, the telephone network and other networks for making use of information technology, suitable for effecting the transition to a market economy at the start of the 1990s. The general point may be made that the Soviet transport and communications infrastructure was built for centralised, raw material-exploiting industrial production, while the infrastructure appropriate to modern knowledge-based and customer-friendly industrial production and to the information processing service sector was almost entirely absent.

For large firms, the new banks and the more or less illegal sector, this has constituted a marginal problem since they have had resources to build the infrastructure they needed themselves. On the other hand it is highly probable that the shortcomings of the public infrastructure with respect to transmission of information have formed a very serious hindrance to the emergence of small businesses. The weak development of the mobile telephone network in Russia during the 1990s may be taken as an example of the problems encountered by small-scale enterprise.

Brunswick Warburg state, in a report of 16 July 1998, 'Despite licensing many of the cellular operators as early as 1991, Russia has seen excruciatingly slow development in the cellular market. To date, there are no more than a handful of viable cellular networks beyond Moscow and St Petersburg with more than 1000–2000 subscribers.' The very uneven regional diffusion is revealed by the fact that, whereas about 15 per cent of Russia's total population are resident in Moscow or St Petersburg, these two cities had about 75 per cent of Russia's mobile telephone subscribers in 1997. The backwardness of the mobile telephone market in Russia and Moscow compared with Western Europe and the United States is shown in Figure 5.1. Despite the fact that income per head in Moscow is more than half that of Portugal, the latter country has ten times as many subscribers per inhabitant as Moscow.

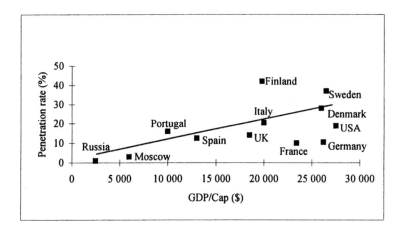

Source: Warburg Dillon Read, Brunswick Warburg.

Figure 5.1   Cellular penetration rates in Russia and industrialised countries in the West

Figure 5.2 shows Russia and Moscow compared with some growing markets in Eastern Europe, Latin America and Asia. Here, too, Russia and Moscow lie considerably lower than what might be expected from the level of GDP per head.

What, then, are the causes of the poor growth of the mobile telephone system in Russia? Brunswick Warburg's report cites an economic and a technical reason. The latter is that the allotted spectrum is too small, especially for GSM 900, although this factor has actually only been of importance in Moscow. What is considerably more significant is the regional distribution of operators created by the prevailing licensing system. Instead of a system of competing operators covering the whole of Russia being created, licences were allotted by regions for the respective standards (NMT450, GSM and AMPS/D-AMPS). In this way Russia has acquired a mobile telephone system with 226 licences dispersed among 140 operators, which may be compared with the 64 licences and 40 operators to be found in *the whole of the rest of Europe*. Thus the consequence has been regional monopolies for the respective standards, which has made Russia one of the dearest mobile telephone markets in the world.

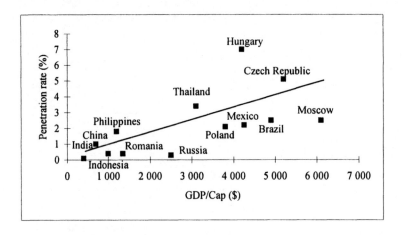

Source: Warburg Dillon Read, Brunswick Warburg.

Figure 5.2   Cellular penetration rates in Russia and other emerging markets

Brunswick Warburg state that there are signs that the mobile telephone market in Russia is going to be restructured and that competing national operators will emerge as a result. They therefore predict rapid growth, bearing in mind Russia's, especially Moscow's, relatively high level of GDP per head. However, the connections between other factors (for example, the structural–economic and cultural–historical factors) and new enterprise and economic growth are not discussed in the report.

On the other hand another important structural economic factor – the educational level – cannot be considered generally speaking to have placed any very important impediments in the way of expansion of the market economy (cf. Lewin, 1988; Hough, 1988). Russia has a very high educational level compared with many Asiatic countries which have displayed remarkable growth during the 1990s. Even though the human capital theory deems this factor crucial to long-term high growth, it is evident that it does not constitute a sufficient condition.

In the discussion above of a possible territorial collapse of Russia, a critical role was assigned to the sluggishness with which cultural–historical factors change. So what role do these factors play in terms of the possibilities of getting economic growth started? In those regions which are being shaken by ethnic and associated conflicts (of language, religion and, to some extent, mentality) it is more or less self-evident that these conflicts, if they become strong enough, have stunting effects on the economy. As we have seen, however, these regions form a very limited part of Russia in terms of both area and population. But certain of the potential breakaway regions have important natural resources, notably oil, which means that they also possess a degree of economic importance for Russia as a whole. However, unless the ethnic antagonisms were to be greatly intensified and wars of national liberation were to break out in several regions simultaneously, the ethnic factors would probably not have any major influence on Russia's overall potential for economic development.

Population density is generally considered to be of importance to the development potential of regions. Generally speaking, densely populated regions have a more diversified economy, a diversified local market and high access to strategic developmental factors such as R&D. From this perspective Russia, with its high degree of urbanisation and its multi-million city populations such as in Moscow and St Petersburg, ought to enjoy good conditions for economic growth. However, certain of the cultural–historical factors definitely exercise a serious negative influence on Russia's scope for economic development. These consist of power structures and property rights, and partly also of the mentality factor. What we have in mind here are conditions which, unlike legislation and other political and administrative factors, change very sluggishly (cf. Snyder, 1994).

The Russian power structure, property rights situation and economic mentality are all products of Russia's history. Compared with the majority of other European countries, including even those of Eastern Europe, two peculiarities are especially characteristic of Russia. First, *Russia is one of the European countries which, along with the Ukraine and White Russia, are most lacking in a capitalist tradition.* The fact that serfdom survived right up to 1861 is the chief indication of the economic backwardness then prevailing. The industrialisation which took place in Russia prior to the First World War differed markedly from West European industrialisation inasmuch as it was not based on small businesses which gradually grew and became big. The Russian state's strategy took the form of a deliberate striving to assist large-scale industrial projects. Russia established large-scale industry without having any small-scale industry, a situation which the Bolsheviks naturally found no reason to change after they assumed power. Although capitalism in the rest of Eastern Europe prior to 1914 was not as developed as in the West, it had greater elements of small-scale enterprise than did Russia. Moreover, capitalism was able to continue developing in the East European countries up to 1945, in spite of war and the depression of the 1930s. In socialist Poland agriculture actually remained under private ownership. Thus, whereas several generations in Eastern Europe were brought up under 'practical capitalism', the embryonic capitalist environments which emerged in Russia were swiftly crushed by Stalin after the NEP period and replaced by the figure of *homo sovieticus*, 'Soviet Man'. All in all, this means that Russia's traditional backwardness (cf. Gerschenkron, 1962) in this respect reflects an absence of capitalist mentality, making it much more difficult for a market economy to emerge successfully.[2]

Second, *Russia largely lacks capitalist institutions and property rights*. A direct consequence of the absence of capitalistic traditions is the lack of institutions and property rights favourable to capitalist development. On the 1997 Transparency International rating of 52 countries, Russia ranked fourth highest in corruption (cf. Sachs and Pistor, 1997). Manifestations of this are to be found throughout the national life as well as in a more limited economic sphere. As regards the latter, the economic activities customarily ascribed to the mafia are a primitive pirate capitalism. By forming a state within the state, raising interaction costs and thereby upsetting the way the market functions, corruption and the mafia have a generally dampening effect on economic growth potential in Russia. The absence of capitalistic institutions and property rights confronts the nation at large with problems on a still broader scale. Because Russia lacks popularly accepted 'rules of the game' for private enterprise and ownership, there is also a lack of trust and of the social capital on which such institutions must build.[3] One of many manifestations of the lack of trust are the many reports of the investments of capital in the West by the 'new Russians'. To create these institutions is a long drawn-out process requiring active popular participation, as was the case in Western Europe and the United States. Legislation should probably be regarded primarily as a confirmation that the process has been successful rather than as an end in itself. Until these institutions have emerged, private enterprise in Russia will require risk premiums at a quite different level from what is the case in countries with established capital institutions. This circumstance may well exercise a detrimental influence on economic growth in Russia for a long time.

The conclusion is that the group of factors which work strongly in favour of Russia's unity, that is the cultural–historical factors, are also the ones which constitute the greatest hindrance to stable economic growth. However, we must be careful to point out that even within this group there are large differences in the propensity for change. Ethnic changes are among the most sluggish of processes. Russians are Russians and will remain so for centuries. On the other hand differences with regard to power structure, the property rights situation and economic mentality are probably more a question of one or two generations.

It has already become evident that Russia's road to 'popular' capitalism is a more difficult one than that of many other countries. As the present survey has shown, however, in a perspective longer than the purely cyclical, Russia has many factors which suggest economic growth. The most crucial questions will probably be whether the heritage from the Soviet period of a 'dual society', where people completely distrust the authorities and rely only on their own informal networks, can be broken down and replaced by a growing trust between the different layers of society (cf. Rose, 1998).

In economic respects this becomes a question of whether the 'virtual' economy, with falling productivity, frequent negative value added, and barter transactions between firms, can be broken down and replaced by functioning markets with monetary means of transaction. The mafia's monetary exactions and the state's demands for tax revenue, paradoxically enough, have provoked a return to the barter transactions common during the Soviet epoch. When wages are not paid, a family's cultivation of its own dadzja (summer cottage) becomes vital to its physical survival. The scope of the 'virtual' economy has been growing during the major part of the 1990s and is regarded by Gaddy and Ickes (1998, 1999) as the primary cause of the August crisis of 1998 and Russia's inability to establish functioning capitalism.

Karl Polanyi (1944) once described how the various parties active during the industrial revolution attempted to defend themselves against the upheavals inflicted on society by the free market. Russia's economic actors have behaved in a similar fashion during the 1990s. But whereas the 19th century actors of the West formed trade unions and other interest groups and articulated demands for state intervention, Russia's economic actors are resorting to the only weapon they have. The economic and social networks formed under the Soviet system still constitute the main alternative to private individuals and business firms alike. The task of gradually breaking this pattern, of creating a modern economy with a deposit of modern social capital capable of providing a foundation of solid property rights, will be a very protracted process.

NOTES

1. Compare Coase's fundamental theorem that the institutional structure of the economy is created by the endeavours of economic actors to hold down collective production, transaction and administrative costs.
2. Cf. Rose (1998) who shows differences between 'anti-modern' Russian/Ukrainian and 'modern' East European behaviour (in the Czech Republic) in the 1990s.
3. It is important to underline that Russia suffers from a lack of social capital in precisely *this* respect. The social capital which manifests itself in popular participation in formal and informal decision-making processes is weak. On the other hand, of course, there are strong social networks in parts of Russian society, from 'evil' networks like the mafia's to small 'virtuous' networks such as non-governmental organisations and consumer cooperatives (Sätre Åhlander, 1999).

Bibliography

ARCHIVES

Rossiiskii Gosudarstvennyi Arkhiv Ekonomiki (RGAE) (Russian State Archive of the Economy), Moscow

File 1562, cat. 8, doc. 1440. Reference book in colour and metallurgic industry 1935. Gosplan, statistical office.

File 4086, cat. 2, doc. 887. Steel Trust, Annual Report.

File 4372, cat. 33, doc. 355. Control Figures of Production for the People's Commissariat for Heavy Industry. Gosplan.

File 4372, cat. 33, doc. 358. Reference book in black, metallurgic, iron industry for 1928–34. Gosplan, Metallurgic Dept.

File 7297, cat. 28, doc. 310. 'Heavy Industry in the USSR 1934'. People's Commissariat for Heavy Industry. Dept. of Accounts and Economy. (Secret classified printed book.)

Personal File of Former Archive Director V. Tsaplin

Tsaplin, V. (1990). 'On certain results of the Soviet Union's economic development under the second Five-Year Plan' (manuscript in Russian).

INTERNET

CIA World Factbook 1995 (www.odci.gov/cia/publications/95fact/index.html).

INTERVIEW

Interview with former director of RGAE (Russian State Archive of the Economy), V. Tsaplin, 23 March 1994.

PUBLICATIONS

Academia Nauk (1940), *Economic Geography of the USSR* (title translated from Russian), Moscow: Socekgiz.

Academia Nauk (1961), *History of the Great Patriotic War of the Soviet Union 1941–1945* (title translated from Russian), Vol. 2, Moscow: Voenizdat.

Academia Nauk (1966a), *Echelons are going to the East: from the History of Relocating Productive Forces of the USSR in 1941–1945* (title translated from Russian), Moscow: USSR Academy of Science.

Academia Nauk (1966b), *Methods of Technical–Economic Calculations in Energetics* (title translated from Russian), Moscow: USSR Academy of Science.

Academia Nauk (1966c), 'Standard methods for the estimation of economic efficiency of capital investments' (title translated from Russian), Moscow: USSR Academy of Science (rotaprint).

Academia Nauk (1967), *Methodical Provisions on Optimum Sectoral Planning in Industry* (title translated from Russian), Novosibirsk: USSR Academy of Science.

Academia Nauk (1969), *Main Provisions of Optimisation of Development and Allocation of Production* (title translated from Russian), Moscow and Novosibirsk: USSR Academy of Science.

Academia Nauk (1974), *Methodical Instructions on the Elaboration of State Plans of National Economy Development* (title translated from Russian), Moscow: Ekonomika.

Academia Nauk (1976), *Modelling of Territorial-Production Complexes Formation* (title translated from Russian), Novosibirsk: USSR Academy of Science.

Academia Nauk (1977), *Methods (main Provisions) for Estimation of Economic Efficiency of the Use of New Machinery, Inventions and Rationalisations Proposals in the National Economy* (title translated from Russian), Moscow: USSR Academy of Science.

Academia Nauk (1978), *Main Methodical Provisions on the Optimisation of Production Development and Allocation* (title translated from Russian), Moscow: USSR Academy of Science.

Academia Nauk (1980a), *Methods for the Estimation of Economic Efficiency of Allocation of Industrial Enterprises* (title translated from Russian), Moscow: USSR Academy of Science.

Academia Nauk (1980b), *Siberia in the Single Complex of the National Economy* (title translated from Russian), Novosibirsk: USSR Academy of Science.

Academia Nauk (1994), *Methodical Recommendations on the Estimation of Investment Projects Efficiency and their Selection for Financing* (title translated from Russian), Moscow: USSR Academy of Science.

Adirim, I.G., Y.A. Yanov and A.Y. Pochs (1975), *System of Models of Forecasting Growth of the National Economy of the Republic* (title translated from Russian), Riga: Zinatne.

Agyanbegyan, A.G. (1982), 'Regional economic modelling in the USSR', in M.M. Albegov, Å.E. Andersson and F. Snickars (eds), *Regional Development Modelling: Theory and Practice*, Amsterdam: North-Holland.

Agyanbegyan, A.G. (ed.) (1984), *BAM: Construction and Economic Development* (title translated from Russian), Moscow: Ekonomika.

Alampiev, P.M. (1959), *Economic Zoning in the USSR* (title translated from Russian), Moscow: Gospolitizdat.

Albegov, M.M. (1975), 'Inter-branch interregional model of production allocation' (title translated from Russian), in Academia Nauk, *Models of Production Allocation* (title translated from Russian), Moscow: USSR Academy of Science.

Albegov, M.M. (1982), 'A simplified system of regional models', in M.M., Albegov, Å.E. Andersson and F. Snickars (eds), *Regional Development Modelling: Theory and Practice*, Amsterdam: North-Holland.

Albegov, M.M., Å.E. Andersson and F. Snickars (eds) (1982), *Regional Development Modelling: Theory and Practice*, Amsterdam: North-Holland.

Albegov, M.M., M.V. Golubitskaya and D.G. Petukhov (1975), 'Optimisation of intra-regional production allocation' (title translated from Russian), in Academia Nauk, *Models of Production Allocation* (title translated from Russian), Moscow: USSR Academy of Science.

Amann, R., J. Cooper and R.W Davies (1977), *The Technological Level of Soviet Industry*, New Haven: Yale University Press.

Artobolevskiy, S.S. (1997), *Regional Policy in Europe*, London and Bristol: Jessica Kingsley Publishers.

Bandera, V.N. and Z.L. Melnyk (eds) (1973), *The Soviet Economy in Regional Perspective*, New York and London: Praeger.

Bandman, M.K. (1980), *Territorial-Production Complexes: Theory and Practice of Pre-plan Studies* (title translated from Russian), Novosibirsk: USSR Academy of Science.

Bandman, M.K. (1982), 'Territorial production complexes: The spatial organisation of production', in M.M., Albegov, Å.E. Andersson and F. Snickars (eds), *Regional Development Modelling: Theory and Practice*, Amsterdam: North-Holland.

Bandman, M.K., O.L. Bandman and T.N. Yesikova (1990), *Territorial-Production Complexes: Formation Process Forecasting with the use of Petri Networks* (title translated from Russian), Novosibirsk: USSR Academy of Science.

Baranov, E.F., V.I. Danilov-Danilyan and M.G. Zavelsky (1971), 'On the system of models of optimum perspective planning', *Economics and Mathematical Methods*, **VII** (3).

Blum, D.W. (1994), *Russia's Future. Consolidation or Disintegration?*, Boulder: Westview Press.

Bradshaw, M.J. (ed.) (1991), *The Soviet Union. A New Regional Geography?* London: Belhaven Press.

Bromlei, Iu. and O.I. Shkaratan (1983), 'National' nye trudovye traditsii – vazhhnyi faktor intensifikatsii proizvodstva', *Sovetskoe Gosudarstvo i Pravo* 2.

Brown, A., M. Kaser and G.S. Smith (eds) (1992), *The Cambridge Encyclopaedia of Russia and the Soviet Union*, Cambridge: Cambridge University Press.

Brunswick Warburg (1998), *Telecoms Russia. The hidden value of cellular. Regional telecoms' cellular exposure underestimated*, Moscow and New York: Brunswick Warburg.

Carlsson, L. and M.-O. Olsson (eds) (1998), *Initial Analyses of the Institutional Framework of the Russian Forest Sector*, IIASA Interim report IR-98-027, Laxenburg, Austria: International Institute for Applied Systems Analysis.

Carlsson, L., N.-G Lundgren, M.-O. Olsson and M.Y. Varakin (1999), *Institutions and the Emergence of Markets – Transition in the Arkhangelsk Forest Sector*, IIASA Interim report IR-99, Laxenburg, Austria: International Institute for Applied Systems Analysis.

Central Statistics Bureau (1936), *Statistical Abstract* (title translated from Russian), Moscow.

Chayanov, A.V. (1921), *Conception of Profitability of Socialist Economy. Methods of non-monetary account of economic enterprises* (title translated from Russian), Moscow.

Dadayan, V.S. and V.V. Kossov (1962), *Input–Output Tables of Economic Region as an Instrument of Plan Calculations* (title translated from Russian), Moscow: USSR Academy of Science.

Danilov-Danilyan, V.I. and M.G. Zavelsky (1975), *System of Optimum Perspective Planning of the National Economy* (title translated from Russian), Moscow: USSR Academy of Science.

Dellenbrant, J.-Å. (1986), *The Soviet Regional Dilemma. Planning, People, and Natural Resources*, Armonk, NY and London: M.E. Sharp Inc.

de Souza, P. (1989), *Territorial Production Complexes in the Soviet Union – with special focus on Siberia*, Gothenburg: Department of Geography, University of Gothenburg.

De Spiegeleire (1994), 'Raspad: The Further Disintegration of the Russian Federation and its Policy Implications for the West', in K. Segbers (ed.), *Rußlands Zukunft: Räume und Regionen*, Baden-Baden: Nomos Verlagsgesellschaft.

Dimitriev, V.K. (1904), *Economic Essays* (title translated from Russian), Moscow: SPB.

Dmitrieva, O. (1996), *Regional Development. The USSR and after*, London: London University College Press.

Dobb, M. (1966), *Soviet Economic Development since 1917*, London: Routledge & Kegan Paul.

Dyker, D.A. (1983), *The Process of Investment in the Soviet Union*, Cambridge: Cambridge University Press.

Energia (1973), *Instructions on the Estimation of Economic Efficiency of Capital Investments in the Development of Power Economy: Generation, transfer and distribution of electric and heat power* (title translated from Russian), Moscow: Energia.

Escoe, G.M. (1995), 'The demise of Soviet industry: A regional perspective', *Journal of Comparative Economics*, **21**, 336–53.

Feigin, Y.G. (1954), *Location of Production under Capitalism and Socialism* (title translated from Russian), Moscow: Gospolitizdat.

Feigin, Y.G. (ed.) (1965), *Regularities and Factors of the USSR Economic Regions' Development* (title translated from Russian), Moscow: USSR Academy of Science.

Financy i statistika (1988), Moscow.

Fukuyama, F. (1995), *Trust. The Social Virtues and the Creation of Prosperity*, London: Hamish Hamilton.

Gaddy, C. and B.W. Ickes (1998), 'Beyond a bailout: time to face reality about Russia's "virtual economy"', *Foreign Affairs*, **77** (5).

Gaddy, C. and B.W. Ickes (1999), 'A simple four-sector model of the virtual economy', *Post-Soviet Geography and Economics*, **40** (2).

Gerschenkron, A. (1962), *Economic Backwardness in Historical Perspective*, Cambridge, Mass.: Belknap Press.

Gladkov, I.A. (1935), 'On the history of the first five-year plan', *Planovoye Khozyaistvo*, no. 4.

Gosplan (1926), *Balance of the National Economy of the USSR for 1923–24*, Moscow: USSR Central Statistics Bureau, Proceedings, vol. XXIX.

Gosplan (1931), 'Principles of geographic location of heavy industry in the 2nd five-year plan', *Planovoye Khozyaistvo*, no. 4, Moscow: Gosplanizdat.

Gosplan (1933), *Second five-year plan for the development of the USSR national economy (1933–1937)* (title translated from Russian), vol. I, Moscow: Gosplanizdat.

Gosplan (1939), *Third Five-Year Plan for the Development of the USSR National Economy (1938–1942)* (title translated from Russian), Moscow: Gosplanizdat.

Gosplan (1950), *Five-Year Plan for the USSR National Economy Building* (title translated from Russian), vol. III, Moscow.

Gosplan (1969), *General Methods for the Elaboration of the General Scheme of Allocation of Productive Forces of the USSR for 1971–90* (title translated from Russian), Moscow.

Gosplan (1977), *Methods (Main Provisions) for Estimation of Economic Efficiency of the use of New Machinery, Inventions and Rationalisation Proposals in the National Economy* (title translated from Russian), Moscow.

Gosplan (1985), *Planning of the USSR Productive Forces' Location* (title translated from Russian), part I, Moscow: Ekonomika.

Gosplan (1986), *Planning of the USSR Productive Forces' Location* (title translated from Russian), part II, Moscow: Ekonomika.

Granberg, A.G. (1973), *Optimisation of Territorial Proportions in the National Economy* (title translated from Russian), Moscow: Ekonomika.

Granberg, A.G. (1982), 'Regional Economic Interactions in the USSR', in M.M. Albegov, Å.E. Andersson and F. Snickars (eds), *Regional Development Modelling: Theory and Practice*, Amsterdam: North-Holland.

Granberg, A.G. (1988), *Modelling of the Socialist Economy* (title translated from Russian), Moscow: Ekonomika.

Hausladen, G. (1991), 'Perestroyka and Siberia: Frontier Resource Development', in M.J. Bradshaw (ed.), *The Soviet Union. A New Regional Geography?*, London: Belhaven Press.

Hirschmann, A.O. (1958), *The Strategy of Economic Development*, New Haven: Yale University Press.

Holubnychy, V. (1982), *Selected Works of Vsevolod Holubnychy*, ed. I.S. Koropeckyj, Edmonton, Alberta: Canadian Institute of Ukrainian Studies, University of Alberta.

Hough, J. (1988), *Opening Up the Soviet Economy*, Washington, DC: Brookings.

Issaev, B.M. (1982), 'Integrated Material–Financial Balances in Regional Economic Analysis', in M.M. Albegov, Å.E. Andersson and F. Snickars (eds), *Regional Development Modelling: Theory and Practice*, Amsterdam: North-Holland.

Issaev, B.M., P. Nijkamp, Rietveld P. and F. Snickars (eds) (1982), *Multiregional Economic Modelling: Practice and Prospect*, Amsterdam: North-Holland.

Jarygina, T. and G. Marcenko (1994), 'Regionale Prozesse in der ehemaligen UdSSR und im neuen Rußland', in K. Segbers (ed.), *Rußlands Zukunft: Räume und Regionen*, Baden-Baden: Nomos Verlagsgesellschaft.

Kaiser, R.J. (1991), 'Nationalism: The Challenge to Soviet Federalism', in M.J. Bradshaw (ed.), *The Soviet Union. A New Regional Geography?*, London: Belhaven Press.

Kantorovich, L.V. (1960), *Economic Calculation of Optimum use of Resources* (title translated from Russian), Moscow: USSR Academy of Science.

Khruschev, A.T. (1979), *Geography of the USSR Industry* (title translated from Russian), 2nd edn, Moscow: Mysl.

Khrushchev, S. (1994), 'The Political Economy of Russia's Regional Fragmentation', in D.W. Blum (ed.), *Russia's Future. Consolidation or Disintegration?*, Boulder: Westview Press.

Kistanov, V.V. (1968), *Complex Development and Specialisation of the USSR Economic Regions* (title translated from Russian), Moscow: Ekonomika.

Kolosovsky, N.N. (1947), *Production-Territorial Combinations (Complexes) in Soviet Economic Geography* (title translated from Russian), Geographical Issues, vol. 6, Moscow: Geografizdat.

Kondratiev, N.D. (1922), *World Economy and its Conjuncture During and After the War* (title translated from Russian), Moscow.

Korobov, A. (1939), 'Socialist location of productive forces', *Planovoye Khozyaistvo*, no. 3.

Korobov, A. (1940), 'Tasks of complex territorial planning', *Planovoye Khozyaistvo*, no. 11.

Koropeckyj, I.S. (1967), 'The development of Soviet location theory before the Second World War – I', *Soviet Studies*, **19** (1).

Koropeckyj, I.S. (1972), 'Equalization of regional development in socialist countries: an empirical study', *Economic Development and Cultural Change*, **21**, October, 68–86.

Kovalevsky, N.A. (1932), *Location of Productive Forces on the Territory of the USSR in the Second Five-Year Plan and General Plan* (title translated from Russian), Moscow: Gostransizdat.

Kowalski, J.S. (1986), 'Regional conflicts in Poland: spatial polarization in a centrally planned economy', *Environment and Planning A*, **18**, 599–617.

Kuibyshev, V.V. (1937), *Articles and Speeches* (title translated from Russian), vol V, Moscow: Partizdat.

Kursky, A. and S. Slavin (1936), 'Regional aspect of the economic plan' (title translated from Russian), *Planovoye Khozyaistvo*, no. 3.

Lenin, V.I. 1918 (1965), *Draft plan of scientific and technical work*, in *Collected Works*, vol. 26, Moscow: Progress.

Leontiev, V. and D. Ford (1972), 'Inter-branch analysis of economic structure impact on the environment. Economics and mathematical methods' (title translated from Russian), *Economics and Mathematical Methods*, **VIII** (3).

Lewin, M. (1988), *The Gorbachev Phenomenon*, Berkeley: University of California Press.

Liebowitz, R.D. (1991), 'Spatial Inequality under Gorbachev', in M.J. Bradshaw (ed.), *The Soviet Union. A New Regional Geography?*, London: Belhaven Press.

Livshitz, R.S. (1954), *Essays on Location of the USSR Industry* (title translated from Russian), Moscow: Gospolitizdat.

Lydolph, P.E. (1979), *Geography of the USSR; Topical Analysis*, Elkhart Lake, Wisconsin: Misty Walley.

McAuley, A. (1979), *Economic Welfare in the Soviet Union. Poverty, Living Standards and Inequality*, Madison: University of Wisconsin Press.

Maddison, A. (1995), *Monitoring the World Economy 1820–1992*, Paris: OECD.

Metallurgizdat (1959), *Methods of technical–economic calculations in energetics* (title translated from Russian), Moscow: Metallurgizdat.

Metallurgizdat (1966), *Methods of technical–economic calculations in energetics* (title translated from Russian), Moscow: Metallurgizdat.

Mezhlauk, V.K. (1934), 'On the adjustment of planning bodies activity (title translated from Russian)', *Planovoye Khozyaistvo*, no. 3.

Myrdal, G. (1957), *Economic Theory and Underdeveloped Regions*, London: Duckworth & co.

Nekrasov, N.N. (1978), *Regional Economy (Theory, Problems, Methods)* (title translated from Russian), Moscow: Ekonomika.

Nemchinov, V.S. (1962), *Economic–Mathematical Methods and Models* (title translated from Russian), Moscow: Socekgiz.

North, D.C. (1981), *Structure and Change in Economic History*, New York: Norton.

North, D.C. and R. Thomas (1973), *The Rise of the Western World*, Cambridge: Cambridge University Press.

Nove, A. (1977), *The Soviet economic system*, London: G. Allen & Unwin.

Nove, A. (1986), *An Economic History of the USSR*, Harmondsworth: Penguin.

Olsson, M-O. (1980), 'De sovjetiska unionsrepublikernas nationalinkomst. En studie om nationalinkomstens värde som indikator på republikernas ekonomiska utvecklingsnivåer', *Nordic Committee for Soviet and East European Research. Contributions to Soviet and East European Research*, 8 (2), Uppsala.

Pallot, J. (1991), 'The countryside under Gorbachev', in M.J. Bradshaw (ed.), *The Soviet Union. A New Regional Geography?*, London: Belhaven Press.

Pallot, J. and D.J.B. Shaw (1981), *Planning in the Soviet Union*, London: CroomHelm

Pavlenko, V.F. (1975), *Territorial Planning in the USSR* (title translated from Russian), Moscow: Ekonomika.

Pavlenko, V.F. (1984), *Planning of Territorial Development* (title translated from Russian), Moscow: Ekonomika.

Polanyi, K. (1944), *The Great Transformation: The political and economic origins of our time*, Boston: Beacon Press.

Probst, A.E. (1971), *Issues of Location of the Socialist Industry* (title translated from Russian), Moscow: USSR Academy of Science.

Putnam, R. (1993), *Making Democracy Work. Civic Traditions in Modern Italy*, Princeton: Princeton University Press.

Rayatskas, R.L. (1982), 'System of models of forecasting and planning of summary indices of national economy development (case study for the union republic) (title translated from Russian)', in Academia Nauk, *System of Models of National Economic Planning* (title translated from Russian), Moscow.

Regional Development in the USSR: Trends and Prospects, Colloquium 25–27 April 1979 in Brussels. Newtonville, Mass: Oriental Research Partners.

Rose, R. (1998), 'Getting Things Done in an Anti-Modern Society: Social Capital Networks in Russia', The World Bank's Social Capital Initiative Working Paper No. 6.

Rosenberg, N. and L.E. Birdzell (1986), *How the West Grew Rich*, New York: Basic Books.

Sachs, J.D. and K. Pistor (eds) (1997), *The Rule of Law and Economic Reform in Russia*, Boulder: Westview Press.

Salmin, A. (1994), 'Zerfällt Rußland? Analyse und Wandlungsvorschläge', in K. Segbers (ed.), *Rußlands Zukunft: Räume und Regionen*, Baden-Baden: Nomos Verlagsgesellschaft.

Sätre Åhlander, A-M. (1994), *Environmental Problems in the Shortage Economy. The Legacy of Soviet Environmental Policy*, Aldershot, UK and Brookfield, US: Edward Elgar.

Sätre Åhlander, A-M. (1999), 'Women and the social economy in transitional Russia', *Annals of Public and Cooperative Economics*.

Schiffer, J.R. (1989), *Soviet Regional Economic Policy. The East–West Debate over Pacific Siberian Development*, London: Macmillan

Schroeder, G.E. (1974), 'Soviet Wage and Income Policies in Regional Perspective', *The Association for Comparative Economic Studies Bulletin*, **XVI** (2), 3–19.

Schroeder, G.E. (1979), 'Regional Income Differentials: Urban and Rural', in *Regional Development in the USSR: Trends and Prospects*, Colloquium 25–27 April 1979, Brussels/Newtonville, Mass: Oriental Research Partners.

Segbers, K. (ed.) (1994), *Rußlands Zukunft: Räume und Regionen*, Baden-Baden: Nomos Verlagsgesellschaft.

Shaw, D.J.B. (1985), 'Spatial dimensions in Soviet central planning', *Transactions of the Institute of British Geographers*, vol. 10, 401–12.

Shaw, D.J.B. (1991), 'Restructuring the Soviet City', in M.J. Bradshaw (ed.), *The Soviet Union. A New Regional Geography?*, London: Belhaven Press.

Shelest, V.A. (1975), *Regional Power–Economic Issues in the USSR* (title translated from Russian), Moscow: USSR Academy of Science.

Shemetov, P.V. (1978), *Economic Studies at the Novosibirsk Research Centre – Formation and Development* (title translated from Russian), Novosibirsk: USSR Academy of Science.

Shniper, R.I. (1978), *Regional Pre-Plan Studies* (title translated from Russian), Novosibirsk: USSR Academy of Science.

Shtoulberg, B.M. (ed.) (1983), *Planning of Economic and Social Development of an Oblast* (title translated from Russian), Moscow: Ekonomika.

Shtoulberg, B.M. (1988), 'Regional policy and the system of territorial planning' (title translated from Russian), in *Distribution of the Productive Forces: Theory and Practice of General Schemes* (title translated from Russian), Moscow: Progress Publishers.

Sloutsky, E.E. (1915), 'On the theory of balanced budget of the consumer', *Giornale degli Economisti e Revista di Statistica*, no. 1.

Sloutsky, E.E. (1960), 'Composition of occasional reasons as the source of cyclic processes' (title translated from Russian), in Academia Nauk, *Selected Proceedings. Probability Theory and Theory of Mathematical Statistics* (title translated from Russian), Moscow: USSR Academy of Science.

Snickars, F. (1985), 'Siberian Gas and its Role in Soviet Energy Policy', in B. Johansson and T.R. Lakshmanan (eds), *The Assessment of Regional Consequences of Large Scale Energy Developments: Methods and Models*, Amsterdam: North-Holland.

Snyder, J. (1994), 'Russian backwardness and the future of Europe', *Daedalus*, **123** (2).

SOPS (1988), *Distribution of Productive Forces: Theory and practice. General Schemes* (title translated from Russian), Moscow: Progress Publishers.

SOPS and Gosplan (1972), *Programme and General Methods for the Development of the General Scheme of Allocation of Productive Forces of the USSR for 1990* (title translated from Russian), Moscow.

SOPS and Gosplan (1992), *Methodical Recommendations on the Elaboration of Sectoral Schemes of Development and Allocation of Productive Forces (I stage)* (title translated from Russian), Moscow.

Sorokin, G.M. (1961), *Planning of the USSR National Economy: Theory and Organisation* (title translated from Russian), Moscow: Socekgiz.

Spechler, M.C. (1979), *Regional Trends in the USSR 1958–1978*, Jerusalem: Hebrew University of Jerusalem.

Szajkowski, B. (1993), 'Will Russia disintegrate into bantustans?', *The World Today*, **49** (8–9).

Tsaplin, V. (1990), 'Defence-preparedness of the industry before the War' (title translated from Russian), *Historical Review of Ukraine* (title translated from Russian), no 8.

Urinson, M.S. (1963), *Planning of National Economy in Union Republics* (title translated from Russian), Moscow: Ekonomizdat.

Varlamov, V.O., S.P. Ivanov, N.N. Kazansky and P.E. Semenov (1976), *Development of the Economy of Union Republics and Economic Regions* (title translated from Russian), Moscow: Ekonomika.

Verg, N. (1994), *History of the Soviet State*, Moscow: Progress-Academy.

Vogel, H. (1979), 'Regional Differences in Living Standards and the Efficiency of the Distribution Network', in *Regional Development in the USSR: Trends and Prospects*, Colloquium 25–27 April 1979 in Brussels. Newtonville, Mass: Oriental Research Partners.

Volodarsky, L. (1946), *Revival of the USSR Regions which Suffered from German Occupation* (title translated from Russian), Moscow: Gospolitizdat.

von Thünen, J. H. (1966), *Isolated State*, Oxford: Pergamon Press.

Voznesensky, N. (1947), *Military Economy of the USSR in the Period of the Great Patriotic War* (title translated from Russian), Moscow: Gospolitizdat.

Wagener, H-J. (1972), *Wirtschaftswachstum in unterentwickelten Gebieten. Ansätze zu einer Regionalanalyse der Sowjetunion*, Berlin: Duncker & Humblot.

Weber, A. (1957), *Theory of the Location of Industries*, Chicago: University of Chicago Press.

Westlund, H. (1998), 'The limits of spatial planning: regional experiences of the Soviet epoch', *Papers in Regional Science: The Journal of the RSAI*, **77** (3).

Westlund, H. (1999), 'An Interaction-Cost Perspective on Networks and Territory', *Annals of Regional Science*, **33** (1).

Williamson, J.G. (1965), 'Regional inequality and the process of national development: a description of the patterns', *Economic Development and Cultural Change*, **13**, 3–45.

Yaremenko, Y.V., E.B. Yershov and A.S. Smyshlyaev (1975), 'Models of inter-branch interactions' (title translated from Russian), in Academia Nauk, *Economics and Mathematical Methods* (title translated from Russian), **XI** (3).

Zalkind, A.I. and B.P. Miroshnichenko (1980), *Essays on the Development of Economic Planning* (title translated from Russian), Moscow: Ekonomika.

Zhdanov, B.N. (1927), *Territorial Organisation of Industry* (title translated from Russian), Moscow: Promizdat.

Index